She Who Speaks Through Silence
An Anthology for Nephthys

Edited by Chelsea Luellon Bolton

She Who Speaks Through Silence: An Anthology for Nephthys

Copyright ©2018 by Chelsea Luellon Bolton
Cover Art Papyrus Reproduction Image
©2018 by Barbara Ann Richter. Used with permission.

Cover and Interior Design ©2018 by Stargazer Design
www.stargazerdesign.net

Works from previously published material are copyrighted by their respective publishers and translators and are included here with permission. Any other material included is covered under the Fair Use Clause, Section 107-108 of the Copyright Act of 1976.

All contributors retain the copyright to their own work. They are included here with permission.

All rights reserved. This book or any portion thereof may not be reproduced or used in any manner whatsoever without the express written permission of the publisher except for the use of brief quotations in a book review.

DISCLAIMER AND/OR LEGAL NOTICES:
This work is not intended for financial, legal, medical, spiritual, or any other advice. This book is for information purposes only.

Printed in the United States of America
First Printing, 2018
ISBN: 9781796836141
http://fiercelybrightone.com

Dedication

This work is of course dedicated to the Goddess Nebet Het (Nephthys).

Image: "Nebet-Het at My Shrine"

©2017, Rev. Anna Applegate

Contents

DEDICATION 3
   Image: "Nebet-Het At My Shrine" by Rev. Anna Applegate 3
ACKNOWLEDGEMENTS 11
INTRODUCTION 12
ESSAYS AND ARTICLES 13
   Who is Nebet Het? by Chelsea Luellon Bolton 14
   The Lady of the Limit and Her Sister by M. Isidora Forrest 30
   Damn You Plutarch, or How I nearly Missed the Chance
   to Get to Know My Lady by Secondgenerationimmigrant 36
   Into the *Duat*: Who is Nephthys? by Rev. Anna Applegate 39
RITUAL AND MAGIC 40
   Morning Ritual to Nebet Het by Chelsea Luellon Bolton 41
   Daily Solar Prayers by Chelsea Luellon Bolton 42
   Offering Ritual to Nebet Het by Chelsea Luellon Bolton 43
   Chant Her Name by Chelsea Luellon Bolton 45
   Candlelighting and Water Purification for Nebet Het by Chelsea
   Luellon Bolton 46
   Sistrum House Cleansing by Chelsea Luellon Bolton 48
   Heka: Pillar of Support, Pillar of Strength by Taqerisenu 49
   Into the *Duat*: A Devotional Ritual to Nebet-Het by Rev. Anna
   Applegate 51
   Nebet Het Rite for Shadow Work by Emily K. Jones 62
POETRY OF NEBET HET BY CHELSEA LUELLON BOLTON 66
   Nebet Het 67
   Desert's Bride 67
   Violence Follows Despair 67
   Passage 68

Thunderstorm's Lullaby..68

Tombstone..69

Veiled Silence..69

Flame...70

Nebet Het Speaks Through Silence...70

Through the Passage..71

Unseen Eye...71

Voices Echo..72

As Dawn Breaks..72

Temple, Tomb, and Home...74

Lady of the Temple...75

Animal Forms of Nebet Het..76

Strong One..77

Royal Lady..78

Sorceress of Transformation..80

Travel to Me...81

Shadow Illumination...82

Lady, Sister, and Mistress...82

Shadow and Light...83

Never Be Afraid..83

Soul Renewal..85

Guide and Illumination...86

Call on Her Today..86

I lead...87

Flow..88

Star Goddess...89

Nebet Het, Daughter of Ra...89

Lady of the Veil..90

Healer..90

Please Reside in Our Hearts...90

Lady of Strength, Goddess Who Beguiles	91
More Than My Sister's Shadow	92
Nebet Het is the Goddess	93
Battered Wife, the Strong One	94
Guiding Light	96
Papyrus, Necklace, and Harpoon	97
Tread Upon Nebet Het	98
Dirge	98
Nebet Het, of the Graves	99
Lady of Sorrow	100
Wipe Away Your Tears	101
Personal Goddess: Nebet Het	102
Nebet Het's Advice on Community	102
Nebet Het's Advice	103
Nebet Het's Rage, Nebet Het's Promise	104
Liberator	105
For All Eternity	107
Hidden One	107
Nebet Het-Seshat	108
Nebet Het-Seshat: Her Sacred Time	110
Nebet Het-Seshat: Recorder of Scrolls	111
Nebet Het-Seshat: Blessings of the Goddess	112
Nebet Het-Seshat: Forever	113
Nebet Het-Nit: Creator, Warrior, and Guide of the Dead	114
Nebet Het-Nit: Uraeus and Guard	116
Nebet Het-Nit-Seshat	117
Nebet Het-Nit-Seshat: Three as One	118
Nebet Het-Nit-Seshat: Three Poems	119
Nebet Het-Hethert: Lady of Beauty	121
Nebet Het-Mehet Weret: Nebet Het, the Celestial Cow	122

Nebet Het-Nut: Heaven, Nile, and Underworld 123
Nebet Het-Nut: Sky 123
Names and Syncretisms: A Poem 124

POETRY OF NEBET HET AND SET BY CHELSEA LUELLON BOLTON 125

Red Lady and Lord 125
Light in Darkness 126
Flood, Rain, and Storm 127
Land's Purge 129
Rain Renews the Land 130
Great of Strength, Lady of Strength 131
Call on Us 132
Choose Your Life by Set and Nebet Het 134
Firestorm and Lightning 136
Change Brings A Little Death 138

POETRY OF NEBET HET, ASET, AND RA BY CHELSEA LUELLON BOLTON 139

Power of My Light 139
Fire and Magic 140

POETRY OF NEBET HET AND WESIR BY CHELSEA LUELLON BOLTON 142

Nebet Het, Wife of Wesir 142
With One Who Grieves 143
King and Lady of the Dead 144
Offering Sacrifice to Nebet Het and Wesir 145
Brother, Husband, and King 146
Lord of the Oasis 148
Aset, Nebet Het, and Wesir 150
Wife and Mourner of Wesir 150

POETRY OF NEBET HET AND YINEPU BY CHELSEA LUELLON BOLTON 151

Guide of Souls 151
Son of Ra and Nebet Het 151
POETRY OF ASET AND NEBET HET BY CHELSEA LUELLON BOLTON
 152
　The Twins, The Dyad 152
　Way of the Two Sisters 152
　Way of the Heart 154
　The Two Sisters Call 156
　Sistrum-Goddess 157
　Magic Gateway 159
　Enraged Widows 161
　Savior Goddesses 162
　Throne and House Goddesses 163
　Lady of the Crossroads 164
　Rhyme for the Two Goddesses 165
　Throne and Throne Shrines 168
　Veiled Magic 169
　Aset-Nebet Het 169
　Wake of Sorrow and Rage 171
　We are Breath 172
　Partners and Twins 173
　Life from Death 174
　Call on the Two Mourners 175
　Creation's Goddess 176
　Goddesses of Creation 177
　Watch Over Your Life 180
　Manifest Your Power 181
　Solar Cycle as a Star 182
　Blazing Goddess of the Star 183
　Burning Fiercely Bright 184

    Uraeus 186

    Star Goddess, Eye of Ra 188

    Celestial Goddess 189

    Eye in the Storm 190

    Her Wrath 193

    Eyes of Ra 194

    Nut, Our Mother 195

    Geb, the Earth God 196

    Ra, Our Father 197

    Wesir, Our Husband, the Fiercely Bright 198

    Those Who Renew 200

    Guide and Guard 201

    Lioness and Leopard 203

    Light of the Panther Goddess 204

    Soul-Bringer 205

    This is Your Star 206

    Aset-Serqet, Nebet Het-Serqet: Expeller of Poison 207

HYMNS, PRAYERS, AND ADORATIONS 208

    Awaken in Peace, Nebet Hwt by Jonathan Sousa 209

    Prayer to Nephthys I by Rebecca Buchanan 210

    Hymn to Nephthys I by Rebecca Buchanan 210

    Twenty-One Adorations of Nephthys by Rebecca Buchanan 211

    Descend With Me by Amanda Artemisia Forrester 212

    You Are Welcome Here by Amanda Artemisia Forrester 214

    Nephthys, In Five Senses by Amanda Artemisia Forrester 214

    To the Two Sisters by Amanda Artemisia Forrester 215

    A Call to Nephthys by Tina Georgitsis 216

    Evocation to Nephthys by Frances Billinghurst 217

    Nebthet by Taqerisenu 218

    The Sorrows of Nebet-Het by Rev. Anna Applegate 219

Prayer to Nebet-Het by Robin Penn 222
Hymn to Nephthys by Hearthstone 223
Poetry of Nebet-Het by Robin Penn 224
FICTION 225
The Queen of the Birds: an Egyptian Tale by Darius Matthias Klein
.... 226
EPILOGUE 229
APPENDIX A 230
Festivals of Nebet Het by Chelsea Luellon Bolton 230
Her Correspondences by Chelsea Luellon Bolton 234
APPENDIX B 237
Gods and Godddesses Name List 237
Contributor Biographies 238
References 241
Glossary 245
About the Author 250
Other Books by Chelsea Luellon Bolton 250

Acknowledgements

Thank you to Tamara L. Siuda for translating the Dawn Prayer, a New Year Prayer, the Canopic Chest Hymn, and Nebet Het's Birthday Prayer for this book, and for also giving me permission to include her material from *The Ancient Egyptian Prayerbook*, *The Ancient Egyptian Daybook*, and *Nebt-Het: Lady of the House*.

Thank you to Dr. Jessica Levai for permission to include her material from her dissertation *Aspects of the Goddess Nephthys, Especially During the Graeco-Roman Period in Egypt*.

Thank you to all the contributors who submitted their works to be included in the book.

I would like to thank these people for helping me with this project:
Thank you to Stargazer Design for designing the interior pages;
Thank you to Andrew S. Meit for designing the cover;
Thank you to Rebecca Buchanan for giving me publishing and editorial advice;
Thank you to Ashley Horn for giving me formatting advice;
Thank you to Natalie Baan for helping me with permissions and publishing;
Thank you to Tamara L. Siuda and Astrid Tanebet for their help with some translations;
Thank you to Rev. Sehedjef, Priest of Nebet Het and Serqet of the House of Netjer;
Thank you to Rev. Anna Applegate, Priestess of Nebet Het, Bast, and Hekate Khthonia of the Fellowship of Isis.

Thank you to all of the Egyptologists who worked so hard to make the information about Nebet Het available to all.

Thank you to my Patrons on Patreon! Thank you to Christie B.

Introduction

In this book, there are essays, oracles, devotional poetry, and prose about the ancient Egyptian Goddess Nebet Het (Nephthys). The contributors of this volume come from various backgrounds and thus, each contributor refers to Nebet Het with their own version of Her name. There are various ways to spell the name of the Goddess: in ancient Egyptian, it is Nebet Het or Nebt Het /nebet-HET/ or Nebet Hwt /neb-ET HOOT/ and in ancient Greek, it is Nephthys /Nef-this/.[1] Each contributor's unique spelling of her name has been retained within their works.

If anyone is interested in the ancient hymns or epithets of Nebet Het, please see my book, *Lady of the Temple: Ancient Hymns for Nephthys*.

Her name Nebet Het can be translated to "Lady or Mistress of the Palace, Temple, Tomb, or Home." As Lady of the Palace, She is the protector of the King, the King's residence and the mother of Heru. As Lady of the House or Temple, She governs over holy places such as temples and shrines as a guard who protects against impurities. As Lady of the Home, She governs the household: its occupants and upkeep. As Lady of the Tomb, She is the goddess over the burial and remembrance of the dead.

As the second wife and mourner of Wesir (Osiris), Nebet Het is the Goddess of the inundation of the Nile, the rainfall, and the fertility of crops. She is a Goddess of the Underworld who helps the dead transform. As wife of Set, She is a warlike Goddess of the edges of the desert and an averter of evil forces.

She is often paired with her sister Aset (Isis) in various roles and functions such as an Eye of Ra and Great of Magic; a protector of the shrines and temples; and a mourner and wife of Wesir. Together, the Two Sisters bring the rain for the Nile's flood, bring the sunrise and sunset, are mothers of Heru and Yinepu (Anubis), are averters of evil, and protect the Gods Ra, Heru (Horus), and Wesir.

---

[1] Siuda, Tamara L. The Ancient Egyptian Prayerbook. (Illinois: Stargazer Design, 2009), 132.

Not much is known about Nebet Het outside of the Wesir mythos or Her association with her sister Aset. She does have two epithets which describe two aspects of her character: *Kherseket* (She Who Wipes Away Tears) and *Merkhetes* (She Whose Flame is Painful). She is the goddess who comforts those who suffer and is the fierce protective deity who destroys enemies with flame.

May these pages help you glimpse into the diverse aspects of this otherwise elusive Goddess.

Best Regards,
Chelsea Luellon Bolton

Essays and Articles

Figure 2: Anubis and Nephthys.

By S F-E-Cameron [GFDL (http://www.gnu.org/copyleft/fdl.html) or CC BY-SA 3.0 (https://creativecommons.org/licenses/by-sa/3.0)], from Wikimedia Commons

Who is Nebet Het?
by Chelsea Luellon Bolton

Nebet Het is an ancient Egyptian Goddess whose origins are lost in time. Wainwright believes that Nebet Het was originally Goddess of the Sky, due to her association with Set, the god of storms in the Pyramid Texts; and the fertility god Min, as the god of the thunderbolt. In the Pyramid Texts, Seshat is mentioned as a name of Nebet Het. She is also associated with Serqet, the scorpion goddess.[2]

From the Pyramid Texts onward, Nebet Het was the Daughter of Ra and an Eye of Ra.[3]

Nebet Het is the companion of Aset throughout ancient Egyptian history. They also mourn Wesir together within the Mysteries of Wesir as to Two Sisters and Two Widows of the God.

Her Family and the Mother of Yinepu (Anubis)

Nebet Het (also Nebt Het; Greek *Nephthys*) is the daughter of Geb, the Earth God; and Nut, the Sky Goddess. Her siblings are Aset, Wesir, Set, and Heru Wer. She is also a daughter of Ra.

She has a few consorts and children throughout ancient Egyptian history. In the *Lamentations of Aset and Nebet Het*, Nebet Het is a Wife and Widow of Wesir.[4] Within Plutarch's work, Nebet Het and Wesir are the parents of Yinepu.[5] In the Roman Period, Nebet Het was called "Wife of Wennefer (Wesir)" and "Mother of Heru" in a hymn from the Temple of Komir.[6]

In the New Kingdom Harris Magical Papyrus, Ra and Nebet Het are named as parents of Yinepu.[7]

Nebet Het is paired with Set, especially during the 18th Dynasty, the Ramessid period, and in the Dakhla and Kharga Oases during the

---

[2] Wainwright, Gerald A. "Seshat and the Pharaoh." In The Journal of Egyptian Archaeology 26, no. 1 (1941), 30.
[3] Wainwright, Gerald A. "Seshat and the Pharaoh," 30.
[4] Levai, Jessica. Aspects of the Goddess Nephthys, Especially During the Graeco-Roman Period in Egypt. (Brown University Dissertation, 2007), 147 and 157-160.
[5] Levai, Jessica. Aspects of the Goddess Nephthys, 160; El-Saghir, Mohamed and Dominique Valbelle. "Komir. I. The Discovery of Komir Temple. Preliminary Report. - II. Deux hymnes aux divinités de Komir: Anoukis et Nephthys." In *BIFAO 83* (1983), 164-166; and Levai, Jessica. Aspects of the Goddess Nephthys, 161-162.
[6] El-Saghir, Mohamed and Dominique Valbelle. "Komir," 164-166.
[7] Levai, Jessica. Aspects of the Goddess Nephthys, 90.

Roman Period.⁸ In one ancient text, Nebet Het abandoned a child she had with Set, for the sake of Heru.⁹ In Plutarch's work, Nebet Het did abandon Yinepu, although Wesir was the father in this version — so this other text may be alluding to Yinepu being Set and Nebet Het's child, but this is not conclusive.

Nebet Het is the Mother of Yinepu. Within the Harris Magical Papyrus, Nebet Het and Ra are mentioned as the parents of Yinepu. Another ancient text mentions Nebet Het had a child with Set that she abandoned. Te Velde says this child is Yinepu, given that he is named as Nebet Het's son in previous sources.¹⁰ According to Plutarch, Nebet Het abandoned Yinepu, so there is some plausibility to this claim. Plutarch's work was filled with Greek customs and mores. Infanticide is not normally an ancient Egyptian practice, but it was an ancient Greek one.

In one papyrus, Inpu-Sopdu (Anubis-Sopdu) is the son of Nebet Het.¹¹ Nebet Het is the Mother of Ihy, with either Ra or Heru as the father.¹² Nebet Het was attested to have a daughter by Heru Hemen.¹³ Nebet Het can be the Mother of Ra in her aspect as the Akhet, or the Celestial Cow.¹⁴ She is also called "Great Mother of Amun" and "Mother of Heru."¹⁵

In Nubia, Nebet Het's consort is Yinepu.¹⁶

Her Name

Nebet Het is normally translated as "Lady or Mistress of the House," where *Nbt* or the basket glyph means "Lady or Mistress," and

---

[8] Levai, Jessica. Aspects of the Goddess Nephthys, 181.
[9] Borghouts, J.F. The Magical texts of papyrus Leiden I 34. (Brill, 1971), 38.
[10] Grenier, Jean Claude. Anubis Alexandrin et Romain *Vol. 57*. (Brill, 1977), 19-20; and Te Velde, Herman. Seth, God of Confusion: A Study of His Role in Egyptian Mythology and Religion. Vol. 6. (Brill Archive, 1977), 29-30.
[11] Borghouts, J.F. The Magical texts of papyrus Leiden I 34. (Brill, 1971), 38.
[12] Tyldesley, Joyce. The Penguin Book of Myths and Legends of Ancient Egypt. (Penguin Books, 2011), 180.
[13] Doxey, Denise M. "Nephthys," in The Ancient Gods Speak: A Guide to Egyptian Religion, edited by Donald Redford. (Oxford University Press, 2002), 276.
[14] Leitz, Christian, ed. *Lexicon der Aegyptischen Goetter und Goetterbezeichnungen* (LAGG, OLA 129, Band 8). (Peeters, 2003), 287.
[15] Leitz, Christian, ed. *Lexicon der Aegyptischen Goetter und Goetterbezeichnungen*. (LAGG, OLA 129, Band 8). (Peeters, 2003), 289.
[16] Levai, Jessica. Aspects of the Goddess Nephthys, 184-185.

Hwt or *Het* means "House."[17] There are other translations of the name of the goddess. Jessica Levai within her dissertation *Aspects of the Goddess Nephthys, Especially During the Graeco-Roman Period in Egypt* goes into further detail about the goddess's name. One possibility cited by Levai is "That Which Rules Inside the House."[18] Other possible translations for *Hwt* are temple, sky, grave, and palace.

Another translation of her name is "Lady of the Temple." Due to her name, Erik Hornung believes that Nebet Het may be the patron of all temples.[19] She and Aset represent the flagstaffs outside of temples as a boundary against evil. Nebet Het herself is also at the "corners or ends" of shrines to protect the holy place itself.[20] This would link her function and her name as "Lady of the Temple."

One possible translation is due to Nebet Het's association with Set. Her name would then be "Lady of the Ombite [Set]" as a possible translation. Given that Hethert means "House of Heru" alluding to the sky god Heru, Nebet Het's name can mean "Lady of the Sky." Since Set is god of thunderstorms, then Nebet Het's "sky" would be during a storm. Given Nebet Het's late association with Set, this association is unlikely.[21]

Due to her association with death, the *Hwt* in Nebet Het's name could mean "tomb" or "grave." Thus, her name could translate as "Lady of the Grave," "Lady of the Funerary Chapel," and "Lady of the Tomb."[22] Levai states that these words are from compound words such as *hwt-ka* for "tomb" and *hwt-netjer* for "temple." While they are a possible translation of her name, Levai thinks there is a better option.[23]

As Aset and Nebet Het were complimentary to each other from early in the Pyramid Texts onward, maybe their names were also complimentary. Aset means "throne" and as Nebet Het's glyph is a depiction of a building, then as Nebet Het as a royal goddess like her sister, then Nebet Het could mean "Lady of the Palace."[24] As Aset was

---

[17] Levai, Jessica. Aspects of the Goddess Nephthys, 20-21.
[18] Levai, Jessica. Aspects of the Goddess Nephthys, 24.
[19] Levai, Jessica. Aspects of the Goddess Nephthys, 26; and Hornung, Erik. Conceptions of God in Ancient Egypt: the One and the Many, trans. John Baines (Cornell University Press, 1996), 186.
[20] Wilkinson, Richard H. The Complete Gods and Goddesses of Ancient Egypt. (Thames and Hudson, 2003), 160.
[21] Levai, Jessica. Aspects of the Goddess Nephthys, 30-32 and 34.
[22] Levai, Jessica. Aspects of the Goddess Nephthys, 27-29.
[23] Levai, Jessica. Aspects of the Goddess Nephthys, 35.

goddess of the throne, Nebet Het would be the goddess of the royal residence. According to Levai, all of these possible translations contain elements of Nebet Het's attributes such as a goddess of royalty, a goddess of mourning and funerals, and a goddess associated with religion.[25] According to Levai, "Mistress of the Palace" is the best translation of Nebet Het's name.[26]

During the Late and Greco-Roman periods, there are spelling variations of Nebet Het's name. There is the three-stepped throne called the *ast* throne, which forms the name of Aset. There is a depiction of Nebet Het's name where her basket (Nebet) is placed upon the throne glyph (Aset). Here the throne glyph can be a determinative for "to destroy" or "destruction," so her name could be read as "Lady of Destruction" (*Nbt htm*).[27] It is likely that this is a depiction of Aset-Nebet Het, but Nebet Het's name is spelled with her usual *hwt* glyph in the text on the stela.[28]

There is one instance in which Nebet Het's name is written with the glyph for "gold" (*nbw*). This is from a coffin from the Greco-Roman period.[29] Another variation of her name is when it is spelled with the word for arm (*rmn*), which can be found at the Temple of Edfu. Both spellings of her name with gold and arm are most likely a phonetic form of wordplay, rather than a different meaning of her name due to the fact that the words were still pronounced the same.[30]

Goddess of Royal Power

Nebet Het, like her sister Aset, is associated with royal lineage and royal power. Jessica Levai presents evidence of Nebet Het's royal role through a few of her epithets, "Lady of the White Crown, Ruler of the Red Crown" and "Excellent Ruler in the Office of Wesir."[31] Other epithets listed by Levai are "Princess of All the Gods" and "She Who Commands the Ennead."[32] Levai also notes that Nebet Het was depicted as one who granted a good reign and royal power to the King.[33]

---

[24] Levai, Jessica. Aspects of the Goddess Nephthys, 20-21, 24-25, and 45.
[25] Levai, Jessica. Aspects of the Goddess Nephthys, 24 and 45.
[26] Levai, Jessica. Aspects of the Goddess Nephthys, 24 and 45.
[27] Levai, Jessica. Aspects of the Goddess Nephthys, 37-38 and 45-46.
[28] Levai, Jessica. Aspects of the Goddess Nephthys, 37-38 and 45-46.
[29] Levai, Jessica. Aspects of the Goddess Nephthys, 39.
[30] Levai, Jessica. Aspects of the Goddess Nephthys, 40-41.
[31] Levai, Jessica. Aspects of the Goddess Nephthys, 51. From the Temples of Bigga and Edfu, respectively.

Also, Nebet Het is related to the family of Gods associated with royalty, namely Aset, Wesir, and Heru-sa-Aset. So, she in turn would have to be of a royal lineage herself.[34]

The Grave and Tomb

According to Egyptologist Tamara L. Siuda, Nebet Het along with her son Yinepu was associated with "death and the deceased, tombs, embalming, and liminality."[35] She protects the sacred ground of the dead. This patronage includes her being offended if someone were to desecrate a grave. A passage in the Pyramid Texts states that one who desecrates a grave will have offended Nebet Het.[36]

As caretaker of the dead, she attends to the deceased, yet she also cares for those who are left behind to grieve and tend the graves.[37] In the Underworld, she was identified with the Night Bark and the linen wrappings which trapped the deceased.[38] She is depicted standing at the head of the mummy while Aset stands at the feet.[39]

This goddess helped the dead cross over to the other side.[40] In the Pyramid Texts she is even compared to the afterlife itself: "the West calls to you as Nebet Het."[41] She was also referred to as the "East Wind" when opening up the sky for the deceased in the Book of the Dead.[42]

---

[32] Levai, Jessica. Aspects of the Goddess Nephthys, 52. From the Temples of Hibis and Edfu, respectively.
[33] Levai, Jessica. Aspects of the Goddess Nephthys, 52-53.
[34] Levai, Jessica. Aspects of the Goddess Nephthys, 51.
[35] Siuda, Tamara L. Nebt Het: Lady of the House. (Imhotep Kemetic Orthodox Seminary, 2004), 17.
[36] Faulkner, R.O. The Ancient Egyptian Pyramid Texts. (Oxford University Press, 1998), 201. Pyramid Text 534; and Siuda, Tamara L. Nebt Het: Lady of the House, (Stargazer Design, 2010 Second Edition), 7.
[37] Siuda, Tamara L. Nebt Het: Lady of the House. (2010), 3.
[38] Faulkner, R.O. The Ancient Egyptian Pyramid Texts, 43. Pyramid Text 216; and Hart, George. The Dictionary of Egyptian Gods and Goddesses (Routledge and Kegan Paul Inc, 1986), 136.
[39] Doxey, Denise M. "Nephthys," in The Ancient Gods Speak, 276.
[40] Faulkner, R.O. The Ancient Egyptian Pyramid Texts, 213 and 289. Pyramid Texts 553 and 676.
[41] Siuda, Tamara L. Nebt Het: Lady of the House, (2010), 3, quoting Pyramid Text 720.
[42] Allen, T.G. The Book of the Dead or Going Forth By Day: Ideas of the Ancient Egyptians Concerning the Hereafter as Expressed in Their Own Terms. (Studies of Ancient Oriental Civilization #37). (University of Chicago Press, 1974), 157. Spell 161.

Nebet Het also has control over ghosts called *mut* (plural *muuet*).[43] An amulet of Nebet Het is used to summon a spirit in a Demotic papyri spell: "If you wish to bring in a dead man, you put ass's dung with an amulet of Nebet Het on the brazier. He will come." To send the spirit away it states to put ape's dung on the brazier while reciting, "Go well, go in joy!"[44]

Nebet Het is the transition between life to death and death to life. She also comforts those in mourning. She guards the sarcophagus and the canopic jars.[45]

She was not only the goddess of the dead; she also aided the living with her protective powers and comforting the bereaved.

Kherseket and Merkhetes

Two of Nebet Het's distinguished epithets are her titles of *Kherseket* (She Who Wipes Away Tears) and *Merkhetes* (She Whose Flame is Painful).[46] These two titles describe her dual functions as both a comforter of the bereaved and as a fierce protector.

Within an inscription from the Temple of Dendera, Nebet Het is described as a primordial being, who is exalted among goddesses. Her title "Kherseket," or "She Who Wipes Away Tears," is mentioned here before her associations with love and being a unique lady among the gods:

> Excellent in Dendera, Primordial and Venerable among the Goddesses.
> Kherseket, Whose love is sweet, Unique among the Ennead.[47]

---

[43] Siuda, Tamara L. Nebt Het: Lady of the House. (2010), 7.
[44] Betz, Hans Dieter. The Greek Magical Papyri: In Translation including the Demotic Spells, Vol 1. (University of Chicago Press, 1996), 200.; F. Ll. Griffith and Herbert Thompson, ed. The Leyden Papyrus: An Egyptian Magical Book. (Dover Publications, 1974), 37; and Siuda, Tamara L. Nebt Het: Lady of the House. (2010), 6-7.
[45] Doxey, Denise M. "Nephthys," in The Ancient Gods Speak, 276; and Siuda, Tamara L. Nebt Het: Lady of the House, (2010), 12.
[46] El-Saghir, Mohamed and Dominique Valbelle. "Komir," 164-166; and Leitz, Christian, ed. Lexikon der Aegyptischen Goetter und Goetterbezeichnungen (LAGG, OLA 129, Band 8). (Peeters, 2003), 292. Thank you to Tamara L. Siuda for the English translation of Kherseket.
[47] Cauville, Sylvie. Dendara II: Traduction. (Peeters, 1999), 181. Translated by Chelsea Bolton.

As a primordial goddess, she also has associations with the Akhet-Cow (or the Celestial Cow) and the goddess Nebetuu.[48]

Nebet Het is called Merkhetes in conjunction with Aset as Shentayet. At the Temple of Edfu, there is a text that states:

> His Two Sisters are with him (Osiris)
> They order His protection,
> It is Aset with Nebet Het,
> It is Shentayet with Merkhetes
> Who exalt the perfection of their brother.[49]

The Two Sisters in their aspects as *Shentayet* (Widow) and Merkhetes (She Whose Flame is Painful) protect Wesir.

Aset-Shentayet has the epithets such as "Mother of God, Sovereign, Lady of the Sky, Mistress of the City, Daughter of Geb, and Daughter of Nut."[50] Cauville states that Nebet Het's epithet of Merkhetes describes a fierce, dangerous, and fiery form of the goddess as protector of Wesir.[51]

According to Cauville, Nebet Het Merkhetes has an additional epithet that can be translated two ways. The epithet is "She Whose Heart is Painful" (*mr ib*); its two translations are "One Who Suffers the Aching Heart" and "the Painful Hearts."[52] Nebet Het Merkhetes is also called "Daughter of Nut."[53]

Another inscription describes her as:

> Nebet Het, Sister of God
> Who Resides in Edfu;
> Merkhetes, Who protects Her brother.[54]

---

[48] Leitz, Christian, ed. Lexikon der Aegyptischen Goetter und Goetterbezeichnungen (Band 8), 292 and 287; 281.
[49] Cauville, Sylvie. "Chentayt et Merkhetes, des avatars d'Isis et Nephthys." In Bulletin de l'Institut Français d'Archéologie Orientale Le Caire 81 (1981): 23.
[50] Cauville, Sylvie. "Chentayt et Merkhetes, des avatars d'Isis et Nephthys," 23-24.
[51] Cauville, Sylvie. "Chentayt et Merkhetes, des avatars d'Isis et Nephthys," 24.
[52] Cauville, Sylvie. "Chentayt et Merkhetes, des avatars d'Isis et Nephthys," 24; footnote 3.
[53] Cauville, Sylvie. "Chentayt et Merkhetes, des avatars d'Isis et Nephthys," 37.
[54] Cauville, Sylvie. "Chentayt et Merkhetes, des avatars d'Isis et Nephthys," 28.

Nebet Het *Kherseket* is the goddess who comforts the bereaved and anyone who suffers any loss. She is the mourner of Wesir. Nebet Het *Kherseket* is the comforter and the refuge for the suffering of both the Gods and the people.

Nebet Het *Merkhetes* is the fierce goddess who spits fire at the enemies of Wesir. She is also the one who personifies the aching heart of those who suffer. She is a protective goddess and one who looks out for those who grieve.

Consort of Wesir

According to Levai, in the *Song of Aset and Nebet Het* (4th century BCE) and the *Lamentations of Aset and Nebet Het*, Nebet Het along with Her sister Aset are named as the "Two Women," "Two Wives," and "Two Widows" of Wesir. Their son Heru is called the "Sisters' child," which would make both goddesses his mother.[55] At the Temple of Philae, Aset is called the "First Wife" of Wesir.[56] Levai asserts with the evidence given here, that Nebet Het had a relationship with Wesir that was not an illegitimate one. According to Levai, Aset and Nebet Het could be co-wives of Wesir, since in the ancient Egyptian culture, kings could have multiple wives.[57] The Egyptian and Hellenistic cultures had different mores about marriage and women's roles.[58] So for Plutarch, Wesir having more than one wife would make his relations with Nebet Het an affair, rather than those of a King with his consort.

According to Plutarch, Nebet Het is the mother of Yinepu with Wesir as the father. However, Plutarch's mention of the relations between Wesir (Osiris) and Nebet Het within the *Iside et Osiride* is only alluded to, and not specifically mentioned within the text itself.

During the Roman Period, Nebet Het was called the "Mother of Heru" and the "Divine Wife of Wennefer (Wesir)" at the Temple of Komir.[59] The only actual mention of the affair between Nebet Het and Wesir comes from an Old Coptic love spell from the 4th century, where Aset is telling her "Father Thoth" about the affair.[60]

---

[55] Levai, Jessica. Aspects of the Goddess Nephthys, 147 and 157-160.
[56] Levai, Jessica. Aspects of the Goddess Nephthys, 154.
[57] Levai, Jessica. Aspects of the Goddess Nephthys, 165.
[58] Levai, Jessica. Aspects of the Goddess Nephthys, 165.
[59] Levai, Jessica. Aspects of the Goddess Nephthys, 160; and El-Saghir, Mohamed and Dominique Valbelle. "Komir," 164-166.
[60] Levai, Jessica. Aspects of the Goddess Nephthys, 161-162.

There is also the instance where in a Greek papyrus, the Warren Magical Papyrus, Wesir "fell in love with his own sister, Senephthys." Senephthys here could be a Greek name for the *dyad*, or the composite deity, of Aset-Nebet Het (Isis-Nephthys).[61]

Nebet Het was a mourner of Wesir and his protector. Given the evidence, it is possible that Nebet Het is also a consort of Wesir.

The Nile Flood and Protector of Her Brother

As a mourner and possible consort of Wesir, Nebet Het had a part in the flooding of the Nile, the rain, and the fertility of the land. She joined Aset in her search for Wesir and helped rejuvenate him.[62]

Along with Aset, she was one of the *Djerety* or "Two Kites."[63] She was known as the *Djeret Nedjeset* "Lesser Kite" and was represented by a woman in the ritual for the preparation and burial of the dead.[64]

Nebet Het has epithets in which she is described as one who protects Wesir. Levai lists a few of them as:

> Protector of Her Brother's Flesh
> Protector of the King in the Great House of Heru
> Protector of Her Brother[65]

She also protects her brother Wesir with flame with epithets such as "She Who Burns the Enemy of Her Brother Wesir" and "Who sends flame around Her Brother."[66]

The Two Sisters

Aset and Nebet Het are twins; they mirror each other in their actions or functions. They can even be a *dyad*, two deities who act as one or as a complimentary pair. They even fuse to form the syncretic deity Aset-Nebet Het.[67]

---

[61] Levai, Jessica. Aspects of the Goddess Nephthys, 174.
[62] Levai, Jessica. Aspects of the Goddess Nephthys, 3.
[63] Wilkinson, Richard. Symbol and Magic in Egyptian Art. (Thames and Hudson, 1994), 199.
[64] Faulkner, R.O. Concise Dictionary of Middle Egyptian. (Griffith Institute Oxford, 1969, 2002), 323.
[65] Levai, Jessica. Aspects of the Goddess Nephthys, 56.
[66] Levai, Jessica. Aspects of the Goddess Nephthys, 59.
[67] Levai, Jessica. Aspects of the Goddess Nephthys, 151-152.

They are goddesses of royal power, the solar power and the flood of the Nile. They are sisters, wives and widows of Wesir. They share many epithets such as:

>
> Two Cobras/Two Uraei[68]
> Two Cows[69]
> Two Female Companions[70]
> Two Goddesses[71]
> Two Great Goddesses of the West[72]
> Two Kites[73]
> Two Mourners[74]
> Two Sisters[75]
> Two Songstresses[76]
> Two Widows[77]
> Two Women[78]

The throne which is Aset's name glyph is the throne of kings. There is a second throne called the *hwt* throne which is a throne with a rectangle in it resembling the *hwt* glyph.[79] Just as the two goddesses

---

[68] Allen, T.G. The Book of the Dead or Going Forth By Day, 28. Spell 17:6.
[69] Dennis, James Teackle. Burden of Isis: Being the Laments of Isis and Nephthys. (J. Murray, 1918), 31.
[70] Allen, T.G. The Book of the Dead or Going Forth By Day, 59. Spell 64; Shennum, David. English-Egyptian Index of Faulkner's Concise Dictionary of Middle Egyptian. (Undena Publications, 1977), 164; and Faulkner, R.O., Concise Dictionary of Middle Egyptian, 151.
[71] Levai, Jessica. Aspects of the Goddess Nephthys, 52.
[72] Piankoff, Alexandre. Tomb of Ramesses VI: Bollingen I. (University of Princeton Press, 1954), 52; and Leitz, Christian, ed. Lexikon der Aegyptischen Goetter und Goetterbezeichnungen (Band 8), 287.
[73] Faulkner, R.O. Concise Dictionary of Middle Egyptian, 323; and Zabkar, Louis V. Hymns to Isis in Her Temple at Philae. (University Press of New England, 1988), 131.
[74] Levai, Jessica. Aspects of the Goddess Nephthys, 48.
[75] Lesko, Barbara. The Great Goddesses of Egypt. (University of Oklahoma Press, 1999), 173; Lichtheim, Miriam. Ancient Egyptian Literature Vol 3: The Late Period, (University of California Press, 1980), 117 and 120; and Levai, Jessica. Aspects of the Goddess Nephthys, 159.
[76] Levai, Jessica. Aspects of the Goddess Nephthys, 159.
[77] Levai, Jessica. Aspects of the Goddess Nephthys, 159.
[78] Levai, Jessica. Aspects of the Goddess Nephthys, 159.
[79] Levai, Jessica. Aspects of the Goddess Nephthys, 24.

complement each other, so too would their association with the throne. The *ast* throne was associated with Wesir and the *hwt* throne was associated with Heru.[80] Since Aset is the *ast* throne and Nebet Het is associated with the *hwt* throne, the duality of the Two Sisters would be mirrored in both the Two Lands (*tawy*) and the Two Ladies (*nebty*).[81] Both of them are associated with living and dead kings and the royal power of the throne.

Aset and Nebet Het are both mothers of Heru. Levai cites an excerpt from the Pyramid Texts where Aset and Nebet Het are named the ones who "conceive" and "beget" Heru, respectively.[82] There is also a relief on a Temple wall with Nebet Het and Geb, where Nebet Het is called "She Who Puts Her Son on the Throne."[83] At the Temple of Edfu, both goddesses are depicted giving Heru the two crowns.[84] These illustrate that the Two Sisters both gave birth to Heru and legitimized his royal power through the thrones and crowns.

As the sisters of Wesir, Aset and Nebet Het both search for, find, and mourn their brother.

Both goddesses aid Ra during his nightly journey into the Duat to slay the serpent Apep. Aset and Nebet assist in the rising and setting of the sun.[85]

They represent the flagstaffs of temples.[86] They stand at the foot and the head of both a woman giving birth and the mummy. They aid in the transformation of the deceased into a Justified Ancestor.

Aset and Nebet Het were both Ladies of Heaven, Earth, and the Underworld. They share the epithet *Nebet Amenti* or "Lady of the West." They guide, guard, and nourish the deceased. They are both associated with the Celestial Cow, the star-filled sky, and the ancestors.

Like Aset, Nebet Het was associated with healing. Nebet Het is mentioned in a Demotic papyrus spell for a fever. "Doth Nebet Het cease to give health?"[87] This would imply she would be able to cure or

---

[80] Levai, Jessica. Aspects of the Goddess Nephthys, 24-25.
[81] Levai, Jessica. Aspects of the Goddess Nephthys, 48.
[82] Levai, Jessica. Aspects of the Goddess Nephthys, 53. Pyramid Text 1154.
[83] Levai, Jessica. Aspects of the Goddess Nephthys, 54.
[84] Levai, Jessica. Aspects of the Goddess Nephthys, 54-55.
[85] Wilkinson, Richard H. Symbol and Magic in Egyptian Art, 159.
[86] Wilkinson, Richard H. The Complete Gods and Goddesses of Ancient Egypt. (Thames and Hudson, 2003), 160.
[87] Griffith, F.Ll. and Herbert Thompson, ed. The Leyden Papyrus: An Egyptian Magical Book, 205.

prevent illness. Both goddesses are associated with magic and healing. They share the epithet "Great of Magic" and "Sorceress."[88]

Aset and Nebet Het have the epithet Eye of Ra. They are both lioness, leopard/panther, and cobra goddesses. They are associated with the Distant Goddess myth, are the Daughters of Ra, and are the fierce protectors of Ra.

Nebet Het was the caretaker and nurse of Heru.[89] In a myth, Nebet Het, along with Aset, helped during a king's childbirth. She stands at the head, assisting the mother, while Aset helps deliver the baby.[90] The Two Sisters help protect the throne and the canopic jars.[91] According to Witt, sistra found in Pompeii had two sides: one for Aset, which symbolized creation or life; and the other for Nebet Het, which symbolized death or the end.[92]

Aset and Nebet Het have much in common and often mirror each other. They are royal ladies, healers, and magicians; and protectors of Ra, Heru, Wesir, and the ancient Egyptian people.

Uraeus, Eye of Ra, and Warlike Goddess

Nebet Het was associated with the Uraeus at least by the New Kingdom. Levai speculates that by the time of the Graeco-Roman period, Nebet Het became more pronounced as a ferocious goddess.[93]

Nebet Het has a few epithets which describe her as the Uraeus and Eye of Ra. Some of them are:

> Eye of Ra
> August or Noble Uraeus
> Beautiful Uraeus
> She Who is on the Head of Her Brother
> She Who Sends Flame Against Those Who Attack Her Majesty[94]
> She Who is on the Head of Her Father

---

[88] Levai, Jessica. Aspects of the Goddess Nephthys, 173; and Leitz, Christian, ed. Lexikon der Aegyptischen Goetter und Goetterbezeichnungen (Band 8), 287.
[89] Hornung, Erik. Conceptions of God in Ancient Egypt, 144.
[90] Meeks, Dimitri and Christine Farvard-Meeks. Daily Life of the Egyptian Gods. Translated by G. M. Goshgarian. (Cornell University Press, 1996), 121.
[91] Levai, Jessica. Aspects of the Goddess Nephthys, 65.
[92] Witt, R.E. Isis in the Ancient World. (Johns Hopkins University Press, 1997), 34.
[93] Levai, Jessica. Aspects of the Goddess Nephthys, 47 and 56.
[94] Levai, Jessica. Aspects of the Goddess Nephthys, 57-58. These are from the Temples of Edfu and Philae.

Daughter of Ra[95]
She Who burns the enemies of Ra[96]
Who Sends Her Flame Against the Rebels[97]

Nebet Het was an Eye of Ra goddess. The Eye Goddess is a ferocious leopard, lioness, or cobra goddess who protects Ra and all of Egypt from enemies. Nebet Het uses flame, weapons, and magic to destroy the enemies. She also protects Wesir and Heru with these same methods.

As an Eye of Ra, Nebet Het is associated with the Distant Goddess Myth. Nit and Anuket were forms of Nebet Het for the Distant Goddess Myth at the Temple of al-Qal'a.[98] As an Eye of Ra, Nebet Het can be associated with the cycle of the sun, the star Sopdet, solar eclipses, the Morning Star, and the full moon. The Eye Goddess is associated with flame, sunlight, and starlight – in restorative, protective, and destructive capacities.[99]

She is a protector of Wesir and Heru. She guards the sanctity of temples and wards against evil forces. Her other warlike epithets are "Strong Armed"[100] and "Strong of Power."[101] In a spell from the Pyramid Texts, Nebet Het favored those who restrained an adversary.[102] At the Temple of Dendera, Nebet Het is shown holding a lotus scepter with three arrows.[103] Levai calls her the "female counterpart" of Set due to her warlike nature.[104]

Wife of Set

The earliest textual evidences of the marriage of Nebet Het and Set are the Metternich Stela, the Papyrus of Imhotep, and Plutarch's *Iside et Osiride*.[105] Nebet Het and Set were worshipped together in

---

[95] Levai, Jessica. Aspects of the Goddess Nephthys, 57-58; El-Saghir, Mohamed and Dominique Valbelle. "Komir," 164-166.
[96] Levai, Jessica. Aspects of the Goddess Nephthys, 58. From the Temple of Edfu.
[97] Levai, Jessica. Aspects of the Goddess Nephthys, 59.
[98] Levai, Jessica. Aspects of the Goddess Nephthys, 61-62.
[99] Pinch, Geraldine. Egyptian Mythology: A Guide to the Gods, Goddesses and Traditions of Ancient Egypt. (Oxford University Press, 2004), 128-130 and 131-134.
[100] Levai, Jessica. Aspects of the Goddess Nephthys, 63.
[101] Levai, Jessica. Aspects of the Goddess Nephthys, 64.
[102] Siuda, Tamara L. Nebt Het: Lady of the House. (2010), 6: ref. Pyramid Text 222.
[103] Levai, Jessica. Aspects of the Goddess Nephthys, 16, 27 and 64-66.
[104] Levai, Jessica. Aspects of the Goddess Nephthys, 104.
[105] Levai, Jessica. Aspects of the Goddess Nephthys, 83-84.

Oxyrhynchus during the New Kingdom.[106] In the Metternich Stela, Nebet Het is described as "In the House of Set," which would mean they are married.[107] There is a papyrus in which Nebet Het says she had a child by Set: "Remember what I did for you, the child of Set, I left to save you."[108]

They are mentioned in some magical papyri as being either married or a couple. Levai states:

> The later evidence especially suggests that while Nephthys's marriage to Set was a part of Egyptian mythology, it was not a part of the myth of the murder and resurrection of Osiris. She was not paired with Set the villain, but with Set's other aspect, the benevolent figure who was the killer of Apophis. This was the aspect of Set worshiped in the western oases during the Roman period, where he is depicted with Nephthys as co-ruler.[109]

She is often paired with him especially in the Dakhla Oasis area during the Roman Period. They are given offerings together in the Deir al-Hagar temple. Nebet Het is portrayed as a woman with the crown of her glyph resting on top of the sundisk surrounded by horns resting on top of the vulture headdress., while Set is depicted with the head of a falcon wearing the Double Crown.[110] Another depiction has Nebet Het in the vulture headdress with a sundisk between two cow horns; her name glyph sits on top of the sundisk, and she has two plumes. Set is depicted with a falcon head with the "double crown, ram's horns, a sundisk and two *uraeii*, both with their own sundisks."[111]

Set in the Oases is depicted as destroying evil, defending Ra, and slaying Apep. He is depicted slaying scorpions and serpents, two symbols of harmful forces. Nebet Het is his consort here, especially in

---

[106] Levai, Jessica. Aspects of the Goddess Nephthys, 113.
[107] Levai, Jessica. Aspects of the Goddess Nephthys, 82. The Metternich Stela dates from the 30th Dynasty.
[108] Levai, Jessica. Aspects of the Goddess Nephthys, 89.
[109] Levai, Jessica. "Nephthys and Seth: Anatomy of a Mythical Marriage." Paper presented at the 58th Annual Meeting of the American Research Center in Egypt, Wyndham Toledo Hotel, Toledo, Ohio, April 20, 2007. It is on page 64 in the Abstract and Programs. http://www.allacademic.com/meta/p176897_index.html
[110] Levai, Jessica. Aspects of the Goddess Nephthys, 107.
[111] Levai, Jessica. Aspects of the Goddess Nephthys, 108.

her role as an averter of evil.[112] In an inscription from Dakhla Oasis, Set is called "Set, Great of Strength, the Great God, Lord of the Oasis." Nebet Het is called, "the Great..." and the rest of her inscription is illegible. In another temple in the Oasis, Nebet Het is called "Mistress of Mut el-Kharab, Mistress of the Gods, Who resides in Deir el-Hagar." A slightly damaged inscription from the same temple in Mut el-Kharab says "Set, Lord of Mut el-Kharab, He who stabs the Apophis-Snake."[113]

There is a goddess statue which was found in the Temple of Set at Deir el-Hagar. The statue has only a small inscription on it and the particular goddess has not been identified, but since it was found in the Temple of Set, many believe this to be Nebet Het. The inscription reads, "Eye of Ra, Mistress of All the Gods, May She give a long life-span, and a high old age...to the Priest of Set, Penbast."[114] These epithets could belong to Nebet Het.

Associations with Other Goddesses

Egyptologist Tamara L. Siuda notes that Nebet Het is heavily associated with Nit (Neith) and Seshat. In her book, *Nebt-Het, Lady of the House*, Siuda gives evidence for connections between these three goddesses,[115] one of which is that these goddesses were connected in the texts of the Temple of Esna.[116]

Seshat

Seshat is the patron goddess of writing, architecture, mathematics, astrology, astronomy, record-keeping, book-keeping, building, knowledge, and libraries. She is the patron of the "stretching of the cord" ritual that was done before temples were built. She is often depicted as a woman wearing a panther-skin dress, holding a stylus and a reed pen. The spots of the panther represent stars and the night sky; this association makes Seshat the goddess of time, astronomy, and the dead. Her head is adorned with a seven-pointed star with two horns pointed downward. The two horns used to be a crescent moon. She is oftentimes the daughter or wife of Djehuty (Thoth).

---

[112] Levai, Jessica. Aspects of the Goddess Nephthys, 106-107.
[113] Levai, Jessica. Aspects of the Goddess Nephthys, 107-108.
[114] Levai, Jessica. Aspects of the Goddess Nephthys, 111.
[115] Siuda, Tamara L. Nebt Het: Lady of the House. (2010), 8-11.
[116] Siuda, Tamara L. Nebt Het: Lady of the House. (2010), 11.

Within both the Pyramid and Coffin Texts, Nebet Het is identified with Seshat as Nebet Het-Seshat: "Nebet Het has collected all your members for you in her name of Seshat, Lady of Builders."[117] According to Siuda, this passage from the Pyramid Texts "blatantly" mentions Seshat as a form of Nebet Het.[118] And in the Coffin Texts, again:

> (O Name of Deceased Person),
> Heru protects you,
> He causes Nebet Het to hold you together,
> To create you in Her Name of Seshat, Mistress of Potters
> She is a Great Lady, Great of Life in the Night-boat,
> Who raises Heru up.[119]

Nebet Het is given titles associated with books, pottery, and builders: "Lady of Books," "Lady of Builders," and "Mistress of Potters."[120] Nebet Het and Seshat share other epithets and functions such as "Lady of the Library" and "Lady of Writing."[121] Nebet Het was even identified with different aspects of Seshat, like Seshat, Seshat the Great, and the Small Seshat.[122] There is also a syncretic deity Nebet Het-Seshat.

Nit (Neith)

Nit is depicted as a woman wearing either of these two headdresses: the Red Crown of Lower Egypt, or a shield with two crossed arrows. She is an ancient Egyptian goddess who was associated through early Dynastic Queens via their names. She is a goddess

---

[117] Siuda, Tamara L. Nebt Het: Lady of the House. (2010), 14; and Faulkner, R.O. The Ancient Egyptian Pyramid Texts, 119. Pyramid Text 364.
[118] Siuda, Tamara L. Nebt Het: Lady of the House. (2010), 14; Wainwright, Gerald A. "Seshat and the Pharaoh," 30, 33, and 39.
[119] Translation by Siuda, Tamara L. in The Ancient Egyptian Prayerbook. (Stargazer Design, 2009), 73.
[120] Faulkner, R.O. The Ancient Egyptian Pyramid Texts, 119. Pyramid Text 364; and Siuda, Tamara L. Nebt Het: Lady of the House. (2010), 14; and Faulkner, R.O. The Ancient Egyptian Coffin Texts Vol 1-3. Translated by R.O. Faulkner. (Aris & Phillips, Ltd., 2004), 304. Coffin Text 778.
[121] Leitz, Christian, ed. Lexikon der Aegyptischen Goetter und Goetterbezeichnungen (Band 8), 286; and Siuda, Tamara L. Nebt Het: Lady of the House. (2010), 30.
[122] Leitz, Christian, ed. Lexikon der Aegyptischen Goetter und Goetterbezeichnungen (Band 8), 292.

associated with hunting, war, and the creation of the world; and as a guide and guard of the dead. She has an aspect as the Celestial Cow who is the creator goddess, the Mother of Ra, and a guide to the deceased. Nit is also an Eye of Ra, a Daughter of Ra, and a fierce lioness within the Myth of the Distant Goddess. She is a consort of Set and the Mother or Daughter of Sobek.[123] Nit is called the "Father of Fathers and Mother of Mothers" as a creator deity, emphasizing a more androgynous nature.[124]

Siuda mentions that there are some instances in the Pyramid Texts, the Book of the Dead, and the Demotic Magical Papyri where Nit takes the place of Nebet Het in scenes where one would expect to see Nebet Het. Also, both Nebet Het and Nit are associated with Set as wives and both are Eyes of Ra.[125] Levai also notes that Nebet Het may be identified with Nit.[126] There is a composite deity Nebet Het-Nit. Both goddesses guard the Canopic Jars.[127]

Within the Temple of el-Qal'a, Nebet Het has "distant" forms of herself in the forms of Nit and Anuket; these forms are connected to Nebet Het via the Myth of the Distant Goddess. These forms of Nebet Het are Nebet Het-Nit, Nebet Het-Anuket, or Nebet Het as Nit-Anuket. In this myth, the Goddess is enraged and leaves, transforming into a raging lioness and then later, she returns and is pacified with beer. These "distant" forms of Nebet Het are probably limited to that temple only.[128] Nebet Het is also identified with Anuket in other instances.[129]

Anuket (Anukis)

Anuket (Anukis, Anoukis) is a goddess of the Nile, a daughter of Khnum, and daughter of Satet (Satis). She is an Eye of Ra and a Daughter of Ra and is associated with bow and arrows. Her sacred animal is the gazelle. She is often depicted as a woman with a feather-

---

[123] Stadler, Martin Andreas. Théologie et culte au temple de Soknopaios: Etudes sur la Religion d'un Village Egyptien Pendant l'Epoque Romaine. (Cybele, 2017), 66.
[124] Lesko, Barbara. The Great Goddesses of Egypt, 61.
[125] Siuda, Tamara L. Nebt Het: Lady of the House. (2010), 13 and 23. Examples include Pyramid Text 577, Book of the Dead Spells 172s3 and 185k, and PDM xiv 260 (IX, 22).
[126] Levai, Jessica. Aspects of the Goddess Nephthys, 64-65 and 67-68.
[127] Siuda, Tamara L. Nebt Het: Lady of the House. (2010), 12.
[128] Levai, Jessica. Aspects of the Goddess Nephthys, 61-62.
[129] Griffiths, J. Gwyn. "Isis." In The Ancient Gods Speak, 171.

plumed headdress and was honored with Nebet Het in the Komir Temple.

Anuket can be syncretized with Nebet Het as Nebet Het-Anuket or Anuket-Nebet Het. Nebet Het's titles of "Kherseket" and "Kherseket, the Great" are also Anuket's.[130] Anuket-Nebet Het's titles in the Temple of Aswan are "Sister of God, the Beneficial Goddess, the Sovereign and Lady of Nubia."[131] At the Temple of Komir, Nebet Het can be honored as Nebet Het-Anuket or Nebet Het as Anuket.[132] Nebet Het can take the form of Anuket in the Distant Goddess myth at the Temple of el-Qal'a.

Hethert (Hathor)

Nebet Het shares some epithets and functions with the goddess Hethert. Hethert is the goddess of joy, love, beauty, motherhood, a creator goddess, a patron of the arts, music, dance, and prosperity, a goddess who guards the dead, and protector of the sun god. She is associated with the Celestial Cow, the cobra or Uraeus, the lioness, and the falcon. Hethert is also associated with the *menat*-necklace, the papyrus scepter, and the sistrum. She is the Distant Goddess, who transforms into a raging lioness and is called back to Egypt by one of the other gods. She transforms into Hethert and is placated with offerings and a procession along an *Isheru*-lake. Hethert can be syncretized with many goddesses such as Mut, Nut, Sekhmet, Tefnut, Aset, and Nebet Het.

Nebet Het shares epithets with Hethert such as "Daughter of Ra," "Mistress of Beer," and "Lady of Drunkenness." Nebet Het may share in Hethert's attributes of joy and the need to be placated with beer. Nebet Het was associated with the "Young Lioness."[133]

Siuda notes that the title of *Tasenetnofret* or "The Good Sister" is "shared by both Nebet Het and Hethert, joyous sistrum-goddesses of the city of Hut Sekhem (Classical Diaspolis Parva, modern Hiw)," and that both are consorts of Sobek-Heru worshipped at Kom Ombo.[134]

---

[130] Leitz, Christian, ed. Lexikon der Aegyptischen Goetter und Goetterbezeichnungen (Band 8), 124.
[131] Bresciani, E. and S. Pernigotti. Il tempio tolemaico di Isi ad Assuan. (Giardini Editori E. Stampatori, 1978), 117.
[132] Siuda, Tamara L. Nebt Het: Lady of the House. (2010), 8.
[133] Cauville, Sylvie. Dendara II: Traduction. (Peeters, 1999), 164-165. Translated by Chelsea Bolton.
[134] Siuda, Tamara L. Nebt Het: Lady of the House. (2010), 16-17.

Within the Temple of Dendera, Nebet Het is described as a goddess full of beauty and love:

> She is the Beautiful Woman, Whose love is sweet,
> With the Beautiful Face, Whose eyes are painted.[135]

She is also described as one who nourishes her child, and who provides milk for the country:

> She of Dendera…a Young Lioness, without Her Likeness…,
> Who rejuvenates Her child, Who feeds the country with Her milk.[136]

Nebet Het is associated with many of Hethert's attributes, including childrearing, beauty, love, and nourishment through milk. She is also associated with Hethert's more ferocious attributes as an Eye of Ra, a Lioness, Daughter of Ra, and the Lady of Drunkenness within the Myth of the Distant Goddess.

Both Nebet Het and Hethert have the title of *Nebet Amenti* or "Lady of the West." They can both be associated with the Ancestors, the Celestial Cow, the star Sopdet (Sirius), and as the Lady of Heaven and the Underworld.

Tefnut

Tefnut is the Daughter of Ra and the Sister and Wife of Shu, the god of wind and light. Tefnut is one of the goddesses in the Distant Goddess myth, an Eye of Ra, and a fierce lioness, and is placated with offerings at a processional with an *Isheru*-lake. In one creation myth, she is created by Ra-Atum or Atum as his first daughter, along with Shu as his first son. Tefnut is goddess of the sun, the solar Eye, moisture, and rain. She is the Mother of Nut and Geb, and Grandmother to all of Nut's children. Tefnut can be depicted as a lioness, or as a lioness-headed woman with a uraeus or with a sundisk and uraeus on top of her head.

---

[135] Cauville, Sylvie. Dendara II: Traduction, 162-163 and 164-165. Translated by Chelsea Bolton.

[136] Cauville, Sylvie. Dendara II: Traduction, 162-163 and 164-165. Translated by Chelsea Bolton. Feline here can be translated as Lioness. In ancient Egyptian, it is *hwnt*, specifically a young lioness. Thank you to Tamara L. Siuda for this clarification.

Levai notes that Nebet Het is identified with Tefnut in the Komir Hymn, and they share the epithet *Tasenetnofret* (Beautiful/Good Sister).[137]

Serqet (Serket, Selkis)

Serqet is a goddess depicted as a woman with a scorpion on her head, or in her zoomorphic form as a scorpion. Her name means "She Who Causes the Throat to Breathe." She is a goddess of healing and protection. She protected against venom, snakebite, scorpion stings, and other poisons and harmful creatures. She is an Eye of Ra, a Daughter of Ra, and a Protector of the Dead.

According to Wainwright, Nebet Het was associated with the scorpion goddess Serqet.[138] There is a composite deity Nebet Het-Serqet.[139] The Four Goddesses of the Canopic Jars are Aset, Nebet Het, Serqet, and Nit.[140] Nebet Het and Serqet both belong to this group of goddesses.

Sopdet (Sothis, Sirius)

Nebet Het is associated with Sopdet. In one inscription, she is called "Nebet Het the Great, Mistress of Women; Sopdet, Lady of Life of the Two Lands."[141] Through Nebet Het's association with the stellar cow goddesses Nebetuu and the Akhet-Cow (Celestial Cow), she can also be associated with Sopdet.[142] When Nebet Het is syncretized with Anuket, she can also be associated with Sopdet.[143]

---

[137] Levai, Jessica. Aspects of the Goddess Nephthys, 62; and El-Saghir, Mohamed and Dominique Valbelle. "Komir," 164-166.

[138] Wainwright, Gerald A. "Seshat and the Pharaoh." *The Journal of Egyptian Archaeology* 26, no. 1 (1941): 30.

[139] Leitz, Christian, ed. Lexikon der Aegyptischen Goetter und Goetterbezeichnungen (Band 8), 292.

[140] Siuda, Tamara L. Nebt Het: Lady of the House. (2010), 12.

[141] Wilkinson, John Gardner. The Manners and Customs of the Ancient Egyptians. Vol. 2. (J. Murray, 1878), 439; Bunsen, Christian Karl Josias, and Samuel Birch. Egypt's place in universal history: an historical investigation in five books. Vol. 1. (Longman, Brown, Green, and Longmans, 1848), 435; Arundale, Francis, and Joseph Bonomi. Gallery of antiquities selected from the British Museum. (J. Weale, 1842), 35. Object = British Museum Number EA8539, translated by Tamara L. Siuda.

[142] Leitz, Christian, ed. Lexikon der Aegyptischen Goetter und Goetterbezeichnungen (Band 8), 292 and 287, 281, entries for Nebetuu-Sopdet. Thank you to Tamara L. Siuda for additional interpretation and information.

[143] Leitz, Christian, ed. Lexikon der Aegyptischen Goetter und Goetterbezeichnungen

Nebet Het is associated with Sopdet as an Eye of Ra. The stellar cycle was analogous to the sun's cycle through the Eye Goddess myth.

Akhet Cow/Celestial Cow

Nebet Het is called the "Akhet Cow in Every District."[144] Like many other goddesses, Nebet Het is a heavenly cow goddess. The Akhet or Celestial Cow is creator goddess at the beginning of the world. She is mother of Ra, goddess of the star-filled night sky, and the Underworld goddess who greets the deceased.

Foreign Goddesses

Within the Greco-Roman periods, both Plutarch and Diodorus Siculus identify Nebet Het with Aphrodite, the Greek Goddess of Heavenly love, sex, war, the sea, and the harbor. The Greeks identified Hathor with Aphrodite.[145] Plutarch also calls Nebet Het *Teleute* or "end," and this can mean the "boundaries, the ends of the earth, and probably equated with the horizon."[146] Plutarch also identifies Nike, the Greek goddess of victory, with Nebet Het.[147] Within some Greek inscriptions, it is possible that the name *Neotera* is an epithet or by-name for Nebet Het.[148] Levai states that Nebet Het could also be identified with the Canaanite Goddess Anat.[149]

Cult Centers

Nebet Het was the chief divinity of Hut-Sekhem (Diospolis Parva), the capital of the 7th Nome of Upper Egypt, whose heraldic symbol was associated with the sistrum.[150] Her cult centers are Per Meru (Komir), Hut-Sekhem (Diospolis Parva), and Sepermeru. She had

---

(Band 8), 121 and 124.
[144] Leitz, Christian, ed. Lexikon der Aegyptischen Goetter und Goetterbezeichnungen (Band 8), 287.
[145] Levai, Jessica. Aspects of the Goddess Nephthys, 11-12.
[146] Levai, Jessica. Aspects of the Goddess Nephthys, 32.
[147] Levai, Jessica. Aspects of the Goddess Nephthys, 47.
[148] Bricault, Laurent, Miguel John Versluys, and Paul GP Meyboom. Nile into Tiber: Egypt in the Roman World: Proceedings of the 3rd International Conference of Isis Studies, Leiden, May 11-14 2005. (Brill, 2006), 25-26.
[149] Levai, Jessica. Aspects of the Goddess Nephthys, 64-65 and 67-68.
[150] Siuda, Tamara L. Nebt Het: Lady of the House. (2010), 8.

chapels at Heliopolis, Behbeit el-Hagar, el-Qal'a, Antaeopolis, Dendera,[151] and Edfu.[152]

In the Roman period, Nebet Het was honored along with Set in the Dakhla and Kharga Oases. She was also honored at the Temple of Shanhur, with the epithet "Lady of Joy."[153]

Sacred Symbols

Nebet Het's animals are the kite, hawk, cobra, falcon, and ibis.[154] Some of her other sacred animals are the duck, the panther or leopard, the female dog, the hippopotamus, the female donkey, the Akhet-cow or Celestial Cow, the black kite, the tilapia, and the dolphin.[155] At the Temple of Dendera, Nebet Het was associated with the "Young Lioness."[156]

Nebet Het was associated with the *tyet* amulet in conjunction with "resurrection and eternal life."[157] She is also associated with the sistrum. According to Baring and Cashford, Nebet Het's symbols were the dark moon and twilight.[158]

Nebet Het's Images and Depictions

She is often depicted as a young woman wearing her name in glyphs (a basket atop a house glyph,)[159] or as a woman with a vulture headdress and a sundisk with horns as well as her name glyph.[160] She is

---

[151] Siuda, Tamara L. Nebt Het: Lady of the House. (2010), 8.
[152] Siuda, Tamara L. The Ancient Egyptian Daybook. (Stargazer Design, 2016), 217 = pWilbour, Dynasty 20; LA, Edfu.
[153] Willems, Harco, and Filip Coppens, Marleen De Meyer and Peter Dils. The Temple of Shanhur: Volume 1. (Peeters, 2003), 23 and 28.
[154] Doxey, Denise M. "Nephthys," in The Ancient Gods Speak, 276; Wilkinson, Richard H. Symbol and Magic in Egyptian Art, 12; Witt, R.E. Isis in the Ancient World, 30; and Wilkinson, Richard. Reading Egyptian Art. (Thames and Hudson, 1992), 89.
[155] Leitz, Christian, ed. Lexikon der Aegyptischen Goetter und Goetterbezeichnungen (Band 8), 287.
[156] Cauville, Sylvie. Dendara II: Traduction, 164-165. Translated by Chelsea Bolton.
[157] Wilkinson, Richard. Reading Egyptian Art, 102.
[158] Baring, Anne and Jules Cashford. "Isis of Egypt: Queen of Heaven, Earth and the Underworld," in The Myth of the Goddess: Evolution of an Image. Anne Baring and Jules Cashford, ed. (Penguin, 1993), 235.
[159] Hart, George. The Dictionary of Egyptian Gods and Goddesses, 136.
[160] Levai, Jessica. Aspects of the Goddess Nephthys , 43.

also portrayed with wings on her outstretched arms or with a *rishi*, a feather patterned dress.[161] Nebet Het was depicted wearing the throne/basket glyph as her crown in some depictions from the Greco-Roman Period.[162]

Nebet Het also has some zoomorphic forms. She can be depicted as a black kite with her normal crown,[163] or as a serpent (uraeus) or ibis with her name glyph headdress. She is also pictured as a woman with a serpent's head with her name glyph crown.[164]

Conclusions

Nebet Het is a complex and multi-faceted goddess. Hopefully, this paper has shed some light on this elusive goddess. She is a guardian, a guide, and a protector. She is also a goddess of beauty and joy. Nebet Het is the fierce Eye of Ra, the Lioness, and the Cobra Goddess. She is the Celestial Cow – the Creator, the Star-filled Sky, and the Mother of Ra. She is the Mistress of the Palace, the Temple, the Home, and the Tomb. She is the mourner, consort, and widow of Wesir. She is the consort of Set and Mother of Yinepu. She is the Nile River and the rain that brings the flood. She is the star Sopdet, who announces the beginning of the year and the inundation. She is the Mistress of the Year and Lady of the Life-Span. She is the Lady of Books and Writing. She is the leopard, the black kite, the female dog, and the female donkey.

But most of all, She is as an inscription from the Temple of Edfu would attest:

> Nebet Het, Sister of God in Edfu,
> Effective One, Young One,
> Who is Great in Edfu,
> One with the Beautiful Face,
> Bright Eyes,
> Kind and Full of Love.[165]

---

[161] Doxey, Denise M. "Nephthys," in The Ancient Gods Speak, 276.
[162] Levai, Jessica. Aspects of the Goddess Nephthys, 37-38.
[163] Pyramid Text 532 (Faulkner, 199-200); and Doxey, Denise M. "Nephthys," in The Ancient Gods Speak, 276.
[164] Levai, Jessica. Aspects of the Goddess Nephthys, 42.
[165] Bergman, Jan. "Nephthys découverte dans un papyrus magique." In *Melanges Adolphe Gutbub*. (Institut d'égyptologie, Université Paul Valéry, 1984), 7.

Bibliography

1. Allen, T.G. *The Book of the Dead or Going Forth By Day: Ideas of the Ancient Egyptians concerning the hereafter as expressed in their own terms.* Oriental Institute of the University of Chicago, Studies in Ancient Oriental Civilization (SAOC) 37, 1974.
2. Arundale, Francis and J. Bonomi. *Gallery of antiquities selected from the British Museum.* J. Weale, 1842.
3. Baring, Anne and Jules Cashford. "Isis of Egypt: Queen of Heaven, Earth and the Underworld," In *The Myth of the Goddess: Evolution of an Image.* Anne Baring and Jules Cashford, eds. New York: Penguin, 1993, 225-272.
4. Betz, Hans Dieter. *The Greek Magical Papyri In Translation including the Demotic Spells, Vol 1.* University of Chicago Press, 1996.
5. Bergman, Jan. "Nephthys découverte dans un papyrus magique." In *Melanges Adolphe Gutbub.* Institut d'égyptologie Université Paul Valéry, 1984, 1-12.
6. Bresciani, E. and S. Pernigotti. *Il tempio tolemaico di Isi ad Assuan.* Pisa: Giardini Editori E. Stampatori, 1978.
7. Bricault, Laurent, Miguel John Versluys and Paul G.P. Meyboom. *Nile into Tiber: Egypt in the Roman World: Proceedings of the 3rd International Conference of Isis Studies, Leiden, May 11-14 2005.* Brill, 2006.
8. Bunsen, Christian Karl Josias and Samuel Birch. *Egypt's place in universal history: an historical investigation in five books.* Vol. 1. Longman, Brown, Green, and Longmans, 1848.
9. Cauville, Sylvie. *Dendara II: Traduction.* Leuven: Peeters, 1999.
10. Cauville, Sylvie. "Chentayt et Merkhetes, des avatars d'Isis et Nephthys." In *Bulletin de l'Institut Français d'Archéologie Orientale Le Caire (BIFAO)* 81 (1981), 21-40.
11. Dennis, James Teackle. *Burden of Isis: Being the Laments of Isis and Nephthys.* London: J. Murray, 1918.
12. Doxey, Denise M. "Nephthys." In *The Ancient Gods Speak: A Guide to Egyptian Religion.* Donald Redford, ed. New York: Oxford University Press, 2002, 275-276.
13. Faulkner, R.O. *The Ancient Egyptian Pyramid Texts.* London: Oxford University Press, 1998.
14. Faulkner, R.O. *The Ancient Egyptian Coffin Texts Vols 1-3.* England: Aris & Phillips, Ltd., 2004.

15. Faulkner, Raymond. *Concise Dictionary of Middle Egyptian*. London: Griffith Institute Oxford, 1972. Reprint, London: Butler and Tanner Ltd., 2002.
16. Grenier, Jean Claude. *Anubis Alexandrin et Romain Vol. 57*. Brill, 1977.
17. Griffith, F.Ll. and Herbert Thompson, eds. *The Leyden Papyrus: An Egyptian Magical Book*. New York: Dover Publications, 1974.
18. Griffiths, J. Gwyn. "Isis." In *The Ancient Gods Speak: A Guide to Egyptian Religion*. Donald Redford, ed. New York: Oxford University Press, 2002, 169-172.
19. Hart, George. *The Dictionary of Egyptian Gods and Goddesses*. New York: Routledge and Kegan Paul Inc., 1986.
20. Hornung, Erik. *Conceptions of God in Ancient Egypt: The One and the Many*. Translated by John Baines. Cornell University Press, 1996.
21. Leitz, Christian, ed. *Lexicon der Aegyptischen Goetter und Goetterbezeichnungen* (LAGG), (OLA 129, Band 8). Peeters, 2003.
22. Lesko, Barbara. *The Great Goddesses of Egypt*. Oklahoma: University of Oklahoma Press, 1999.
23. Levai, Jessica. *Aspects of the Goddess Nephthys, Especially During the Graeco-Roman Period in Egypt*. Rhode Island: Brown University Dissertation, 2007.
24. Lichtheim, Miriam. *Ancient Egyptian Literature Vol 3: The Late Period*. Los Angeles: University of California Press, 1980.
25. Meeks, Dimitri and Christine Favard-Meeks. *Daily Life of the Egyptian Gods*. Translated by G.M. Goshgarian. Ithaca: Cornell University Press, 1996.
26. Piankoff, Alexandre. *Tomb of Ramesses VI: Bollingen I*. University of Princeton Press, 1954.
27. Pinch, Geraldine. *Egyptian Mythology: A Guide to the Gods, Goddesses and Traditions of Ancient Egypt*. Oxford University Press, 2004.
28. Shennum, David. *English-Egyptian Index of Faulkner's Concise Dictionary of Middle Egyptian*. Malibu: Undena Publications, 1977.
29. Siuda, Tamara L. *Nebt-Het: Lady of the House*. Illinois: Stargazer Design, 2010.
30. Siuda, Tamara L. *The Ancient Egyptian Daybook*. Portland: Stargazer Design, 2017.
31. Siuda, Tamara L. *The Ancient Egyptian Prayerbook*. Illinois: Stargazer Design, 2009.
32. Te Velde, Herman. *Seth, God of Confusion: A Study of His Role in Egyptian Mythology and Religion. Vol. 6*. Brill Archive, 1977.

33. Wainwright, Gerald A. "Seshat and the Pharaoh." In *The Journal of Egyptian Archaeology* 26, no. 1 (1941), 30-40.
34. Wilkinson, Richard H. *The Complete Gods and Goddesses of Ancient Egypt*. New York: Thames and Hudson, 2003.
35. Wilkinson, Richard H. *Reading Egyptian Art*. New York: Thames and Hudson, 1992.
36. Wilkinson, Richard H. *Symbol and Magic in Egyptian Art*. New York: Thames and Hudson, 1994.
37. Witt, R.E. *Isis in the Ancient World*. Baltimore: Johns Hopkins University Press, 1997.
38. Zabkar, Louis V. *Hymns to Isis in Her Temple at Philae*. London: University Press of New England, 1988.

The Lady of the Limit and Her Sister
by M. Isidora Forrest

The Two Ladies

As Twin Goddesses, Isis and Nephthys are complements of each other and are often called "the two" this or that. They are the Two Kites, the Two Women, the Two Goddesses of the Hall of Truth, the Two Long-Haired Ones, the Two Uraeus Serpents, the Two Spirits, the Two Nurses, the Two Weavers, the Two Feathers, the Two Birds, the Two Cows, the Two Divine Mothers, the Two Eyes of God, the Two Wise Ones, the Two Weepers, the Two Great-Great Ones, the Two Uniters, and the Twins.[166]

We often think of Isis as the Bright Twin and Nephthys as the Dark Twin. And it's true. Sort of. For instance, the Pyramid Texts instruct the deceased king to

> Ascend and descend; descend with Nephthys, sink into darkness with the Night-barque. Ascend and descend; ascend with Isis, rise with the Day-barque.[167]

The Two Goddesses bear light and dark children to the same God. Osiris fathers the bright God, Horus, with Isis, while with Nephthys, He fathers the dark God, Anubis. The Two Goddesses also manifest their Divine power differently. While Isis guides and sheds light on the hidden paths of the Otherworld, the Coffin Texts tell us that Nephthys speaks and they are obscured.

> Hidden are the ways for those who pass by; light is perished and darkness comes into being, so says Nephthys.[168]

While Isis summons the Barque of the Day, Nephthys is "possessor of life in the Night-barque."[169] As in Pyramid Text 217,

---

[166] Various sources collected in E.A. Wallis Budge, *An Egyptian Hieroglyphic Dictionary* (New York: Dover, 1978).
[167] Faulkner, R.O. *The Ancient Egyptian Pyramid Texts.* (London: Oxford University Press, 1998), p. 50. Pyramid Text 222, Faulkner trans.
[168] Faulkner, R.O. *The Ancient Egyptian Coffin Texts.* (Warminster, Wiltshire [UK]: Aris & Phillips, Ltd., 1994), vol. II, p. 9. Coffin Text 373, Faulkner trans.

Nephthys is paired with Set, a God of dark moods and dark reputation associated with Upper Egypt, while Isis is paired with the benevolent God Osiris and connected to Lower Egypt. In the tomb of Tuthmosis III, Nephthys is said to be the Lady of the Bed of Life, by which was meant the embalming table. She is also Queen of the Embalmer's Shop. Plutarch preserves the tradition that Nephthys was associated with the dry and infertile desert, while Isis is that part of the earth made wet and fertile by the Nile.

But wait. As with most Things Egyptian, it's not that simple. It's not that black and white — nor that dark and light.

Isis is not just about rebirth and sunrise. She is also the Great Mooring Post, the one Who calls each of us to our deaths. She is the Goddess "ruling in the perfect blackness"[170] of the Otherworld, and She has Her own wrathful and fiery moods. Nephthys, on the other hand, is not only about descent in the Night-barque. She is right there with Isis at the sunrise's rebirth. And She is a Goddess for Whom festivals of drunkenness and joy were celebrated. She is the Lady of Beer and while Isis, too, can be so called, I know of no festivals of Divine inebriation celebrated for Isis, even given Her close connection with Hathor, the original Queen of Divine Drunkenness.

It is also interesting that the Two Sisters seem to have become attached to different aspects of Hathor in Their association with Her. Nephthys became connected with Hathor, Lady of Joy and Divine Intoxication, while Isis became connected with Hathor the soft-eyed Cow Mother, the Mother of the God, and the Lady of Amentet. Yet, as always, these roles are fluid and the Two Sisters flow into one another, even as They express different aspects of Their Divinity.

Older Egyptological books informed us that Nephthys had no temples of Her own. But that was only because they hadn't found any yet. We now know of several surviving Nephthys temples, including a New Kingdom temple within a Set precinct at Sepermeru, halfway between Heracleopolis and Oxyrhynchus (where that huge cache of texts, including magical texts and a praise of Isis was found), and a Ptolemaic and Roman-era temple at Komir, near Esna.

In Her Komir (Egy. *Pr Mer*) temple, there is a lengthy hymn to Nephthys that calls Her

---

[169] *Ibid.*, p. 304. Coffin Text 778, Faulkner trans.
[170] Meyer, Marvin and Richard Smith, eds. *Ancient Christian Magic: Coptic Texts of Ritual Power*, (HarperSanFrancisco, 1994), p. 84. Papyrus Michigan 136, Meyer & Smith trans.

The Great, Excellent One, residing in the Beautiful Countryside, the dwelling of Her brother Wesir [Osiris], Who comes to life again in Her, She renews for Him the Body of this One in Her Name of Renewal of Life.[171]

And just as Isis is many-named, so the Komir hymn identifies Nephthys with many other Goddesses. She is invoked as Meshkenet, the Birth Goddess; Hathor, Mistress of Drunkenness and Joy; Tefnut "when She appears in anger"; and Seshat, Lady of Writing and "of the Entire Library." She is Mut and Mafdet and Meret and Heket. She is the Beneficent One and unites Herself with Ma'et. She is the Mother of Amun and the Daughter of Re. She is Venerable, Formidable, Beautiful.[172]

In a papyrus sometimes known as the *Book of Hours* — Ptolemaic and probably from Memphis —praises are recorded for a select group of Deities, including Nephthys. There She is called Kindly of Heart, Mistress of Women, the Valiant, the Strong-Armed, Who Begat Horus, Potent of Deeds, the Wise, the Acute of Counsel, and the Sad at Heart.[173]

Interestingly, Her epithets in this papyrus do not parallel those of Isis in the text. In contrast, Isis is In All that Comes Into Being at Her Command, Lady of What Exists, Sharp of Flame, Who Fills the Land with Her Governance, Who Pleases the Gods with What She Says, the Savior, Isis-Bast and Isis-Sekhmet, the Sister of the Great One [Osiris], Who Comes at Call, and the Living North Wind.[174]

The Strange One, the Hidden One

In an afterlife text known as the *Book of Caverns*, Nephthys is described as the one Whose "head is hidden."[175] Yet Nephthys reveals Herself when we pay attention, when we search, when we ask. Then it

---

[171] El-Saghir, Mohamed and Dominique Valbelle. "Komir. I. - The Discovery of Komir Temple. Preliminary Report. II. - Deux hymnes aux divinités de Komir : Anoukis et Nephthys." *BIFAO 83* (1983), pp. 164-166. Translated by Chelsea Bolton.
[172] *Ibid.*
[173] Faulkner, R.O. *An Ancient Egyptian Book of Hours (Pap. Brit. Mus. 10569).* (Oxford: Printed for the Griffith Institute at the University Press by Charles Batey, 1958), pp. 13-15 (Nephthys) and pp. 12-13 (Isis). Faulkner trans.
[174] *Ibid.*
[175] Piankoff, Alexandre and N. Rambova. *The Tomb of Rameses VI.* (New York: Pantheon Books [Bollingen Foundation], 1954), p. 112, Piankoff and Rambova trans.

turns out that Nephthys is stranger, more intriguing, more unexpected, and indeed more beautiful and powerful than we might, at first, think.

For when we first read our Egyptian mythology, we see loyal Nephthys always in Her more dramatic sister's shadow. She assists Isis with Osiris and Horus; She gets stuck with the troublesome, rowdy, and too-dry-to-be-fertile Set for a husband. She is the Dark Lady in the Barque of the Night. She speaks, and the pathways of the Otherworld are obscured. The one being reborn is advised to throw off the tresses of Nephthys like she throws off her mummy wrappings at her rebirth. Nephthys is sometimes called *Keku*, Darkness itself. She is the Lady of the West, She is "in the Cemetery," She is Lady of the *Duat* (the Underworld), the Mourner and, like Her mother Nuet, She is called "Coffin."[176]

Some see Her darknesses and consider Sad-at-Heart Nephthys to be Death Itself or even Dying Itself, for entering into death does indeed make us sad at heart. Plutarch records that one side of the sistrum was decorated with Isis' face while the other side had Nephthys' face, symbolizing creation and death, respectively.[177]

It is an interesting and useful identification — and you can certainly make a good case for it. Yet, it doesn't quite satisfy me. Not that Death isn't a Big Thing. Death is possibly the Biggest Thing we face in our lives, outside of being born. But because it is so big, *many* of the Egyptian Deities are Death Deities. For instance, we could certainly consider Amentet to be Death Herself for Amentet means "The West," that is, the Egyptian Land of the Dead, and Amentet is often called the Beautiful West and welcomes the dead to Her realm. And, of course, Isis and Osiris are a Goddess and God intimately associated with death. Death is among the concerns of many Deities and it is indeed a concern of Nephthys.

But we're not quite there yet. There must be more we can discover about this Lady. So where else can we look for Nephthys?

One place some scholars have looked is Her connection with other Deities. One of the more interesting ones is Her surprisingly close association with Seshat, the Lady of Books, the Mistress of Builders. Yes, I know. Not the first connection that would come to mind, is it?

---

[176] Various sources collected in Leitz, Christian, ed. *Lexikon der ägyptischen Götter und Götterbezeichnungen* (Leuven: Peeters, 2002).
[177] Plutarch and J. Gwyn Griffiths. *Plutarch's De Iside Et Osiride* (Cardiff: University of Wales Press, 1970) p. 219, section 63, Griffiths trans.

46 SHE WHO SPEAKS THROUGH SILENCE

As early as the Pyramid Texts (the oldest ones date from 2400-2300 BCE), Nephthys is said to have "collected all your members for you in this Her name of Seshat, Lady of Builders."[178] Her much-later hymn from Komir invokes Nephthys as

> Seshat the Great, Mistress of Men, Mistress of Writing,
> Lady of the Entire Library[;]
> To You, Who commands divine decrees; Great of Magic,
> Who resides in the House
> of the Archivists.[179]

A Ptolemaic text from Denderah says that Nephthys is "She who reckoneth the life-period, Lady of Years, Lady of Fate,"[180] which Seshat also does for the pharaoh by an ancient method of marking notches on a palm rib. The Coffin Texts say

> Horus has protected you, He has caused Nephthys to put you together, and She will put you together; She will mold you in Her name of Seshat, Mistress of Potters, for such is this great lady, a possessor of life in the Night-barque, Who raises up Horus, and She will bring you.[181]

Texts at Edfu and Kom Ombo also record Seshat as a form of Nephthys. (It is well worth noting that Isis and Seshat were assimilated as well; which should remind us that, when it comes to Egyptian Deities and indeed when it comes to spirituality, nothing is ever completely without contradiction or complication.)

The priesthoods of Nephthys and Seshat seem to have overlapped in places, too. In addition, Nephthys is paired with Set and is the mother of Anubis with Osiris; interestingly, we have records of a priest of Seshat who served both Set and Anubis — and who was also in charge of "controlling the foreigners." More on that in a minute.

The most complete discussion of the Nephthys-Seshat connection (that is available in English and accessible via your library, if

---

[178] Faulkner, *Pyramid Texts, op. cit.* p. 119. Pyramid Text 364, Faulkner trans.
[179] El-Saghir, *op. cit*, Bolton trans.
[180] Daumas, François, Émile Chassinat, and Sylvie Cauville. *Le temple de Dendara* (Cairo: l'Institut d'Archeologie Orientale du Caire, 1934), p. 149 and Pl. 131, cited in Wainwright, G.A. "Seshat and the Pharaoh," *JEA*, vol 26, pp. 30-40.
[181] Faulkner, *Coffin Texts, Vol. II, op. cit*, p. 304. Coffin Text 778, Faulkner trans.

your library is subscribed to JSTOR) is in a paper by G.A. Wainwright from the 1940s called "Seshat & the Pharaoh." He proposes that both Seshat and Nephthys were so old by the Old Kingdom that They were already starting to be forgotten and that Nephthys may have originally been rather Hathor-like, having been a Sky Goddess and a Love Goddess and a Victory Bringer (think of Goddesses like Inanna and Ishtar, Who are involved in both love and war and are connected with the planet Venus). Plutarch, in the 2nd-century CE, noted that some called Nephthys Teleutê ("End;" more on that in a minute, too), others Aphrodite, and some Nikê ("Victory").[182] Wainwright says that Nephthys' veneration was renewed by being brought into the Isis-Osiris cycle, while Seshat came into the counting house of pharaoh and became connected with Thoth.

A Nephthys-Seshat connection that doesn't seem to have been made by anyone I've read so far jumped out at me right away. So, with this brief speculation alert, here we go.

As Lady of Builders, one of Seshat's main functions is to lay out the boundaries for new buildings, especially temples, via the ceremony of Stretching the Cord, which was a method of using a cord or rope to measure out straight foundations for a building. She is Goddess of architecture, math, and accounting, as well as being the Divine Scribe. Broadly, these are concerns of delineation, creating limits, setting boundaries, deciding what is in and what is out. Keep that in mind as we go on to the next part.

Next, let's look at Nephthys' name. In Egyptian, it's *Nebet-Hwt*, the Lady (*Nebet*) of the Temple (*Hwt*). You will also see it as Lady of the House. "House" *is* one translation of *hwt*, but that translation has, for most of us at least, connotations of the home or household — yet Nephthys has little in Her of Hestia or Vesta. More often, *hwt* means mansion, temple, or even tomb. (Isis' name can have similar meanings.[183])

The hieroglyph for Nephthys' name combines two other symbols: a *neb* bowl placed on top of the *hwt* sign, which is a rectangular sign with a little square or rectangle in the lower right. The *neb* glyph represents a wickerwork basket and conveys concepts such as "lord" (*neb*) or "lady" (*nebet* with the feminine *t* ending) and "all" or "every." My guess is that because *neb* meant "all" it was also used to refer to the ruler of all, the lord or lady. Alan Gardiner in *Egyptian Grammar* says the *hwt*

---

[182] Griffiths, *op. cit*, p. 137, section 12, Griffiths trans.
[183] See https://isiopolis.com/2012/02/26/what-does-the-name-isis-mean

glyph is an "enclosure seen in plan" — in other words, we're looking down at a blueprint for an enclosure or building.

What better name glyph for the Lady of Builders than one that represents the blueprint of a building? The Lady of the House — the Goddess with a blueprint in Her name — is also the architecture Goddess Who delineates the foundations of all buildings, but especially the sacred houses of the Deities, the temples. At Denderah, we even find an ibis-headed Nephthys, which only strengthens the connection between Nephthys and the Divine Scribe, this time with the ibis-headed Divine Male Scribe (*sesh*), Thoth, rather than the Divine Female Scribe, Seshat.

Now, let's go back to Plutarch's comments about what people in his time called Nephthys: Teleutê. In Greek, it means "end" or "completion." Plutarch says

> They give the name Nephthys to the ends of the earth and the regions fringing on mountains and bordering the sea. For this reason, they call Her Teleutê and say She cohabits with Typhon [Set].[184]

Later he says that Nephthys is what is "below the earth and invisible" in contrast with Isis Who "is above the earth and manifest."[185] Both statements speak of Nephthys' mystery and liminality. She is the border between here and there, then and now, in and out. And if She is that border, She also controls it. The priest of Seshat mentioned earlier was also "controller of the foreigners" and Nephthys' husband Set is the God of foreigners and foreign lands; thus the Goddess and God delineate or "draw the line" between us and the Other.

An Egyptian epithet of Nephthys calls Her *Nebet-er-Djer Em Netjeru*, which Tamara L. Siuda translates as "Lady to the Limit Under the Gods."[186] There's also a God, Neb-er-Djer, which I've seen translated as Lord to/of the End or Lord to/of the Utmost, so we may also translate this Nephthys epithet as Lady of the End (aha, Teleutê again!) or Lady to the Utmost *Em* ("among") the Deities. Here again, Nephthys is the border, the line, the limit between All of This and whatever is beyond the End, the Limit, the Utmost.

---

[184] Griffiths, *op. cit*, p. 177, section 38, Griffiths trans.
[185] Griffiths, *op. cit*, pp. 187-188, section 44, Griffiths trans.
[186] Siuda, Tamara L., *Nebt-het: Lady of the House* (Illinois: Stargazer Design, 2010) p. 29.

As you've no doubt figured out, *djer* in Egyptian is "end" or "limit." Faulkner in *A Concise Dictionary of Middle Egyptian*, thinks *djeri* may mean an enclosing wall, a *djeru* is a boundary, and the *djerty* are the Two Kites, Isis and Nephthys. This last one, the Djerty, may mean nothing other than being a rather interesting coincidence. On the other hand, perhaps we can think of the Two Djerty circling aloft, delineating a space in the heavens — one that may be reflected on earth, for example, as They protectively encircle the body of Osiris as He awaits rebirth.

Now let us come back once more to the Lady of the Temple. What are temple walls but the boundary and the limit between sacred and profane? Thus, it is Nephthys, the Lady of the Temple, Who founds and builds the temple walls, enclosing the sacred within, and setting it aside as special, protected, and preserved.

Isis and Nephthys: The Point and the Circle

I've written in other places of the idea of Isis, the Goddess Whose name means "Throne," as the first Something that came into Being.

In the Coffin Texts, the Creator God Atum says He was "alone in lassitude" in the Nu, the Primordial Chaos, and describes it as a time "when my throne [or seat] had not yet been put together that I might sit on it."[187] Here, the throne or seat is a symbol of *Being*. With the coming together of the throne is the coming into being of all things. Thus, I suggest that we can consider Isis, the Goddess Throne, as Goddess of Existence. Without a stable base on which to establish All Things, nothing exists but the Primordial Chaos and the Divine consciousness.

The Goddess *Iset* – Throne – is the First Place, the First Holy Point of Being, the Sacred *Some*-thing that Came Into Existence from *No*-thing. She is the point, so to speak, in the center of the circle.

But the circle itself is Nephthys, the holy wall that surrounds and encloses the point. Isis is the Beginning, Nephthys is the End or Limit. And because the space that Nephthys encloses is not just any space, but sacred space – temple space – it is specially set-aside and protected and may serve as a place of contact with the perfection of First Creation as well as with the Goddesses and Gods. And indeed, that is, in many ways, how the ancient Egyptians envisioned their temples.

---

[187] Faulkner, *Coffin Texts, Vol I, op. cit,* pp. 83-87. Coffin Text 80, Faulkner trans.

A Visit to the Temple of Nephthys

Since this is a devotional work dedicated to Nephthys, I'd like to share with you a meditation and vision I had with the Lady of the Limit in Her temple. Here is what I experienced:

> The doors are nearly half-a-story tall, of dark wood, and plainer that I would have expected. As I stand before them, they swing outwards, pivoting smoothly on their hinges. I enter Her temple.
>
> In contrast to the sandstone-red desert outside, inside is a living jungle. Palm trees, lush wetlands, lotus flowers blooming everywhere; they open their inner hearts to me as I pass by. The Great Above is a beautiful shade of twilight in the Temple of Nephthys. The temple ceiling — or is it the sky? — is deep indigo blue, as deep as the most precious lapis lazuli and flecked with diamond stars.
>
> I am immediately aware of all the living creatures around me. An enormous crocodile wanders by, yawning, showing its teeth. A huge serpent moves, seeming to flow past, yet taking no notice of my presence. I am a bit disconcerted by all this dangerous life. But the voice of the Goddess says, "They are satisfied." At the time, these words of the Goddess do not penetrate home to me. Later, they will. At least a little. Since the creatures of Her temple were "satisfied," they felt no need to snack on me; I need not be afraid. And yet, I think that I have not yet quite unpacked that whole interaction. There is a mystery in the satisfaction of the beasts that will come, I think. They live within Her temple. They exist in Her primordial perfection — for indeed, that is what Her temple encloses, encircles, surrounds: Primordial Perfection, Paradise — the Garden, the First Place, the Mound That First Arose from the ancient chaos of the Nun. It is still muddy and moist. And it is beautiful; as beautiful as you could ever want, as beautiful as you

could ever imagine. It exists in dark warmth and deep blue twilight. Life burgeons within. Satisfied.

I know I should go to Her, to find Her within this, Her temple. So I walk on and, of course, soon come to Her throne room, for She is indeed seated upon a throne.

I approach, kiss the ground before Her beautiful face. I can't quite see Her fully. She seems to exist in an indigo cloud. I sense dark blue and black with glimmers of red and gold. She does not leave Her throne as we talk.

I ask Her about Her relationship with Isis and how it came to be. She tells me that, first of all, the Goddesses are all sisters and so, of course, She is the sister of Isis. She also tells me something that, as far as I know, has not been suggested by any scholar to date, so I won't share it for now. More research is required. (I can sense Her laughing a little in my head as I type this.)

Now for this next bit, you have to know that I've been working on shapeshifting and having a certain amount of difficulty with it. And that by "shapeshifting," I mean taking on the imaginal form of a sacred animal, in this case, the sacred kite of Isis and Nephthys, and then employing that form to explore in vision.

Nephthys, in a very sisterly way I may add, says that She is a better shapeshifter than Isis. She shows me a particular, somewhat uncomfortable, posture. And almost instantly I am shapeshifted (all but my feet, which won't. quite. go. there). I am Kite. Glossy brown feathers, sharp beak, weird side-of-the-head vision, light avian bones. Not wanting to leave the Goddess, I don't fly away, but She invites me to come back to Her temple for more lessons. And I will. But for now, I let my form, my *kheper*, melt back to my own.

I've been back to Her temple several times since. I have been trying to sense the differences between Her and Isis. Overall, She feels just a tiny bit wilder, more shamanic, if I may use that term. But even in Her wildness, She does not seem erratic; it's not *that* kind of wildness. She is wild in the way that Her lush temple is wild, She is close to the Primordial, but it's a paradisiacal, encircled and surrounded Primordial that She has created by delimitation in order to interact with us.

And there is one final footnote to all this that actually brings us back to the beginning and the many names of the Two Ladies. Just as I was finishing writing about the vision above, I came across a little piece of paper on which I had scribbled a note long ago. On it was another name for the Two Sisters. They are also called the *Herti*, the Two Pacified, Peaceful, or — wait for it — the Satisfied Ones.

Damn You Plutarch, or How I nearly Missed the Chance to Get to Know My Lady

by Secondgenerationimmigrant

When I was a kid, I caught the Ancient Egypt bug early.

When "The Lion King" was released, I already knew enough about the Myth of Osiris to realise that it was basically a reskin, and then the *Ramesses* Series by Christian Jacq came out in 1997, and I collided with Seth through the pages of the first book. I was low-key pagan ever since, in a sporadic and very informal way.

I read everything I could put my hands on that had a chance of containing even a little bit of Seth, and my parents seconded my inclination, buying me fairly advanced books, such as George Hart's *Egyptian Myths* and Prof Dimitri Meeks and Christine Favard Meeks' *Daily Lives of the Egyptian Gods*. I knew the myths involving Seth by heart and back-to-front, and I had strong opinions about them.

There was only one problem: Plutarch and his influence on much of the literature. Through him, I had the impression that Nebt-Het was a secondary, supporting character, a shadowy figure that paled in comparison with Her sister Aset and with Seth's other partners. Hidden and undefined, she slipped from my attention, leaving center stage to her showier relatives.

For years, I didn't give her much thought.

Fast forward to 2015.

Looking for inspirations for a creative project on Ancient Egyptian mythology, I started lurking in the Kemetic community on Tumblr and then at some point instead of lurking I was engaging and participating and before I knew, I had jumped the gun and declared for the NTRW. At first, I openly worshipped only Seth and his consorts Ash Neb Tehenu and Anat of Ugarit, but as I interacted with other

Seth-kids I noticed that many of them worshipped Seth and Nebt-Het as couple. At first the idea seemed a bit outlandish to me: after reading Plutarch (and in the original Greek too thanks to my Liceo Classico schooling), I just couldn't imagine it, but I was curious, as usual.

Henadology opened my eyes to the fact that there was more to Nebt-Het than the helpmate of Aset and a Mistress of the House, as Her name would indicate. Through him I came to know Her as the Lady of Terrible Gaze, Beautiful and Terrible Like Ra Rising From The Gates, as the Lady of Joy and Drunkenness. Not just a shadow then, but full of life and power in Her own right, ready and willing to stand up to the enemies of Ma'at and even to Her redoubtable husband and kick his backside. She was even considered non-binary by some!

Then through her worshippers on Tumblr, and especially through Pajamapartyonrasbarque, I got a glimpse of Her love for Her husband and learned how They'd stand together at the prow of Ra's Barque and fight together against the enemies of Ma'at. I was made to notice how many epithets They shared and in how many temples They were worshipped together and finally it clicked. Plutarch had lied, but not intentionally, no. At the time of his writing, Seth had been thoroughly demonised in most parts of Egypt, except the Oases, and the Greco-Roman cult of Isis had thoroughly erased the idea that Seth and Nebt-Het had once been a loving, royal couple as much as their twin siblings, and I had fallen for it, much to my chagrin. I silently apologised to Her for the many years of turning a cold shoulder on Her and during my first Wep Ronpet Festival I gave Her offerings for the first time, imagining She would ignore me in turn.

And then it happened: one morning I went to the lab to start an experiment, full of caffeine to the tips of my hair, and as I sat there in the dark and cold doing superresolution imaging, it happened. Suddenly She was all I could think and feel and the words to a short poem were ringing in my head. I ripped a sheet from the laser log and jotted it down, hands trembling, eyes full of tears.

You shattered my heart into pieces,
I broke yours into shards,

But I still hold you against it,
With trembling, loving hands.

We bleed
We hurt
We cry

Pieces of our hearts
Slice into our flesh
Digging deep
Down to the core

They grind against each other
These broken hearts of ours
But the pain of loving you
Is nothing to the agony
Of going on without you.

Love and heartbreak, the pain of the separation and the joy at the reconciliation, so many different feelings poured through me and I understood that maybe it wasn't a fairytale, but They were very much a thing still (always and forever) and if I wanted to worship Him, I had to make room for Her too, because They were pretty much a package deal and She wanted in. Slightly confused, awed and wondering how I would manage to recompose myself before going out of the lab, I went "Yes, of course."

Ever since that day, Nebt-Het has found her place in my heart, bringing some needed balance in my spiritual life until then dominated by Her overactive, impulsive Consorts. Through my work as support scientist in a facility, I came to appreciate her role as Helpmate and Friend to Isis and understand how wearying but ultimately satisfying it is to contribute to other people's victories from the backstage.

Hers is my coffee in the mornings, and every time I have to perform a Western Blot I pray to Her as Mistress of the Healing Laboratory and Most Excellent and Useful Goddess, in hopes that She will grant me Her help and Her patience.

To me She is the smell of books in the library, the feel of paper after it has been written on, and overcaffeinated nerdy rants. She is the strawberry smell of Virkon in the lab, the darkness of the microscope rooms, the satisfaction of a job well done.

She is there when I can't help but dance, when I am so happy I end up crying, when I miss home, when I squee in delight at something nerdy. She is loving your friends so much that you want to adopt them. She is standing beside your loved ones and helping them pick up the pieces when things go wrong. She is the pleasure of cooking good food for your guests and seeing them smile appreciatively, but She is

also fury and blood and fear against all those who seek to harm Her loved ones and go against what She believes in.

Sometimes I wonder what would have happened if I had figured Her out earlier, but the point is ultimately moot. She came to me when I was ready for Her, and my life is much richer for it.

Into the *Duat:* Who is Nephthys?

by Rev. Anna Applegate

Notes from June 17, 2014 Workshop at Pagan Spirit Gathering (Stone House Park, Illinois).

- She's mentioned first in Old Kingdom funerary literature (2649-2150 B.C.E.), where she rides the night boat of the Unseen World *(Duat)*, meeting a deceased king's spirit and accompanying him into the *Duat*.
- She is often identified as the Night Boat itself within which the god Ra makes His nightly journey into the land of the dead, and She is compared to the West itself.
- As with many other Deities from other pantheons, Nephthys' name is more of a title: it means "Mistress of the Temple" or "Lady of the House." The hieroglyph for her name atop her head depicts a libation bowl as would be found in a temple, and in terms of iconography, it matches Her with depictions of other divinities She is often paired with Aset (Isis), Nit (Neith), and Serqet (Selket).

Attributes and Imagery

- Associated with death and mourning throughout Egyptian history and today venerated not simply as the process of death itself, but as a companion who gives guidance to the newly deceased, and as a winged goddess who comforts the deceased's living relatives

- Earliest depiction gives her a compound name of Nebet-Het-Seshat, the delineator and recorder of Time; prayer from the *Coffin Texts* (beginning in First Intermediate Period of 2191-2055 B.C.E. at end of the Old Kingdom) invokes her to bless the dead:

> • *O [NAME], Heru protects you. He causes Nebt-Het to hold you together, to create you in Her name of Seshat, Mistress of Potters; She is a great lady, great of life in the Night Boat, who raises Heru.*[188]

---

[188] Siuda, Tamara L., *The Ancient Egyptian Prayerbook*, (Stargazer Design, 2009), 73. Translated by Tamara L. Siuda.

- Her hair is metaphorically compared to the strips of cloth shrouding the bodies of the dead
- She can appear in bird form: kite, swallow, even a crow
- In later periods of Egyptian history, Nebt-Het was understood as a deity of liminality – her name extends to the regions fringing on mountains and bordering the sea; the Hellenistic Egyptians called her *Teleute (End)*, probably relating to Her funerary character

<u>Goddess of Liminality</u>
- Dusk and dawn as the liminal times of day
- The Goddess of Welcome at the Liminal Entrance of the Underworld *(Duat)*
- Liminal process of fresh corpse to preserved mummy (Anubis as god of embalming)
- Liminal thresholds: the end of a landscape, where the land meets the sea, or the field meets the mountain
- Liminal states of consciousness: Drunkenness!
- Nebet-Het, like her husband, Set, is associated with the altered, liminal state of drunkenness in a beer offering on the walls of Edfu Temple in Upper Egypt on the West Bank of the Nile. She is said to "give drunkenness without pain [hangovers]."[189]

---

[189] Siuda, Tamara L., *Nebt-het: Lady of the House*, (Illinois: Stargazer Design, 2010), 21, footnote 69.

Ritual and Magic

Figure 2: Shrine of Nebet Het (Nephthys) by Chelsea Luellon Bolton. Photo taken by Monica Hart. Nebet Het icon (left) by SculptSongStudio.

Morning Ritual to Nebet Het
by Chelsea Luellon Bolton

Items for Nebet Het Shrine
- Image or Statue of the Goddess Nebet Het
- White or Purple Altar Cloth
- Two Purple or White Candles
- Incense or Essential Oil
- Offerings
- Water Offering

Say: As Ra rises in the East
So too, do You come to Your shrine.
True is She-Before-the-Red.
Lady Nebet Het, Lady Nephthys
Come to the shrine
and come to Your Image as I praise You.

Light Incense.

Light the Candles. Offer the Water.

Place Offerings on the Shrine.

Say: Awaken in Peace
Lady Nebet Het, Nephthys
Lady of the Temple, Home, and Tomb
Lady of the Shrine, Who Dispels Impurity
Kherseket – She Who Wipes Away Tears
Merkhetes – She Whose Flame is Painful
Wife of Set, Daughter of Ra
Consort of Wesir, Daughter of Nut
Sister of Aset, Mother of Yinepu
Great of Magic, Eye of Ra
Awaken in Peace, Nebet Het
Every day.

Henu or Bow to the Goddess.
Extinguish the candles.
Drink the water.
The rite is done.

Eat Nebet Het's offerings.

Notes:

Henu: a ritual gesture where your arms are outstretched in front of you, with your hands cupped and palms toward the shrine or image of the deity. You can also prostrate yourself after this gesture.

Daily Solar Prayers
by Chelsea Luellon Bolton

The priests in Ancient Egypt performed rituals for the gods every day at dawn, noon, dusk, and midnight. One way to mythically experience this solar cycle is through a goddess. This goddess can be Nut, Aset, Hethert, or Nebet Het as the Celestial Cow, the Eye of Ra, the Lady of the West, and the Tree Goddess. This goddess is the mother giving birth to the sun god at dawn; she is the Eye of Ra at noon; she is Amenti, the Lady of the West at dusk; and she is the Tree Goddess nurturing the dead at midnight.[190]

You can make this as elaborate as you choose. You can light a candle or use an LED candle for light while you pray. You can offer to the Goddess as well.

You can also substitute *us* for *me* in the prayers if there is more than one person.

Dawn Prayer (Celestial Cow)
Nebet Het, Goddess of the Dawn
Lady of Light, Mother of Ra
Heavenly Cow,
Please be with me today and always.

Noon Prayer (Eye of Ra)
Nebet Het, Eye of Ra
Merkhetes, She Whose Flame is Painful
Lady of Fire, Lady of Light
Leopard Goddess, please help me
throughout this day.

Dusk Prayer (Lady of the West)
Nebet Het, Lady of the West
She Who Dispels Darkness with Light

---

[190] Nicoll, Kiya. The Travellers' Guide to the Duat. (Megalithica Books, 2012), 145.

Lady of the Stars, Queen of Heaven
Lady of the Ancestors,
Please watch over me throughout the night.

Midnight Prayer (Tree Goddess)

Nebet Het, Queen of the Ancestors
Sister of Wesir, Star Goddess
Lady of Life, Water Libationer
Tree Goddess,
Please watch over me throughout the night.

Offering Ritual to Nebet Het
by Chelsea Luellon Bolton

Items for Nebet Het Shrine
- Image or Statue of the Goddess Nebet Het
- White or Purple Altar Cloth
- Two White or Purple Candles
- Incense or Essential Oil
- Offerings
- Water Offering

Offering Ideas
- Milk
- Beer
- Wine
- Chocolate
- Cookies, Pastries
- Cakes, Bread
- Tea
- Coke, Pepsi, Sprite
- Pomegranate Juice
- Strawberry Flavored Drinks and Food
- Strawberries
- Fruit and Vegetables
- Water

Flower Offerings: Roses, Lilies, Violets
Stones: Dark Gemstones

Offer water.
Light candles.

Invocation to Nebet Het
Nebet Het, Lady of the Shrine
Protector against impurity,
Goddess of the Crossroads
Lady of the Way.

Guide me.
Protect me.
As You guide and guard
As Yinepu does.
Kind-Hearted Lady
Guardian of the Shrine
Guardian of the Home
Guardian of the Tomb
May You be satisfied with my offering.
Thank you, Lady Nebet Het.

Offer to Nebet Het.
Speak to the Goddess in your own words.

Henu or Bow to the Goddess.
Extinguish the candles.
Drink the water.
The rite is done.

Eat the Offerings to Nebet Het. You can also pour libations out to Her if you wish.

Notes:
Henu: a ritual gesture where your arms are outstretched in front of you, with your hands cupped and palms toward the shrine or image of the deity. You can also prostrate yourself after this gesture.

Chant Her Name
by Chelsea Luellon Bolton

The meaning of Nebet Het's name is up for debate among Egyptologists and other scholars. Here is a list of possible translations of her name. This can be used as a devotional chant or song to the Goddess.

Here are possible translations
    Lady of Destruction*
    Lady of the Grave
    Lady of the Funerary Chapel
    Lady of the House
    Lady of the Ombite (Set)
    Lady of the Palace
    Lady of the Sky
    Lady of the Temple
    Lady of the Tomb
    That Which Rules inside the House[191]

Note:
*This is a late and specialized way to spell Her Name.

---

[191] Levai, Jessica. Aspects of the Goddess Nephthys, Especially During the Greaco-Roman Period in Egypt. (Rhode Island: Brown University Dissertation, 2007), 4, 5, and 21-29.

Candlelighting and Water Purification for Nebet Het

by Chelsea Luellon Bolton

Items Needed
- white or purple candle
- lighter
- cup or bowl of water
- offerings for Nebet Het

1. Light the Candle.

Say: This is the Goddess Nebet Het (Nephthys)
The sacred mound as dawn breaks
The sunlight glittering against the water
The air as you exhale
The rain as it drenches the land
The storm-clouds forming
As death draws near.
Exhale, Inhale
Breathe.
I am there.

I am all around you.
Yes, even you.
I am here.
In the whispers
In the darkness
In the solitude,
I bring the light.

2. Offer water to the Goddess.

Say: I am the waves beneath the wind
I am the river, ever flowing
I am the rain,
Born of tears and rage,
Anguish born from despair,

Yet, never wavering
I am as still as the water in this cup.
I am silence, following despair
I am stillness, following strength
I am the calm, following rage.

Drink the waters of Purification.
Cleanse your Ka.
Cleanse yourself.
And be renewed.

For I am the Lady of Renewal,
Who brings
Strength from sorrow
Who brings
Silence from despair
Who brings
Light from the dark.

3. Drink the water.

Say: Thank you, Lady Nebet Het (Nephthys)
Goddess of Renewal.

Henu or Bow to the Goddess.
Extinguish the candles.
Drink the water.
The rite is done.

Eat the Offerings to Nebet Het. You can also pour libations out to Her if you wish.

Note:
Henu: a ritual gesture where your arms are outstretched in front of you, with your hands cupped and palms toward the shrine or image of the deity. You can also prostrate yourself after this gesture.

Sistrum House Cleansing
by Chelsea Luellon Bolton

Within Judika Illes' book, *The Encyclopedia of 5,000 Spells,* there is a spell to cleanse the home with a sistrum with the goddess Hethert (Hathor).[192] I thought this kind of spell was a wonderful idea for Nebet Het too, as she is both Lady of the Sistrum and Mistress of the Home. If possible, clean your house before this working.

Items Needed
- Shrine or Altar to Nebet Het
- Offering to Nebet Het
- Sistrum

Light a candle. Make an offering.

Then say:
Nebet Het, Lady of the Home
Eye of Ra, Whose Flame is Painful
Who dispels impurity
Who dispels harmful forces
Please cleanse my home.
May this sistrum cleanse this home
of impurity and harmful forces.
May it become.

Take the sistrum and shake it around your home or just in the space where you want the purification. Repeat this prayer as needed.

When you are finished, thank the Goddess:

Thank you.

Extinguish the candle.
If the offering is food or drink, eat the offering.

---

[192] Illes, Judika. The Encyclopedia of 5,000 Spells. (HarperOne, 2009), 200. Inspired by the Hathor spell in this book.

Heka: Pillar of Support, Pillar of Strength
by Taqerisenu

Nebthet supported her sister, Aset, through their mutual grief at the death of Wesir, helping her to gather his scattered remains, so that he could be made whole. This heka draws upon that supportive element of Nebthet's role, asking her to act as a pillar of support and strength in your life, as well as asking her to help you have the strength to support others through strife and grief, when they need it.

Required Materials: a blank piece of paper; a writing instrument in a color other than red (preferably black, green, or blue); cool water; and offerings for Nebthet.

Light the shrine lamp and make a fourfold libation.

On the blank sheet of paper, draw a large image of a house, as it is often pictured (a square, topped by a triangular roof). In the middle of the square wall of the house, draw a rectangle for its front door. On either side of the door, draw a pillar, reaching from the ground to the roof, supporting it.

Write your name on the triangle that forms the roof of the house. Focus on the image of the house. Imagine it vibrant, full of life and color. It is a place you can find comfort, that you can retreat to when needed. It is a place you feel at peace, safe, and loved. The house you have drawn represents your life, as you wish it to be.

Think about the people and things in your life that sustain and support you, that help keep you going during periods of trouble and grief. Write the names of these people and things that support you on the pillar to the left of the door. You may also add people and things that you would like to be able to rely upon for strength and support in the future. Picture the pillar glowing with green energy of strength and renewal. Imagine it as a massive Djed pillar of cedarwood, representing strength and stability. Imagine leaning against it, relaxing, allowing it to support your weight while you rest.

Say, "Nebthet stands behind me, as she stands behind her brother, Wesir. Nebthet stands beside me as she stands beside her sister, Aset. The Lady of Renewal sustains me. The Silent One, Who Hears Prayers, laments and rejoices with me."

Turn your focus to the people and things in your life that you help support, who you stand beside, and lend your strength to. Think about the people in your life you want to be able to help, who may be facing grief, illness, or strife.

Write the names of the people and things you wish to support, to be a pillar of strength to, on the pillar to the right of the door. Picture the pillar overflowing with green energy of strength and stability. Imagine it as a massive Djed pillar of cedarwood. Its earthy, spicy scent relaxes you. You rest your hand on it, and the energy of the pillar flows into you, coalescing around your spine. You feel your spine becoming strong and stable, like the pillar, full of a well of energy resources you can draw upon when you let others rest their weight on you for a time, taking the weight of their grief and anxiety. As you support them, Nebthet's boundless strength and quiet comfort supports you.

Say, "Nebthet is in the House of Life, and her joy is in me. Nebthet is the uraeus on the brow of her brother, and her strength is in me. I raise the Djed pillar. The Ma'ati raise the Djed pillar."

Focus now on the front door of the house. On this door, write all the good things that you want to enter your life. Imagine yourself welcoming them in. They are passing through the doorway to become a part of your life, a part of your day-to-day existence.

Say, "I am in the Beautiful House of Nebthet. I am in the House of Light and Darkness. All good things are supplied to me by the Lady of Heaven. I am protected by She Who Does Not Speak, But Spits Flame. My house is protected by the Lady of Life."

Make offerings of thanks to Nebthet. Place the drawing in your shrine. You may wish to use it as a focus when you need support, or as a reminder of the importance of self-care while one is trying to support those one loves.

Into the *Duat*: A Devotional Ritual to Nebet-Het

by Rev. Anna Applegate, M. A.

Challenge at the Threshold to Participants:
Me: "How is it you come forth shining from the Field of Reeds with *heka?*"
Participant answers: "I am that pure *Heka* who is in the utterance and the body of Ra. I am His *ba, Heka. Hu* is in my mouth, *Sia* is in my heart: my speech is the shrine of *Ma'at.*"
Me: "Enter, blessed one."

Opening Song in Egyptian:

Reχ ḫāāiu
I rejoice
Ma a-á̇ paut neteru
May I look upon the company of the Gods.

Nuk ut'a tep ta χer Rā mena-a nefer
I am strong upon the earth before Ra,

Χer Aus?r
May my arrival be happy before Osiris
Nuk t'a pet
I have sailed over heaven
Nuk ??h
I am the moon
Ba-ā pu neteru bai u en neheh
My soul is the Gods, who are the Souls of Eternity
Au-? ab kua neteri-kuá̇
I myself am pure, I am mighty

    [SHAKE SISTRUM; BOW BEFORE NEBEṬ-HET'S IMAGE]

A net'-hra-k Neben Neferu
Homage to Thee, Lady of Welcome

A net'-hra-ten nebu heh
Homage to Thee, Ye Lords of Eternity

Nuk ab per em seχet
I am the pure one coming forth from the field

☐n-na en Ѳen netersenѲer
I have brought you incense

[BOW BEFORE ANPU'S IMAGE; ARMS IN OSIRIS POSE]

Tu a Anpu
You are Anpu
Suten heh
Lord of Eternity

Ta-k-na uat seś-a em-hetep
Grant to me a way that I may pass in peace
☐n-na kert āb-kua
I am silent, I am pure

I-nā, χerk-k neb Ra
I have come to Thee, O my Lord Ra

Reχ hāā.iu
I rejoice

Reχ hāā.iu
I rejoice

[BOW AND SHAKE SISTRUM]

Lighting Fire Prayer — [TO BE SAID UPON LIGHTING ALTAR CANDLES]
Welcome in peace, Eye of Heru,
Shining, perfect, healed, in peace!
May you shine like Ra-Heruakhety!
Heru's Eye is victorious!
Heru's Eye repels the enemy!

Lighting Incense Prayer — [LIGHT INCENSE AND HOLD SMOKING BRAZIER ALOFT TO THE EAST]

I give incense to the eastern *Ba,*
Heru of the East,
Bull of His Mother in the Aten,
He of Terror Who Shines with two *Udjat* Eyes,
Ra-Heruakhety the great god, Power with Wings,
Foremost of the Southern Heaven.

Censing the Circle Prayer — [CENSE THE AUDIENCE WALKING CLOCKWISE]
It is pure, it is pure for your *ka!*
You are pure for your *ka.*
Your head is pure with sweet incense;
The incense makes you new.
Holy fragrance is on your limbs;
Heru and Set, the Two Great Ones, cleanse you.
I cense you with this Eye of Heru.
I make you holy with this Eye of Heru.
I make you holy,
The Eye makes you holy,
Its scent washes over you,
The perfume of Heru's Eye lies upon you.

And now let us invoke the aid of the Divine Pillars of the Cosmos, the Four Sons of Heru, followed by the Quintessence of Khnum.

[SHAKE SISTRUM]

Hapi, Qebhsennuf, Tuamāutef, Imseti,
☐net' hr☐-tem mebu maāt
t'at'at ha ☐us☐r
t'at'at śat em asfat,

☐miu-Χet hetep-seΧus,

Mā-ten-u☐ i-ku☐ Χer-ten.

Hapi, Qebhsennuf, Tuamāutef, Imseti,
Homage to You, Lords of Right and Truth
Divine Beings who are behind Ausar
Causing to be annihilated defects who are in the following of *hetep-sekhus,*

Grant ye that we may come to you. Companions, let us begin by turning to the South to welcome Hapi.

[ALL FACE SOUTH]

Volunteer 1 / Water Signs: *Neter* Hapi! I welcome You from the South, with Your gift of life-giving water. Welcome, Son of Heru!
ALL: Welcome, Son of Heru!

[VOLUNTEER 1 POURS WATER INTO BOWL]
[ALL TURN AND FACE EAST]

Volunteer 2 / Fire Signs: *Neter* Qebhsennuf! I welcome You from the East, Hawk Who Soars from the Horizon of Light. Welcome, Son of Heru!
ALL: Welcome, Son of Heru!

[VOLUNTEER 2 LIGHTS CANDLE BEFORE QEBHSENNUF'S CANOPIC JAR]
[ALL TURN AND FACE NORTH]

Volunteer 3/Earth Signs: *Neter* Tuamāutef! I welcome You from the North, Jackal of Desert Domain. Welcome, Son of Heru!
ALL: Welcome, Son of Heru!

[VOLUNTEER 3 POURS SAND IN BOWL]
[ALL TURN AND FACE WEST]

Volunteer 4/Air Signs: *Neter* Imseti! I welcome You from the West, Imseti, with the Breath of Life. Welcome, Son of Heru!
ALL: Welcome, Son of Heru!

[VOLUNTEER 4 LIGHTS INCENSE BEFORE IMSETI'S CANOPIC JAR]

Thank you, companions of the Four Pillars. Please take your seats.
Anet' hra-ten nebu maāt! [I GENUFLECT]
ALL: *Anet' hra-ten nebu maāt!* Homage to You, Lords of Right and Truth!

And now let us invoke the aid of ram-headed Khnum, Divine Craftsman seated in the Center of the Pillars, the point from which He cannot err!

Hymn to Khnum (Pronounced "Kuh-NOOM")

Volunteer: Glory to Khnum in the Center! God of the potter's wheel!

He who settled the land by his handiwork;
He who joins in secret, who builds soundly
Who nourishes the nestlings by the breath of His mouth
Who drenches the land with *Nūn!*
He has fashioned gods and men
He has formed flocks and herds
He made birds as well as fishes
Formed all on His potter's wheel!
All Your creatures give You thanks,
You are Ptah-Tatenen, Creator of Creators,
Beneficent God,
God who forms bodies,
God who equips nostrils
God who binds the Two Lands so that they join Their natures.
The Nile rises at Your will.
Architect of All That Is!
Give health to us, to those who toil!
Hail, Khnum!

ALL: Hail!

Thank you, companion. Please take your seat.

> [I PERAMBULATE THE ALTAR, SHAKING SISTRUM]

The Heavens are opened, the Earth is opened, the West is opened, the East is opened,
The Southern Half of Heaven is opened, the doors are opened,
And the gates are thrown wide open to Ra as He Cometh Forth from the Horizon!

And now, at this time, let the one who would invoke our starry mother Nut step forth!

> [FEMALE VOLUNTEER STRETCHES ARMS SKYWARD AND SAYS:]

Hymn to Nut [Pronounced "Noot"]
O Great One, Mother Sky,
You made power and strength,
And filled every place with Your beauty.

All lands belong to You.
You hold Geb and all creation in Your embrace.
Hail, Nut!

ALL: Hail!

Let the one who would invoke Nut's consort step forth!

[MALE VOLUNTEER COMES BEFORE ALTAR AND TOUCHES EARTH BEFORE SAYING:]

Hymn to Geb
O Geb, Son of Shu,
You stand on the earth that You may govern at the head of the Ennead,
For You are the essence of Them All.
Nourish and sustain us in the work we are to do.
Hail, Father Earth!

ALL: Hail!

Invocation of Nebet-Het
Let us awaken Nebet-Het with a call-and-response invocation. I'll speak in Egyptian and you'll reply with the English translation, line by line.

Nehes, nehes, nehes
Awake, awake, awake
Nehes em hotep
Awake in peace
Nehes em neferu
Rise Thou in peace
Nebet hotepet
Lady of peace
Weben em neferu
Rise Thou in beauty
Nutjert en Ankh
Goddess of Life
Nefer em pet!
Beautiful in Heaven!
Pet em hotep
Heaven is in peace

Ta em hotep
Earth is in peace
Nutjert sat Nut,
O goddess,
Daughter of Nut,
Sat Geb,
Daughter of Geb,
Weret, Sedjmet-nebet,
Great One, Lady Who Hears,
Nutjert asha renu!
Goddess rich in names!
Anekh hrak,
All praise to You,
Anekh hrak,
All praise to You,
Tu a atu,
I adore You,
Tu a atu,
I adore You,
Nebet-Het!
Nephthys!

And now let us say the following prayer from the Pyramid Texts together to let the Lady know we come before Her with pure hearts:

I have come to You, Nebet-Het,
I have come to You, Night-Boat,
I have come to You, True Before the Red,
I have come to You, Birth-Brick of Souls.
Remember me.
Gone is Orion, caught by the Underworld,
Yet cleansed and alive in the Beyond;
Gone is Sothis, caught by the Underworld,
Yet cleansed and alive in the Beyond;
Gone am I, caught by the Underworld,
Yet cleansed and alive in the Beyond.
It is well with me and with You
It is peaceful for me and for You,
Within the arms of Our Father,
Within the arms of Atum.

[SHAKE SISTRUM]

Presentation of Offerings to Nebet-Het
Nebet Sekhem, Powerful Lady, with pleasing eyes, accept our offerings of
____, ____, and _____,
O *Nebet-Hotep,* Lady of Offerings,
And deign to comfort us in our hour of need, You who are no stranger to the soul's dark passage,
Mourner of Ausar who gathered His body together, who pulled Him together,
Who split open His mouth for Him.
Nebet Resh, Lady of Watchfulness,
Protect our beloved and blessed dead
Offer them welcome
And grant us fortitude and solace
Until the day we can be reunited again,
Blessed before the throne of Your Brother, Lord of Eternity.
And with Your Wayfinding son, gentle and wise Anpu,
Neb-ta-djeser, Lord of the Sacred Land,
Come to us and witness well the works of healing, remembering, and laying to rest
That which must go to the West.
Praise to You, *Netjeryt!* Holy One! Hail, Nebet-Het!

ALL: Hail!
Let us turn now to Anpu, that Good God whom the Greeks named Anubis.

[SHAKE SISTRUM]

Invocation of Anpu and Presentation of His Offerings
Anet hra-k, Anpu!
Khenty-she-netjer, Imy-ut!
Come to us, O High One, O Mighty One,
O Master of Secrets for those in the Underworld,
O Pharaoh of those in Amenti,
O Chief Physician,
O good son of Ausar,
He whose face is strong among the gods,

You should appear in the Underworld before the hand of Ausar.
You should serve the souls of Abydos in order that they all live through You,
These souls, the ones of the Sacred Underworld.
Come to the earth!
With pleasing eyes, accept our offerings of _____, _____, and _____.

Reveal Yourself to us today,
Opener of the Ways!
Hail, Anpu!
ALL: Hail!
[BOW IN OSIRIS POSE]

MAIN RITUAL ACTIVITY

Nebet-Het and Anpu mark well our words and are here to lend their energies to the workings we are about to commence.

As the corpse of Ausar, also known as Osiris, became encased in a sycamore tree, I invite those of you who have lost a loved one to inscribe their names on scraps of gauze – remember, Nebet-Het's hair is likened to linen wrappings that formed a mummy's shroud – and to those scraps to a branch of our own Tree of Memory Eternal. At the end of the ritual, you may remove those scraps or leave them on the tree, as the bulk of my devotional practice at home is ancestor work and I will add the names on this tree to my own litany of the dead.

The other ritual activity is one of release. If there has been woundedness in your life from some other loss besides physical death – the loss of a relationship, job, friendship, health, even the loss of a dream – I invite you to grab a bay leaf and breathe on it while focusing on the loss in question. Your breath will imprint the leaf with your *sahu*, your vital energy. Once you feel you've charged the leaf and you're ready to let it go, take the leaf and bury it in this pot of soil, which I will take to the huge compost heap in my parents' backyard when PSG is over. That way, you will symbolically bury the loss and make space in your heart and in your life for new and good things to enter.

In honor of Nebet-Het, who speaks with the silence of the tomb, let us do our work in the next few moments in silence.
[DO RITUAL WORK IN SILENCE]

Offerings to the Dead

As Nebet-Het's chief function is to guard our beloved and blessed dead and Anpu to guide them, it is to our ancestors that we now turn.
Children of Heru! Hapi, Qebhśennuf, Tuamāutef, Imseti,
As You spread Your protection over Your father, Ausar, Foremost of the Westerners,
So spread Your protection over us, and over the living *bas* of our beloved and blessed dead.

Hail to our beloved and blessed ancestors, blood of our blood, bones of our bones,
The sky is yours, the earth is yours, the cemetery roads are yours,
Praise to you in peace!
You will not be separated from the Lord of the West.
Nebet-Het spreads Her arms over you,
She grants you peaceful rest forever.
O Gods, grant that the names of those we honor today be true of voice
And among You in the House of Beauty!
Here is your cold water, blessed ones! Refresh yourselves with it!

[POUR SOME ON GROUND AND SPRINKLE TREE]
[ADDRESSING THE AUDIENCE NOW BY OFFERING PITCHER/GOBLET, SAY:]

Drink, and may Memory Eternal be with those you carry in your heart always!

[PASS PITCHER/GOBLET FOR ALL TO TAKE A SIP FROM]
[ONCE RETURNED, PLACE VESSEL OF WATER ON GROUND AND HOLD ALOFT BREAD, SAYING:]

Ancestors, take this bread which we give as your loaf,
Which Heru, great in Upper Kemet, gives you;
Be filled with what we bring.
It is the Eye of Heru.

[TEAR OFF PIECE AND OFFER THE REST;
SHARE ANOTHER WHOLE BREAD WITH AUDIENCE]

Antiphonal Chant
As our ancestors, shining in Amenti, enjoy peace and freedom from fear,

So too may we live our lives in peace, growing in health, abundance, and wisdom,
Protected from evil in all of our undertakings.

ALL: *Nedjen ma sebet! Nedjen ma fa-u!* Protect us from evil!

Laying on of Hands (Optional)
If anyone is feeling stuck in their grief, or if their heart chakras hurt, signal to me and I'll come do a blessing on your head and your heart. I'll place my hands on the crown of your head, forehead, temples, sternum, and nape of your neck, which the Egyptians believed was the most spiritually vulnerable part of a person. I have blessed water and a special concoction formulated to avert evil — it has a citrus base of essential oils and herbs.

Would anyone like to receive a hands-on blessing?

Silent Meditation (Optional)
And now, let us sit for a few moments in silent meditation, honoring Nebet-Het in our hearts and inviting Her to impart any messages to us.

[PAUSE FOR 3 OR 4 MINUTES]

OPENING THE CIRCLE

And now let us thank the Holy Powers we have invoked and send Them our love as our ritual concludes.
Let us turn first to Anpu, gentle guide — the one who shows the way.

[SHAKE SISTRUM]

Thanksgiving to Anpu
Hail, Anpu!
Neb-ta-djeser, Lord of the Sacred Land!
Wise herald and guide, lead us in the ancient ways.
Be with us in our journeys.
And when our time comes to be led into the Hall of the Double Truth,
Be our unfailing wayfinder, illuminating the darkness,
And our steadfast companion, Gentle Weigher of the Heart.
Son of Nebet-Het and Ausar, protect and guide us.
May our arrival be happy in Amenti.
Hail, Anpu!

ALL: Hail!

[SHAKE SISTRUM]

Let us now give our thanks and praise to our Blessed Lady, Exalted in the *Duat!*

Thanksgiving to Nebet-het
Glory unto You, beautiful Nebet-Het!
Lady of the Temple Glorious,
Sister to Aset, with whom You speak the Divine Utterances to unfetter all from evil,
As Heru was unfettered from the blades of Set.
May You deliver us from everything evil, from all diseases of darkness,
As You safeguard the body of Your Brother on His funerary bier,
Calling unto Him in tears!
Merciful Mother of Jackals,
Veil of Brilliance,
May we ever be mindful of Your gifts,
O Revealer of Hidden Things,
As we stand on the threshold of that which is a place, yet not a place.
Ease our hearts of grief as You enfold us within Your indigo wings,
Mistress of Sorrow,
We make open the napes of our necks to You, *Netjeryt.*
Make us receptive to Your voice of silence and its whispered wisdom,
Lady Great in *Heka!*
Goddess of Earth,
Goddess of Heaven,
Goddess in the *Duat,*
Watch over us always!
Hail, Nebet-Het!

ALL: Hail!

[BOW IN OSIRIS POSE AND SHAKE SISTRUM]

And now let us turn to the Earth, to Father Geb, supporter of all our undertakings. May his companion step forth.

Thanksgiving to Geb
Volunteer [TOUCHES EARTH AND THEN RISES TO SAY]:
O Geb, Son of Shu,

Essence of the Gods made manifest,
Swallow not any of us anytime soon
And bless us that we always tread lightly upon You.
Tā-k-na uat seś-a em hetep! Grant us a way that we may pass in peace!
Hail, Father Earth!
ALL: Hail!
[SHAKE SISTRUM]

And now let us stretch arms upward in praise of Mother Sky, Nut! May Her companion please step forth.

Thanksgiving to Nut (Noot)
Volunteer: Great Nut, Starry Vault of Heaven,
We rejoice as our deceased rise to become one with you,
Immortal in Your bosom.
We give thanks knowing that Millions of Years will be born of Your womb on the morrow,
Lady of Divine *Ma'at,*
The Pure One arching over the company of the Gods!
Bless us with pleasure and rest tonight and all nights!
Hail, Sky Mother Nut!

ALL: Hail!
[SHAKE SISTRUM]

And now let us give thanks to Khnum, the Creator. May His companion step forth to praise Him for us.

Thanksgiving to Khnum (Kuh-NOOM)
Volunteer: Great Khnum!
Maker of all forms imbued with *Shemsu,* the Divine Breath of Life,
As we draw towards the close of another year and look forward to the flood of abundance in the new,
May all our works be blessed and empowered by Your shaping hands, Great Creator!
Anet-hra-ten nebu heh! Homage to You, Lord of Eternity!
Hail, Khnum!

ALL: Hail!
[SHAKE SISTRUM]

Thanksgiving to the Four Sons of Heru
And now let the companions who invoked the Four Sons of Heru step forward. We begin in the West with Imseti.
Volunteer 4 [FACING WEST]: Thank You, Imseti, for attending this rite. May the incense lit in Your name carry our prayers to the Heavens. In peace may You ever stand watch in the West.
ALL: Stand watch in peace, Son of Heru!

And now let us turn to the North, to Tuamāutef.

Volunteer 3 [FACING NORTH]: Thank You, Tuamāutef, for attending this rite. Be our unerring pathfinder as we tread across Your domain. In peace may You ever stand watch in the North.
ALL: Stand watch in peace, Son of Heru!

And now let us turn to the East, to hawk-headed Qebhśennuf.

Volunteer 2 [FACING EAST]: Thank You, Qebhśennuf, for attending this rite. May Your flame of righteousness ever burn brightly in our hearts. In peace may You ever stand watch in the East.
ALL: Stand watch in peace, Son of Heru!

And finally we turn to Hapi in the South.

Volunteer 1 [FACING SOUTH]: Thank You, Hapi, for attending this rite. May our lives always be blessed by Your flowing Waters of Life. In peace may You ever stand watch in the South.
ALL: Stand watch in peace, Son of Heru!

[SHAKE SISTRUM]

Final Proclamation
Repeat after me:

Reχ hāāiu	I rejoice!
Ba-ā pu neteru	My soul is the Gods, who are the Souls of Eternity.

There is no part of us that is not of the Gods. Blessed are those who would listen and know.

[BOW REVERENTIALLY TOWARDS AUDIENCE]

Suggested Reading

Baines, J., Leonard H. Lesko, and David P. Silverman. *Religion in Ancient Egypt: Gods, Myths, Personal Practice.* Ithaca, NY: Cornell University Press, 1991.

Betz, H.D., ed. *The Greek Magical Papyri in Translation.* Chicago: University of Chicago Press, 1986.

Budge, E.A. Wallis. *The Egyptian Book of the Dead: (The Papyrus of Ani) Egyptian Text, Transliteration and Translation.* 1895. New York: Dover Publications, 1967.

-----. *The Egyptian Heaven & Hell.* 1905. La Salle, IL: Open Court, 1989.

-----. *The Gods of the Egyptians: Studies in Egyptian Mythology.* Vols. I and II. 1904. New York: Dover, 1969.

Faulker, R.O. *The Ancient Egyptian Coffin Texts.* Aris & Phillips, 1978.

-----. *The Ancient Egyptian Pyramid Texts.* Oxford: Oxford University Press, 1969.

Frankfurter, David. *Religion in Roman Egypt: Assimilation and Resistance.* Princeton University Press, 1998.

Lesko, B. *The Great Goddesses of Egypt.* University of Oklahoma, 1999.

Meyer, M. and Smith, R., eds. *Ancient Christian Magic: Coptic Texts of Ritual Power.* HarperSanFrancisco, 1994.

Müller, W. Max. *Egyptian Mythology.* Mineola, NY: Dover Publications, 2004.

Page, Judith and Ken Biles. *Invoking the Egyptian Gods.* Woodbury, MN: Llewellyn Publications, 2011.

Pinch, Geraldine. *Magic in Ancient Egypt.* Austin, TX: University of Texas Press, 1994.

Siuda, Tamara L. *The Ancient Egyptian Prayerbook.* New Lenox, IL: Stargazer Design, 2009.

-----. *Nebt-Het: Lady of the House.* New Lenox, IL: Stargazer Design, 2010.

Nebet Het Rite for Shadow Work

by Emily K. Jones

Nephthys is a complex and somewhat hidden goddess who can offer powerful assistance in shadow work. In some ways, she can be seen as the shadow or the mirror of her sister Isis. Isis is the devoted wife and good mother, while Nephthys is the deceptive adulterer who abandons her own child. Isis is celebrated in a multitude of stories and prayers while Nephthys is somewhat shrouded in obscurity, glimpses of her peeking through in the stories of other gods.

Because Nephthys does not have her own stories, she can be somewhat hard to find. She is mentioned primarily in the stories of her more well-known siblings Isis and Osiris. She is a funerary Goddess probably most well-known for assisting Isis in the revival of Osiris. She is also the neglected wife of her brother Set, a brutal husband who is more interested in conquest than anything else. Out of her loneliness, she disguises herself as her sister in order to trick Osiris into loving her.

When Anubis is born out of that union, depending on the story, she either abandons him in the desert out of fear of retribution from her husband and brother Set, or else Set takes her child from her and leaves him in the desert. Either way, she ends up as a mother without her child, stuck in a loveless and barren marriage before rejecting her husband and aligning herself with her sister Isis to restore Osiris and protect Horus.

Working with Nephthys can be a challenge precisely because it can be so difficult to find her. Her mythology resides in fragments found in the stories of other gods and goddesses. In this way, she seems very much a goddess of women, particularly all of the women throughout patriarchal history that never had their stories told. She is defined through her relationships, rather than recognized as her own unique self.

She is also a goddess for anyone who feels stuck in loveless or abusive relationships. Nephthys understands loneliness and desperation and need because she has experienced those things herself. She understands making difficult choices and behaving in ways others might perceive as less than honorable because of her experiences. The best way to discover more about Nephthys is to work with her directly.

Here is a rite to help you do so. This rite may be more effective if performed at the threshold moments of sunset or midnight. In addition to your usual altar tools, you will need a scrying bowl or scrying mirror to most effectively perform this rite. Cast circle in your usual way. You might want to use quarter calls with an Egyptian theme, such as those following which call on the sons of Horus as elemental guardians. If you prefer, substitute your own quarter calls.

>Ladies and Lords of the North,
>Guardians of Earth,
>Great Lord Hapi,
>protected by Nephthys,
>please throw open the gates
>of your firm and earthly realms
>and come forth to guard and witness this rite.
>Hail and welcome!
>
>Lords and Ladies of the East,
>Guardians of Fire,
>Great Lord Duamutef,
>protected by Neith,
>please throw open the gates
>of your hot and fiery realms
>and come forth to guard and witness this rite.
>Hail and welcome!
>
>Lords and Ladies of the South,
>Guardians of Air,
>Great Lord Qebhsennuf,
>protected by Isis, please throw open the gates
>of your light and airy realms
>and come forth to guard and witness this rite.
>Hail and welcome!
>
>Ladies and Lords of the West,
>Guardians of Water,

Great Lord Imsety,
protected by Serket, please throw open the gates
of your cool and watery realms
and come forth to guard and witness this rite.
Hail and welcome!

Light a black candle as you invoke Nephthys.

Lady Nephthys, Mistress of the House,
Hidden Nephthys, Mistress of Shadows,
Great Lady of Mystery,
I invite your sacred presence
as I seek to know both you and myself better.
Welcome Nephthys!

At this time, it would be appropriate to light some kyphi or jasmine incense as an offering to Nephthys. Once you have invoked Nephthys and made your incense offering, state your intentions and speak your heart.

If you are more comfortable writing rather than speaking, write her a letter of petition and then burn it in your cauldron or some other fireproof container.

If you are burning incense or a petition letter, you can use the smoke for scrying if you prefer that to the bowl or mirror.

Ask to get to know Nephthys better. Tell her how her experiences speak directly to you. As you talk with her, position your scrying mirror or bowl so that you can see into it without seeing your own reflection. Soften your gaze and let yourself relax. Focus on the candle flame if that helps. If you will count yourself down to your meditative state, you may have a better scrying experience.

You may substitute another form of divination, such as tarot or runes, but scrying tends to be the most effective type of divination in this particular rite.

Ask Nephthys to reveal herself to you and to send you any messages that you are ready to hear at this time.

Once you sense her presence and feel like you have established a connection to her, ask if she is willing and able to assist you in doing some shadow work.

Continue scrying, asking her to help you see clearly the darker areas of your life where you are afraid to look.

Think about any wounds you have been carrying around in your soul. Look at the areas where you feel loss, loneliness, regret, or guilt. Be willing to honestly examine and accept your shadow.

If this becomes too difficult, be willing to lean on Nephthys for her assistance. Remember that she understands and that she is here to help you integrate these shadow areas and move forward into wholeness. She will not judge or condemn you, and she urges you not to judge or condemn yourself.

Honestly acknowledge your shadow side, your past painful experiences, your less than pleasant emotions, and any guilt you have been carrying.

Ask her assistance in determining what you have tried to repress and in understanding why you made choices you now regret. Think about the changes you want to make, and if you are unsure about how to make them, ask Nephthys for her guidance.

Take as long as you need to do this. Just as Nephthys aided Isis in restoring Osiris, she will assist you in restoring you to yourself.

Feel her love, understanding, and acceptance. Know that you are not alone in your darkness. Feel her wings descend around you in her loving, healing embrace. Feel yourself becoming joyful and whole in your heart as you are held in the wings of Nephthys.

Allow the powerful magick of this goddess to course through you, transmuting the poisons of your pains and regrets into emotional energy that better serves you. Let those parts of yourself that you fear are unlovable and destined to be alone soak up all of the love and acceptance offered to you by Nephthys. Know that you are never truly alone, no matter how lonely you might feel.

Hold the knowledge in your mind and your heart that you have had the courage to look into the darkest places of yourself in order to understand and transform them.

When you feel that your shadow work is complete for now, count yourself up from your meditative state. Take some time to journal about your experience and the work you did with Nephthys. When you are ready, prepare to say your farewell to Nephthys.

> Lady Nephthys, Mistress of the House,
> Hidden Nephthys, Mistress of Shadows,
> Great Lady of Mystery,
> I thank you for your presence in this rite
> and in my life.
> Please help me in the ongoing work
> of knowing and loving myself.
> Now stay if you will or go if you must
> as I offer my thanks and farewell.
> Farewell Nephthys.
>
> Ladies and Lords of the West, Guardians of Water,
> Great Lord Imsety,
> please return now to your cool and watery realms,
> taking with you my thanks.
> Hail and farewell.
>
> Lords and Ladies of the South,
> Guardians of Air,
> Great Lord Qebhsennuf,
> please return now to your light and airy realms,
> taking with you my thanks.
> Hail and farewell.
>
> Lords and Ladies of the East,
> Guardians of Fire,
> Great Lord Duamutef,
> please return now to your hot and fiery realms,
> taking with you my thanks.
> Hail and farewell.

> Ladies and Lords of the North,
> Guardians of Earth, Great Lord Hapi,
> please return now to your firm and earthly realms,
> taking with you my thanks.
> Hail and farewell.

Open circle, remembering that you can repeat this rite any time you feel the need to connect with Nephthys or continue your shadow work.

After completing this rite, be sure to take care of yourself. Go out with friends, treat yourself to your favorite dinner, buy yourself flowers, take a hot bubble bath or pamper yourself in some other way that will make you feel special.

Do something to show that you know, love, and accept yourself. Remember to be gentle and compassionate with yourself and with others.

If doing this shadow work has caused too much emotional upheaval, consider seeking out a counselor or therapist.

And most importantly, remember that you have established a powerful connection with Nephthys, and that you can return to her at any time for help dealing with the shadow areas of your life.

Poetry of Nebet Het

Figure 5: Nephthys from the Sarcophagus of Ramses III. Width on northern side. (Louvre museum, Paris, France).

By Tangopaso [Public domain], from Wikimedia Commons.

Note: Many of these poems by Chelsea Luellon Bolton were previously published in *Sun, Star and Desert Sand: Poems for the Egyptian Gods*. Lulu Press, 2017.

Nebet Het

by Chelsea Luellon Bolton

Wailing when mourners cry for the dead
Soft hug at a bittersweet ending of a poem
Shadows that hold the darkest secrets and
the quiet that comes from just listening
Hidden like the new moon and
Always there
Waiting to hold those who are in tears

Desert's Bride

by Chelsea Luellon Bolton

Mourner
Nurturer
House Holder
Mistress of the Home
Seldom heard
Powerful in Voice
Death's Companion
Desert's Bride
Subtle Messenger
Of the Unseen
and the Unknown

Violence Follows Despair

by Chelsea Luellon Bolton

Dry wind
Twirls, stirring up the foliage
Desert storm
Sparks flame
Chaos burns inhabitants' houses
Desolation left in its wake
Mother, You are there
Tears stream down
Among the charred ruins
Of lost homes and lives
Violence follows Despair

Passage

by Chelsea Luellon Bolton

Hallowed Winds
Tear
Between the Worlds
Of Invisibility and the Seen
Death waits at the Threshold
Where cries are heard
Only by those who listen to the weary of heart
The world waits to pass through
The Threshold
Bending and flowing like a veil
Consistent and yet ever moving
Untamable in Its Wrath
Unmovable in Its Peace
Solid and Liquid
It moves
Unseen and Unheard

Thunderstorm's Lullaby

by Chelsea Luellon Bolton

Trembling
Step forward
Fire burns below
Empty footsteps behind
Ahead the clouds rumble
Storm brews like a boiling pot
Soon explodes quenching the flames
Lightning cracks
Thunder roars
Sky cries of pain
Thunder vibrates in my ears
The lull of thunderclaps
calms my fears
like a lullaby
Rain drenches my skin
Cleansing blanket of droplets
Lightning flashes
Thunder rolls on

Tombstone

by Chelsea Luellon Bolton

I am Death
I am Sorrow
I am the night devoid of the moon
I comfort those who He is forced to change
Why do you not know?
I am with you
Yes, you, Child
I am subtle
I am the whisper you can barely hear
I am holding you in your despair
Come to Me when you grieve
I am the Opener of the Way
I break the tombstone
So passage to the Hall of Ma'at
is possible

Veiled Silence

by Chelsea Luellon Bolton

Morbidly Beautiful
O Shadow Queen
Lurking in Darkness
On the coldest of nights
Thunder shatters the tranquility
Of the rain patting windowsills
Soft as velvet
Opaque as a veil
You come swiftly
And silently slip away

Flame

by Chelsea Luellon Bolton

I am venom laced with flame
I am strength laced with steel
I am shrieking as a mourner
Rocks tumble
Glass shatters
My cries resound
Deafening those that can't hear

Nebet Het Speaks Through Silence

by Chelsea Luellon Bolton

Thoughts, whispers not yet manifest
In form, In Creation
Ideas not yet realized
Tangibility not yet reached
In this liminal space
The Goddess resides
Hidden in motion
Slightly recognized
But not with words
Nebet Het Speaks through silence

Through the Passage

by Chelsea Luellon Bolton

I am an Eye of Ra
I am the coiling snake,
The slinking serpent
How am I a nice goddess?
I am the leopard who roars
The fierce lioness who protects her cubs
How am I a nice goddess?
I am the magician who protects
I keep the boundary clear
From impurity
From evil
From that which displeases the gods
For I am the line between the sacred and the profane
I guard the temple
I guard the home
I guard the cemetery
and all who dwell in liminal space
From entrance to exit and the mid-point between
I am the threshold
All must pass through Me

Unseen Eye

by Chelsea Luellon Bolton

The Eye slithers across the water
Towering over desert and fertile land
Blistering the earth
Warmth or Scorch
Rumbling heard overhead
Tears of God
Quench the Earth's thirst
Thunder Roars
Sky's Fire Dances
Flashing
Illuminating
Crackling against the Sky
Mystery Concealed in the Darkness
Spark seen only by the Unseen Eye

Voices Echo

by Chelsea Luellon Bolton

Cunt
Fuck
These are just words
But words have meanings, little one.
Words give Voice
to those who do not speak
Words give meaning
to those who have none
Words give magic
to those who would wield such power
And yet, they do not realize the Power of their Voice
Voices carry
Voices linger long after they are silenced
Voices echo
Echoes linger
in the mind, in the heart
Echoes create more voices
More words
More meaning
More magic
Beware, child
Of the magic you create with words

As Dawn Breaks

By Chelsea Luellon Bolton

I am the Kite that shrieks
the Kite that mourns
For I am the mourner
I am the Goddess who heals
The Goddess who bereaves
I am the Goddess who rejoices
For My son is King
Yes, My son
for Heru is Mine as well
As is My husband
for Wesir is Mine as well
I am His wife in death
as My Sister was in life
We are His Widows
We are His Companions
We are His Sisters
We are His Wives
I am also Set's wife
as Aset is also Wepwawet's
Our Partners change
Our Children change
Based on what People need
And what We need as well
I am the Goddess of the Sky
I am the Night and the Dusk and the Dawn
I am the twilight
I am the One who sees who is hidden
I am the One who peers into darkness
I am the One who illuminates the Night
I am one of the Two Cows
I am the Star Goddess
Of Dusk and Dawn
Of Twilight
I am the sun and stars

I am the moon, rising when it cannot be seen
The New Moon is My time
Wesir is slain as the Moon goes dark;
Wesir is revived as the moon is full
This is Our cycle
The sky matching the world below
As rain My tears fall
along with My Sister's
to mourn Our dead brother
I am the Wife
I am the Mourner
I am the One who rejoices
Through the Moon
Through the Stars
Through Sopdet and Rain
and the Nile Flood;
These are all My cycles
as well as My Sister's.
I am Nebet Het.
And I speak through whispers
And I speak through silence
as dawn breaks.

Temple, Tomb, and Home

by Chelsea Luellon Bolton

Royal Lady
of temple and tomb
Royal Mistress
of the Sistrum and Menat
You are the Princess in the Palace
as Royal as Your sister
Lady of the Palace
who rules over the King's home
where he is enshrined on the throne
You are the Lady of the House
Noble Women are named for You
Their title is Your name
Their functions are Yours also
Mistress of the Home
Upkeep of the House
Lady who honors their dead
These duties are Yours also
Lady of the Temple
Lady of the Shrine
Lady of the Sanctuary
Who protects the sacred within
Lady of the Tomb
Who weeps for her husband
Who greets the dead upon arrival
Who helps transform the dead into an ancestor
She who governs the dwelling places of mortals, Gods, and Kings,
And also the dead.
For Her house is also their tomb.
For She is the Goddess of the Temple, Tomb, and Home

Lady of the Temple

by Chelsea Luellon Bolton

I am the Lady of the Temple,
I am the Lady of the Shrine,
Call to Me in your life,
Call for My blessings,
Call for My aid,
I will help those who honor Me,
so honor Me today.
I will come into your life,
I will come into your home,
I will come and put things in order,
Look at a Temple in ancient Egypt,
how organized it was,
with priests and priestesses,
with chanters and singers,
with acrobats and scribes,
with ritualists and record-keepers,
with artisans to make implements
and offerings for the Gods.
Look at how organized
all of those people had to be,
in order to honor at a temple,
in order to honor one God or Goddess.
Smaller shrines had fewer people,
but it still took a community
to honor a deity.
Not so for you.
Not so for you.
You can buy Our implements,
or make them yourself.
You can buy Our statues,
or make them yourself,
or have them commissioned.
It still takes a community
to create a shrine,

but it is a different kind.
And yet the shrines in your home,
and the shrines in your life,
are created with Us in mind.
So listen, child,
and listen well,
Our shrines in your home,
are like small temples.
Guard and tend them well.

Animal Forms of Nebet Het
by Chelsea Luellon Bolton

I am associated with the Dog
because of Sopdet, the Dog Star.
And because of My husband Set.
I am associated with the Donkey
as proclaimed in the spell.
For I am Set's companion and His bride.
Yet, I am also a Donkey,
for I am a Goddess of the wild as well.
For I am the Goddess of the Edges –
of forests, of oases,
of trees and the shade they bring,
of fertile land and desert,
I am the Goddess of these boundaries
and thus of untamed, wild things.
I am a Panther Goddess,
as an Eye of Ra,
as a Goddess of the Heavens,
with the spotted-coat of the Leopard,
being the stars of the night sky,
who are also the Blessed Dead.
I am the Akhet-Cow,
the Celestial Cow of the Horizon
I am the Sky Goddess here,
the Primordial Goddess who came from the Waters
in the First Time,
and gave birth to the sun.
And I am the Goddess who
nourishes the deceased in their time.
I am the Cow Goddess
of the ancestors.
I am the Kite,
soaring in the sky,
wailing and mourning,
keening for My slain Lord,
for My slain husband,
for He was My husband

as well as My sister.
I am the Goddess
of Many Forms.
I am the Cobra and Snake,
as an Eye of Ra,
with Her flame and magic
and might.
And I am the Goddess of the Sun,
as the protector
of Ra, Heru and Wesir.

Strong One

by Chelsea Luellon Bolton

The fires of Ra and Wesir
are My own.
I am the Goddess of *Ka*-Power,
I am the Goddess of the Diadem.
I am Ra's Eye,
spitting cobra,
slithering snake,
I am the Lioness,
and the Panther.
I am the Strong-Armed,
Lady of Strength.
Just as Set is the Great of Strength,
I am its Lady.
I am Nebet Het, the Strong Armed,
I am Nebet Het, Strong in Power,
I am Nebet Het, the Strong One.
I am Nebet Het, *Merkhetes*,
She Whose Flame is Painful.
I am Nebet Het, the Bright One,
burning fiercely, with My light.
I am Nebet Het,
And Strength is My Power.

Royal Lady

by Chelsea Luellon Bolton

I am a Royal Goddess
I am a Royal Wife
I am a Royal Lady
I am a Royal Second Wife.
I am a Royal Princess,
I am a Royal Queen.
I am a Lady and a Goddess
Who commands sunbeams.

I am the Wife of Set,
Lord of the Oasis.
I am the Wife of Wesir,
Lord of the Fields and Underworld
I am the Sister of Wesir,
I am the Sister of Set,
I am the Widow of Wesir,
As My brothers and consorts
are a King and a Lord.
I am a Queen and a Lady.

I am Royal Myself,
I am the one who gives
royal decrees.
I am a Goddess
of Royal birth.
I was born of the Queen of Heaven,
and Lord of the Earth.

I am Royal,
I am the Wife,
I am the Goddess
I am the Ruler
I am the Lady of Life.

I am the Daughter of Ra,

King of the Gods.
I am His *Uraeus*,
and His Eye,
I am the Lady of Stars.

I am the consort of Ra,
for I birthed His son.
Yinepu is Our child,
He is the only one.

I am a Princess,
I am a Queen,
of Stars and the Sky.
I am the Lady who is rarely seen.

I am the shining Lady
on the moonless night.
I am the shining Lady,
burning ever so bright.

I shine in darkness,
more than light.
I shine with radiance,
fiercely bright.

I am dark
when My sister is bright.
And She is dark,
when I am light.

I am the Royal Lady
I am the Royal Wife,
I am the Goddess of Royalty,
I am the Goddess of Life.

Sorceress of Transformation

by Chelsea Luellon Bolton

I am the Sorceress Queen
I am the one who casts spells
I am the one who does divination
I am the one who knows Her spells
Like My sister, Aset.
I am the fashioner of spells
In the *Duat*.
I am the fashioner of spells
In the Unseen Realm.
I make all things possible.
I bring to light what is hidden.
I bring magic from the Unseen to the Seen World.
I bring magic of breath and fire
Rain and water
Ice and snow
I bring the scorching heat
The warmth of flame
For I am the Cobra and the Eye.
I bring protection
I bring resolution
I bring transformation
In spells.
I am the flame on the candle's wick
I am the incense in the air
I am the water with salt and herbs in a bowl
I am fire
I am breath
I am that which you fear,
Yet must face.
For I am the disturber
I am the one who brings revolution
To you,
And to anyone else
Who asks Me for the change of transformation
Of Ra, Heru, and Wesir.

Travel to Me
by Chelsea Luellon Bolton

Who is Nebet Het?
The Sister of Aset?
The Sister of Set?
The Sister of Wesir?
Ra's Daughter?
Ra's Wife?
Yes, and all of these.
I am all of these.
Whether or not you acknowledge Me is unimportant.
I am there.
I am here.
I am everywhere.
You cannot contain Me,
In words or ideas,
They do not alter who I am.
I am the breeze.
I am the Wind.
I am the Hurricane,
along with My husband.
I am Nebet Het,
of the Crossroads.
Between Sky and Earth,
Between Twilight and Dawn,
Between here and there.
I am in between places,
For I am the liminal Goddess
Of Dawn and Dusk,
Of Twilight.
And I am the Sun and Moon
in the sky,
I am the Unseen Moon
And the sun which rises and sets.
For I am Nebet Het,
The Light in the Dark,
Unseen,
Unheard,

Unknown
And yet, to see Me is to disappear
Into the self,
To hear whispers,
To see what must be known,
To glimpse the Truth.
What must be known
Cannot be known,
Without traveling through darkness,
to find the light.

Shadow Illumination

by Chelsea Luellon Bolton

Nebet Het, Nephthys
She is the Goddess of the Dawn
She is the Goddess of Twilight
She is the Goddess of Here and There
She is the Star Goddess
She is the light of dawn
She is the light, blazing forth
repelling darkness
It cowers back
It flees as light illuminates
what is hidden in the shadows
This is the light of dawn
This is the light of Nebet Het
She illuminates shadows
Darkness quakes at Her approach

Lady, Sister, and Mistress

by Chelsea Luellon Bolton

Nebet Het, Lady of the House
Lady of the Home
Lady of the Temple
Lady of the Tomb
Lady, who walks with those who travel
Lady, who walks with souls through the Underworld
Lady, who guards the graves
Lady, who guards the tomb
Lady, who guards the temple
Lady, who guards the home
Lady, Sister and Wife of Set
Lady, Sister and Wife of Wesir
Lady, Daughter and Consort of Ra
Lady, Mother of Yinepu
Lady, Mother of Heru
Lady, Mistress of the Sky, Earth, and the Underworld

Shadow and Light

by Chelsea Luellon Bolton

Nebet Het is *Amenti*
Lady of the West
Lady of the Sycamore
Lady of the Tree
Goddess of Women
Lady, who weaves
And watches
She is an observer
She perceives the hidden things
She sees what cannot be seen
She peers into the hidden night
And sees what cannot be seen
Hidden Lady,
Shadow Princess
Lady and Queen
Lady of the Crossroads
Who illuminates the secrets
Hidden in the night
Lady and Hidden One
Lady who is both
Shadow and Light

Never Be Afraid

by Chelsea Luellon Bolton

Nebet Het
is the Whispers in the Wind
is the sorrow in your despair
is the rage in your grief
is the calm before the storm
and the aftermath in its wake.
I am all the pain in your despair
But fear not,
Know that I am there
Now
I have come before you thought it
I have come before you called My name
I am with you now
Now
Speak to Me

Of your despair
Of your rage
Of your sorrow
I am there
I am here
Now
In the present
Yes, now
So come to Me
Despite your anguish
Despite your rage
For these do not define you
They are a moment in time
In passing,
A fleeting moment that seems like eternity
I assure you, it is not
It is not.
Your rage and your fear

Do not define who you are
Your actions define you
How will you sit with your rage?
How will you express it?
How will you temper it?
How you will accept yourself,
if you cannot own your rage?
It is yours.
Own it.
Possess it.
And then release it.
And then, child,
You will be free
From yourself
And all that holds you back.
Fear is your enemy,
an enemy of your mind.
It holds you back.
If you follow Me,
you need not be afraid
I am with those who follow Me
All the way
For I am Nebet Het,
Who conquers despair

Soul Renewal

by Chelsea Luellon Bolton

Nebet Het
Of the Wishing Well
People make wishes to the Gods
I am the one whom people call upon
To end their despair
To end their sorrow
To end their despair
Which is embedded in their soul
Deeply embedded
It would take an execration
To tear it out
For the soul absorbs what is around it
For the soul in nourished by what one feeds it
Do you feed it rage?
Do you feed it pain or rejection or abusive speech?
Do you feed it excuses or harsh criticism?
Do you feed it sorrow or despair?
Do you feed it joy?
Do you feed it laughter or happiness?
Do you feed it with what you love?
Do you feed it with hard work?
Do you feed it love?
Do you feed it with what you desire?
Decide what you will feed it
And then nourish it.
And your soul will brighten or diminish
By what you choose to feed it.
You can ask Me and My Husband or Sister
For help with this,
But ultimately, it is up to you.

Guide and Illumination

by Chelsea Luellon Bolton

Nebet Het of the Way
Nephthys of the Way
Wepwawet is the Guide
He is the God of your life
He is the Way-shower
He is the Guardian and Guide
He is the one who protects your life
You are lost
You know the way
I am here to illuminate your path
To see what you are missing
What you have lost
You can regain;
What you have sacrificed,
Can be renewed;
Let Him show you the way
He is the Guide and Guard
Of all paths, of all lives
Let Him show you
What your path holds,
What the Gods have in store for you

Call on Her Today

by Chelsea Luellon Bolton

Nebet Het of the Temple
Nebet Het of the Shrine
Nebet Het of the Pathway
Nebet Het, the Divine
Lady of All Roads
Lady of All Paths
Lady, who has set tasks
Lady of the Crossroads
Lady of the Way
Lady of the Life-span
Call on Her today.

I lead

by Chelsea Luellon Bolton

I am Nebet Het, Nephthys
Mistress of the Home and hearth
Mistress of the Lake of Rushes
Mistress of the Sycamore
Mistress of the Tomb
You are nearing your death
You are nearing your transformation
Into the person you will become
And Aset will be with you here
And Nebet Het as well
And the Egyptian Gods
Nebet Het has more to tell you
Nephthys has more to say
Aset is your Goddess for the Egyptian Gods
Aset is your main Goddess overall
I am too, for I am Nephthys
I am Nebet Het
Her Sister
Her Twin
Her Co-Wife
I am Nebet Het of the Shores of Heru
I am Nebet Het of the River
I am Nebet Het of the Two Lands
Aset is here too,
Please don't think She isn't
I am Nebet Het of All possible paths
I am the Guardian of the Road
I am the Guardian of the Paths
I am like Wepwawet
I am like Yinepu, My son
I lead
I guide
I go forth and traverse the paths
I travel
I guide

I lead lost souls
I lead you
Now, through your transformation
Like I lead all through change
For My husband is Set
For My husband is Ra
For My husband is Wesir
I lead them all
I illuminate the path of Set,
When He destroys the Enemy of the Gods

I illuminate the path for Ra,
When He travels the Night-Bark
I illuminate the path for Wesir,
When He changes and transforms in the *Duat*
I illuminate the pathways
Like Wepwawet
I lead the way

Flow

by Chelsea Luellon Bolton

Nebet Het of the River
Nebet Het of the Stream
Nebet Het, who knows your dreams
All possibility is in the water
Outcomes in all shapes and forms are possible
With water
It can flow anywhere
It can form the shape which holds it
It can survive in all worlds
Water and air
Water and heat
Earth and Sky contain it as do the seas
So it is everywhere
Adapt like water
Mold yourself to fit your shape
And be one with your own flow
Flow like water
Adapt to your own way

Star Goddess

by Chelsea Luellon Bolton

Nebet Het of the Stars
Nebet Het of the Night
Nebet Het, of the Northern Skies
Nebet Het, of the *Duat*
Who guards and guides the dead
She is the Star Goddess
As Sopdet
As the Celestial Cow Goddess
As an Eye of Ra
As the Goddess of the Night Sky
She holds the dead in Her embrace
And shelters the living
With the ancestors watching over them from above
She is Nebet Het, the Lady of Stars
Nebet Het, the Goddess of the Ancestors
Nebet Het *Amenti*
And Nebet Het, the Goddess of Stars

Nebet Het, Daughter of Ra

by Chelsea Luellon Bolton

Nebet Het, Daughter of Ra
Eye of Ra, Lady of Flame
Sopdet, Eye of Ra
Lady of the Stars
Leopard Goddess
Cobra Goddess
Lady of Fire
Lady of the Brazier
Lady of Temples and Shrines
Guardian of Holy Spaces from Impurity and Evil Forces
One Who Guides the Sun Boat through the Darkness
Slayer of Evil Spirits and the Serpent-Enemy of the Gods
Eye of Ra, Mistress of Magic
Queen of Renewal
Mother of Yinepu, Fathered by Ra
Daughter of Ra, Sun Goddess
Lady of Mystery and Magic
Lady of the Unknown and the Unseen
Queen of the Dead, Consort of Wesir
Sister and Wife of Set, Lord of the Oasis
Daughter of Ra
Solar Lady,
Queen of the Gods

Lady of the Veil

by Chelsea Luellon Bolton

Nebet Het of the Veil
Nebet Het of the Unseen
Nebet Het, Lady of Tears
Mourning Goddess
Dark Queen
of the Night
Lady of Darkness
Goddess of Shadows
Hidden One
Shining Light
Illuminating what cannot be seen

Healer

by Chelsea Luellon Bolton

Nebet Het of the Outside
Nebet Het of the Hidden One
Nebet Het of the Way-Finder
Nebet Het, the One Who Leads
Who leads the way for the Apothecary,
Who leads the way for the Healer
Who leads the way for the Dead
She guides and leads like Wepwawet
The Apothecary and Healer
The one who leads the way
For healing and mending to begin

Please Reside in Our Hearts

by Chelsea Luellon Bolton

She who speaks through silence
She who speaks through words unheard
She who speaks through the heart
She who doesn't mince Her words
Goddess Nebet Het
Goddess Nebet Het
Please cleanse my soul
Goddess Nebet Het
Goddess Nebet Het
Please make me whole
Goddess Nebet Het
Goddess Nebet Het
Please save my soul
Goddess Nebet Het
Goddess Nebet Het
Please heal my heart
Goddess Nebet Het
Goddess Nebet Het
Please never depart
Goddess Nebet Het
Goddess Nebet Het
Please reside in our hearts

Lady of Strength, Goddess Who Beguiles

by Chelsea Luellon Bolton

I am the Goddess of Strength
I am the Lady of Guile
I am the Goddess of Magic
I am the Lady of the Oasis
As the Wife of Wesir
As the Wife of Set
I am Nephthys
I am Nebet Het
I am the Lady of Strength
One who beguiles through trickery
Like My sister;
When I beguile, I enchant
With words of power and might
While Her voice is Powerful, My Sister Aset
My voice is silence
My voice is the power of the grave
No one can come back from death
And no one can escape Me
For I am the Lady of Strength
Whose word is as immutable as the final resting place,
The Grave.

More Than My Sister's Shadow

by Chelsea Luellon Bolton

I am more than a Goddess of the Dead
I am an Eye of Ra
I am a Wife
I am a Mother
I am a Sister
I am a child of the Sky and Earth, of Nut and Geb
I am the Daughter of Ra
I am a Princess and I am the Eye Goddess in the Court of Ra
These are My titles as befits a Goddess
Of My rank and position within the realms of Gods
I am of Egypt
I am of Africa and other lands which accepted the Egyptian religion
I am of many places and many names,
Like My sister Aset;
Yet I am not as well-known as She
I am as multifaceted as She is — for I am Her twin
Like My Sister
I am the Eye of Ra
I am the Great of Magic
I am the Rain Goddess and the one who brings the Nile's flood
I am the Mourner of Wesir and Wailing Woman
I am Sopdet, the Invisible Star, the Brightest Star in the Sky
I am the Lady of the West, the Lady of the Dead
The Lady of the Ancestors
I am the Celestial Cow
I am the Star Goddess
I am at the Dawn and Dusk of each day
I am all of these things
Along with My Sister
But there is more to Me
Than My role as the Sister of Aset
I am Nebet Het, the Lady of the Temple, Tomb and Home
I am Nebet Het, the Wife of Set
I am Nebet Het, *Kherseket* (Who Wipes Away Tears)
I am Nebet Het, *Merkhetes* (Whose Flame is Painful)
I am Nebet Het, the Panther Goddess, the Leopard Goddess

I am Nebet Het,
who is offered meat on braziers to ward against evil
I am more than My Sister's Twin
I am more than My Sister's Shadow
I am the Hidden Goddess
I am the Dark Goddess
Who will reveal Herself
In Her own time

Nebet Het is the Goddess

by Chelsea Luellon Bolton

Nebet Het is the Goddess
Of the Ancestors, of the Dead
Nebet Het is the Goddess
Of the Sun, of the Star Sopdet
Nebet Het is the Goddess
Of the Nile's flood, of the Rainclouds
Nebet Het is the Goddess
Of Mourning, of Keening
Nebet Het is the Goddess
Of Magic, of Power
Nebet Het is the Goddess
Of Illumination, of Light
Nebet Het is the Goddess
Of Flame, of Fire
Nebet Het is the Goddess
Of the Unseen, of the Secrets
Nebet Het is the Goddess
Of the Coffin, of the Tomb
Nebet Het is the Goddess
Of the Sky, of the Star-filled Night Sky
Nebet Het is the Goddess
Of Malachite, of Beauty
Nebet Het is the Goddess
Of Joy, of the Tambourine
Nebet Het is the Goddess
Of the Leopard, of the Cobra
Nebet Het is the Goddess
Of Her sister Aset, of Her brother Wesir
Nebet Het is the Goddess
Of Her consort Ra, of Her son Yinepu
Nebet Het is the Goddess
Of Her husband Set, of the Oasis
Nebet Het is the Goddess
Of Strength, of Protection
Nebet Het is the Goddess

Of Her People, of Her Devotees
Nebet Het is the Goddess
Of you and of me

Battered Wife, the Strong One

by Chelsea Luellon Bolton

I am not the battered wife.
I am not the victim here.
I am not Set's concubine
or a damsel in distress,
who needs saving.
When Set was vilified,
so was I.
He was the demon.
I was the weak, distressed
victim of a wife.
Do you understand?
To take away His strength,
is to take away Mine.
When you vilify one,
you damage Us all.
For We are built into the system,
even Set has His place.
As do I.
Where is My role,
if you remove His?
Where is His role,
if you remove Me?
My strength and His strength
We are complementary.
We work in tandem,
We work together.
As husband and wife.
I am the Wife of Set.

I am the Wife of Wesir.
I am His second Wife.
I am the Royal Lady,
and the Royal Wife,
along with My sister, Aset.
I am the Widow and Wife.

I am the Mourner and the Weeper,
I am the one who wails,
the death of the King.
I am Nebet Het, the Mourner of Wesir
with Aset.
I am the Widow and the Wife,
along with My sister.
This cycle is Ours.
We weep and mourn,
Our brother slain.
We are the Widows and the Wives.
We are the Goddesses of Life.

In the Myth of Plutarch,
I have a child with My husband.
For Plutarch, it was illegitimate,
for Plutarch's culture would not fathom
a King with more than one wife.
I am the second Wife of Wesir.

And even so, within this myth,
I leave My "abusive" husband, Set.
So how I am a battered wife,
when I leave an abusive relationship?
How am I weak, for leaving,
and going with My sister,
to find Wesir?

I am not the victim.
I am the one who had the strength to leave.

I am the Wife of Wesir,
as a Mourner, as a Widow, as a Wife.
I am His sister too.
I am with My sister here.
We Two are the Wives of Wesir.

I am the Wife of Set,
when He is the Slayer of the Snake,
who is the Enemy of the Gods.

I am the Wife of Set,
as the Averter of Evil
and as one who protects against harm.

But this is only in some time periods
and some temples.

I am the Wife of Wesir,
before I became the Wife of Set.

Even so, I am not the battered wife
of either God.
Both love Me.
Both cherish Me.
And Both treat Me like the Lady
that I am.

I am not the battered wife.
I am the wife,
Who is as strong as both Her husbands.
I am as strong as Wesir, the Strong One
I am as Strong as Set, Great of Strength,
and I am Strength's Lady
as They are its Lord.

This is Who I am
as the Wife of these Two Gods.

I am the Wife of Wesir
I am the Wife of Set.
And I am the Wife of the All-Lord.
I am as strong as He.

I am not a victim.
I am not a battered wife.
I am the Lady of Strength,
along with My husband,
be it Set or Wesir or Ra.

I am the Strong One,

I am the Lady of Power
and I am the Eye of the Solar God.

This is Who I am,
as the Wife or Widow
or the consort of these Gods.

Guiding Light

by Chelsea Luellon Bolton

Hidden One
Blinding Light
Darkness shrinks back
Darkness flees
When You shine Your radiant light
Bright Goddess, Holy One
Nebet Het, Daughter of Ra
Who repels darkness with Her light
She who walks through darkness
Guided by Her own light
She guides Her devotees
Through the darkness
Where the sun shines
As She is the Daughter of Ra
And the Goddess of Sunbeams

Papyrus, Necklace, and Harpoon

by Chelsea Luellon Bolton

I am Nebet Het of the Reeds,
Papyrus stocks growing,
lining up on the riverbank.
Swishing in the wind,
like a sistrum.
I sit and wait
as papyrus blooms
into flowers
and human-made scrolls.
This is the first lesson:
a writer must have something
on which to write.

The necklace is made
of amber, carnelian,
jasper —
red and orange hues,
the sun's carnelian
is the *Tyet* Amulet.
This is Mine,
as it is Aset's.
Sparkling fire,
held in a jewel.

The harpoon
is the weapon
of the Gods of Egypt,
along the Nile.
Spearing fish
to eat.
Spearing larger prey
to eat or ward off.
This is the weapon
of accuracy and precision

Take aim and shoot,
hoping the prey is caught,
to eat supper,
which are offered to the Gods.
hoping the prey is caught,
and enemies felled,
With the might of the harpoon.

Tread Upon Nebet Het

by Chelsea Luellon Bolton

Those who step on graves
Those who tread upon My sacred ground
with carelessness
with thoughtlessness,
are the ones who offend Me.
These are the lands belonging
to the ones who have gone before.
These are the lands belonging to the Dead,
both the Blessed and Restless Dead.
And these people do not care,
if you come to them weeping of your life
if you do not take care to treat their grounds
with respect by the time you leave.
Do not tread on Nephthys.
Do not tread on Nebet Het
if you cannot clean up after yourself.
Do not leave beer bottles or trash in your wake.
Do not leave rotting plants by the tombstones.
Do not leave trash behind.
Clean up after you offer to the Dead.
Pour out libations to the Dead and
the Gods or Spirits who watch over them.
Place the food offerings in a bag and then throw it in the trash bin.
Clean up after yourself.
We will bless you.
If you come to honor us,
We will bless you.
But dear child,
clean up after yourself
at the gravesite or ancestor shrine.
For if you tread upon Nebet Het,
if you tread upon Nephthys,
how can you expect to be blessed by the Goddess
or those She cares for in the *Duat*?

Dirge

by Chelsea Luellon Bolton

I scream and My voice resounds,
echoing in the night.
I wail and glass shatters,
howling as a dirge.
I scream and keen
as the wail deafens the ears.
I speak and thunder rumbles,
I weep and wind wails
at the peak.
I scream and My wailing
shatters, shatters
as I weep.
as I mourn.
as I cry,
as I shriek.
And I mourn as night falls,
and I weep.
And My song
is a requiem for
those in mourning
and those yet to mourn.

Nebet Het, of the Graves

by Chelsea Luellon Bolton

I am Nebet Het of the Graves,
I am Nebet Het of the Tomb,
I bring all to the resting place,
I am with Mehet Weret, here.
I am the Celestial Cow of the starry vault of Heaven,
I am *Amenti*, Lady of the West.
I am the Sycamore Goddess,
nourishing the dead with fruit and water.
I am Nebet Het, Lady of the Sycamore.
I am Nebet Het, Goddess of the West.
The Beautiful Land of creation and life.
I am the one who guards the gates.
I am the one who greets the Dead.
I greet them as they enter *Amenti*.
I greet them as they enter the *Duat*.
I am the Goddess of the Ancestors.
I am the Goddess over their care.
So honor Me and honor them,
Do you dare —
to gaze at the bright stars of Heaven,
to tend to the graves and shrines,
Honor Me at twilight,
where light and darkness meet.

Honor them in the morning,
when you greet the dawn,
or in the evening, at dusk
these are My times.
Honor the Dead among the Living,
and power will flow,
for from the ancestors,
I command,
blessings will flow
to those who honor Me,
to those who honor the Blessed Dead.

Lady of Sorrow

by Chelsea Luellon Bolton

I am the one who sees the gate,
between here and there,
between this and that.
I am the one who sees
the keening
the mourning,
as they weep
over graves and the dying.
Deep in their pain
Deep in their remorse,
Darkness falls,
for those who can't forgive themselves.
For when you die, it is too late.

Death does not release its grip
on those who cross its threshold.
There is nothing you can do.
in this life.
Things change,
things happen.
All is forgiven.
You did your best — as we all must,
as we all do.
Now, listen to your heart beat.
Do you feel the moments between
each pump of blood,
coursing through your veins?
You have all the time in the world,
you tell yourself,
and yet,
you are never guaranteed tomorrow.

Do not sit idly by in your life
and watch and wait for things to come,
for they may not come.

In order to get what you want,
you must act.
There is only today.
None other.
Many tomorrows,
yet to come.
Stop wasting time,
for it is the only commodity
you can't retrieve.

So come to your life,
cherishing this gift.
See what you can accomplish
in one day.
And do what is on your list.

Wipe Away Your Tears

by Chelsea Luellon Bolton

I am Nebet Het.
I am the Mourning Woman.
I am the One who wept.
I am the one who cried.
I am the one who wailed,
when My husband died.
I know the tears you weep,
and the sorrows you feel.
For they are Mine.
I hold this sorrow within Me,
so I know your pain.
so I know your sorrow.
I know your loss, dear child.
I am the One Who Wipes Away Tears.
I am Nebet Het, *Kherseket*.
I am the One Who Wipes Away Tears.
So come to My shrine or altar.
Come to any place you can,
and cry or weep,
and call out to Me,
so I can wipe away your tears.

Personal Goddess: Nebet Het
by Chelsea Luellon Bolton

Nebet Het, Lady of the Gods
Lady of Strength, Goddess of Fortitude
Lady of Kindness, Compassionate One
These are the qualities of Nebet Het
You aspire to possess
You already possess
This Goddess is Aset's twin
Her counterpoise
Her balance
Her mirror self
You need this too
For Aset is your Mother.
And you need Her
To be your best self
To be your true self
To be who you desire to be.
As a Beloved of Nebet Het,
Sister of Aset, Queen of the Gods.

Nebet Het's Advice on Community
by Chelsea Luellon Bolton

Be kind
Everyone has their pain and issues
Everyone has their hiccups and missteps
Everyone has their preferences and needs to honor Us
And these must be respected;
As Our shrines are respected;
As Our offerings are respected;
So too must Our people respect each other
And you don't;
You belittle and bicker
And you mock your teachers
You mock their words
You mock their teachings
You mock their temples and following,
Yet where do you learn to honor Us?
From books?
Those authors are your teachers.
From a temple and community?
Those priests and priestesses are your teachers,
their books and writings aid in their teaching.
Respect them.
Respect yourself and the gods you follow.
Respect all those who honor Us,
Even if their way is not yours.

Nebet Het's Advice

by Chelsea Luellon Bolton

Nebet Het of the Nile
Nebet Het of the stream,
Do you know what you dream?
Nebet Het of the cycles
Nebet Het of your heart,
Do you practice your art?
Nebet Het of the written word
Nebet Het of your art,
Do you know what is in your heart?
Do you know what you dream?
Do you know what you wish?
You do not understand your own soul.
You do not understand your own desires.
You desire a life free of strife
You desire your dream to be manifest
You write and read
And think it means nothing
But you are wrong.
You are so wrong.
You preserve Us.
You record Our names and hymns.
You record Our holidays,
Even obscure ones.
You record Our deeds.
These are not small things.
Give yourself permission to bask in your own glory.
You deserve to be proud of your own accomplishments.
Yet, you brush them aside
as if they mean so little.
They do not.
They mean a lot to Us.
And to you.
So listen,
For this is your task,
when you are done with this,

create something for yourself.
Feed your *Ka*.
Write your stories,
Tend your shrines.
And let Us guide you forward.
These Gods will help you:
Wesir, Aset, Nebet Het, Wepwawet, and Ra.
Take this advice:
You need to honor your commitments.

Nebet Het's Rage, Nebet Het's Promise

by Chelsea Luellon Bolton

I am the Hidden One
I am She Who is Hidden,
I am Nebet Het
Of Darkness
Of the Shade
Of the Stillness of Night with no Moon
No light.
Yet, the stars burn in this darkness,
This luminous light
Brightens the night
as the stars shine in the sky.
I am the Light in Darkness
I am the Twilight at Dawn and Dusk.
I am the Light
in the Darkest of Times.
And this is a dark time for many.
There is fear in their hearts
There is fear in their words
There is righteous anger,
The fury at injustice,
And yet,
I am the Light in the Darkness
I drive away evil
I empower good
I bestow strength on those
who will stand and fight —
any way they can —
with art, with words
with actions,
with kindness,
being intolerant of injustice —
in whatever form it takes.
And here I will stand with those
who March.
For I am a Goddess of Women

as is My sister.
as well as many Goddesses and some Gods.
Injustice won't stand against Our wrath.
Sekhmet, Hethert, and Bast with Their flames and magic,
Nit and Wepwawet with Their arrows and magic,
Aset with Her scimitar and magic,
And I, Nebet Het, with My arrows and magic
Ra with His Eyes,
Hethert's joy will keep the people going,
For joy and rage must balance each other
in the hearts of those who fight.

And yet, I will come
as a snake, as cobra
as a leopard
Whose flame will burn
the shackles of fear which bind you,
the evil around you,
and the injustice against you.
and whose arrows
will strike down the enemies of *ma'at*.
will destroy injustice.
So Ra will be triumphant,
as the Uncreated is destroyed.
So you too will be triumphant,
Against the enemies of health
Against the enemies of life, prosperity, and happiness.
Against the enemies of safety and treating people well.
If We are called upon:
Women who are attacked will be defended,
and healed.
Men who are attacked will be defended,
and healed.
We will save the people who call on Us.
Always.
This is Our promise to you.
So call on Us,
And We will come.
We will march with you.

Liberator

by Chelsea Luellon Bolton

I am Set's Sister
I am Set's Wife,
I am His Partner
in all things.
I am the Wife of Wesir
as a Mourner and a Rain Goddess.
But I am Set's Wife
When I am a liberator
When I am the one who initiates
Transformation.
When I am the one who initiates
Change.
I am come in this form
To aid those who need it.
I come to you
In the form of the swallow
I come to you in the form of
the one who transforms
Rage into power
Sorrow into strength
Despair into joy.
So listen,
All of you — Listen.
You cannot change yourselves
If you cannot love your neighbor
If you cannot stand up for the disenfranchised
If you cannot stand up for the vulnerable —
All of the Vulnerable,
Not just a few.
in your society,
when their lives are at stake,
Then how can you stand up for yourselves?
How can you ask for what you desire?
How can you ask for what you need?
If you have no compassion for others,

You have none for yourself.
How can you ask Us for anything,
if you cannot stand up for your fellow humans?
And where are you then?
Where is your heart?
Does it beat?
Does it move blood through you,
as it did your ancestors?
Does it keep you alive?
Yes?
Good.
Now use your life to honor those before you,
and stand with their descendants.
Rise up and fight for justice.
Rise up against the oppressors.
Rise up and stand with the people
All people,
And stand with the Gods beside you
as you march toward
a better world.

For All Eternity

by Chelsea Luellon Bolton

Time is on your side
Time is on your side
You can accomplish all of your tasks
Just delegate a time to do each one
Work for Aset
Work for Nebet Het
And other Egyptian Gods and Goddesses
Work on your stories
Give room for the Gods in your life
Give Them room to breathe
To be Present
So you can feel Their Presence
All around you
And again be filled
With the love of the Gods and Goddesses
Of your heart
Egypt is here
We are here
And We abide within you and without
Aset, Nebet Het, Wepwawet, Sekhmet-Mut, Ra
And other Egyptian Gods are your Gods
We have not left
We are here
Now
We are Nebet Het
We are Aset
And We say this:
The Gods of Egypt are yours for all Eternity

Hidden One

by Chelsea Luellon Bolton

I am the Hidden Moon
I hide the vast stars
in the veil of darkness
in the Hidden spaces,
I am there
as the Queen of the Crossroads
as the owner of the night.
I am there.
I am there.
With Hekate and Aradia.
With Arianhod and Circe.
I am there.
With Aset.
I am Nebet Het of the Wind
I am Nebet Het of the Moonless Night.
I am Nebet Het of the Gales,
I am Nebet Het of the Dark Moon
I am Nebet Het of the Heavenly Stars
I am Nebet Het, burning, fiercely bright.
I am the Light in the Darkness
I am hidden in plain sight.
I am Nebet Het, the Hidden One.
I am Nebet Het, the Bright One.
Hidden and Seen
in darkness,
by turning on the light.

Nebet Het-Seshat

by Chelsea Luellon Bolton

Nebet Het of the Graves,
Nebet Het of the Shrine,
Nebet Het the Guardian
of both of these places.
Nebet Het, who wards off impurity,
and the forces that offend the Gods.
We are together here,
as Nebet Het-Seshat.
One is the builder,
One is the scribe,
One is the guardian of the holy space.
As one We are the Keeper of Records in the holy spaces
and shrines.
We record the deeds and offerings,
We record the Gods' portions.
We record the deeds of the priest and priestess,
who tends to the shrine and holy spaces.
We record the implements of the Gods.
We record the implements of the priest or priestess,
in charge of the temple or shrine.
We record and We write down,
what We see in the hearts of those who serve Us,
be they priest, or priestess,
or spirit-worker
or devotee.
We see into the hearts of all those who honor Us.
We are the Scribe.
We are the Lady of Time.
and record-keeping.
We are the Lady of Book-keeping
and accounts.
We are the Lady of the Library,
and temple scribes.
We are the Lady of Knowledge,
of all kinds,

of books and scrolls
and the computer too.
We are the knowledge-keepers,
and ones who guard the shrine.
We are the Lady of the Books,
We are the Lady of All Books.
and all knowledge is Mine.

We wear the panther shroud,
of the star-coated leopard.
We are the Lady of Panthers,
for the *Duat* is full of danger,
and this is Our form,
as an Eye of Ra.
as the Leopard Goddess,
of the Sky filled with stars,
as the one who gives birth to dawn,
and as the one who prowls through the night.
We are light in darkness,
We shine so bright.
The starry leopard and panther Goddess,
who rules both day and night.

We are the Panther Goddess
who record the history
of the home and people.
We record what will come
and what has been.
We record the deeds of the disturber.
We record the words of the Gods
and people.
We record the deeds of the Blessed Dead
and the living.
We record the names of Kings,
We record the names of Gods and Goddesses,
We record the names of men and women,
We record dictations and notes
We record prayers and offerings,
We record all these things,
so that all are held accountable,

so that all know their deeds
and are held responsible.
For We are the record-keepers of the Gods
and We record all that the Gods do,
We record the deeds of all people,
and yes,
that includes you.

Nebet Het-Seshat: Her Sacred Time

by Chelsea Luellon Bolton

Twilight.
This is Her sacred time.
The time between light and shadow.
Sunset and Sunrise.
The time where the worlds touch on the Horizon.
This is the sacred time of Nebet Het.
Dawn and Dusk.
The Liminal Spaces.
The In-Betweens.
This is Her sacred time.

Boundaries are Her sacred spaces.
These are the places between two states.
These are the places between two realms.
This is dream and waking.
This is sleep and slumber.
These are two states.
Like two states of Being.
Two ways of acting.
Two ways of becoming.
These are the places between two states.
This is where I reside.
In darkness and shadow.
At the edges and the cusps.
The Edges of the Desert are My sacred Domain.
As are the Edges of Temples.

I am the Flagstaff
guarding the entrance of Temples.
Between the Sacred and the Mundane.
I guard against impurity.
I keep the boundary holy.
This is where I reside.
At the edges.
At the circumference.

At the corners.
I am here and not.
I am there and not.
I am everywhere and nowhere.
This is always My state.
I am always In-Between.
I am here.
I am there.
I am everywhere you look, yet you cannot find me.
For I am hidden in shadow and starlight.
I am at the Edges of Time.
I am with Seshat here.
Nebet Het-Seshat.
I am the Lady of Time.
I write what cannot be written.
I am the word that cannot be spoken.
I am the language that cannot be read.
Yet, I am the Lady of Libraries.
They are My sacred Domain.
As all Houses and all Homes are Mine.
And all of these are on the Edges of My Sacred Time.

Nebet Het-Seshat: Recorder of Scrolls

by Chelsea Luellon Bolton

I am Nebet Het-Seshat
I am the Recorder of Scrolls
I record deeds and accomplishment
And failure too;
You have succeeded
And you have failed
And this is normal
For all people succeed and fail
You succeed when you are happy
You fail when you give up
So don't give up
Don't give in to despair or sorrow
Let your feelings flow
And eradicate what is unnecessary
And cherish what you want and need
What you need is to write
What you need is your joy
This is what you need
This is what needs to transpire
Honor the Gods and Goddesses
Of Egypt
Honor yourself
By honoring your commitments
Doing what you love and need
Honor yourself
By treating yourself better than you treat yourself now
Always improve on how you treat yourself and others
And always honor your heart

Nebet Het-Seshat: Blessings of the Goddess

by Chelsea Luellon Bolton

Do not disregard the blessings of Nephthys,
Do not disregard the blessings of Nebet Het,
the Lady of the Home, Temple, and Shrine.
Do not disregard Her blessings,
of a clean home,
of a healthy life,
of a protected existence.
Do not disregard Her blessings,
as Ruler of the House,
as Ruler of the Home,
as the one who provides blessings,
for the House and Home.
Do you need groceries?
Call to Her.
Do you need nourishment?
Eat Her offerings.
Do you need stability?
Drink of Her nectar of wine, milk, and honey.
Do not disregard the Lady of the House,
for She is the Goddess of all things in your home,
Honor Her.
Honor Her.
And Her blessings will flow.

I am with Seshat,
for an organized home,
from organized shelves and books,
to laundry,
for cleanliness,
I am with the Lady of the Library,
as Nebet Het-Seshat or Myself alone,
as the one who can organize a home.
Look at a library, look at its shelves,
how organized it is,

do you want your home to be
that pristine?
Then call to Us and We will aid you.
Call to Nebet Het,
Call to Nephthys,
Call to Nebet Het-Seshat,
Call to Nephthys-Seshat,
and She will aid you.

Nebet Het-Seshat: Forever

by Chelsea Luellon Bolton

Nebet Het
Nebet Het-Seshat,
Lady of the Road
Lady of Time, Lady of Fate
Lady of Years, Lady of the Life-span
Who records the names and deeds
Of gods and men, of goddesses and women
Who records the deeds of the disturber
Who records the pathway of the gods and goddesses
As the sun boat travels through the *Duat* until dawn
Who aids in the sunrise and birth of the god, Ra
Every day, Aset and Nebet Het, Aset and Nebet Het-Seshat
The two midwives who aid the god of dawn
Who guard the *Bennu* Bird, the Phoenix
Who guard the birth of Kings
Who guard mothers and sons
Who guard mothers and daughters
As the Eye of Ra, as the Lady of Flame
As the Goddess of Fire
We protect the beloved ones of the Gods and Goddesses of *Kemet*
In this world and the next,
Forever

Nebet Het-Nit: Creator, Warrior, and Guide of the Dead

by Chelsea Luellon Bolton

Nebet Het-Nit is the Goddess
Of the Home
An organized home,
A minimalist home
Filled with what you need and want
In an organized way;
She is the Female Wepwawet
She guides and guards
She is the Warrior armed with a bow and arrows
I am here with Her as Lady of the Crossroads
As the Lady of the Roads
I guard and guide the living and the dead
She guards and guides the living and the dead
Both of Us guard the Canopic Jars
Both of Us guard the King
Look to the West
At the graveside,
We are there tending the dead
She tends the dead
As a warrior should, as all wars contains casualties
Comrades die, friends die,
Soldiers and civilians die
So all warriors tend the graves
Of fallen comrades, of fallen heroes
Of fallen martyrs, of fallen friends
Of fallen soldiers, of fallen bystanders
Innocent lives taken too soon
These are the graves that Nebet Het-Nit tends to
As the warrior, the guard and guide for the deceased

Nit is the creator
Nebet Het is the creator
Both are the Female Nun
Both of Them are the Celestial Cow

Heavenly Cow with horns and solar disk
Heavenly Hippopotamus with the blue hide adorned with lotuses
Mother of Ra, Mother of the Gods
Mehet Weret, the Great Flood
The Female Nun, Nunet
And She is the Mother of the Gods
Each day She gives birth to the sun

Eye of Ra, Daughter of Ra
Lady of Flame,
The Lioness, the Leopard, the Cobra
These are the titles and forms of the Eye Goddess
These are the attributes of the Daughters of Ra
Nebet Het-Nit is the Goddess who is angered and leaves
Nebet Het-Nit is the form She takes as the Avenging Leopard,
the Avenging Lioness, the Avenging Cobra
As She leaves Egypt during the Summer Solstice
Nebet Het-Nit returns as the Lioness and Leopard, as the Cobra
And She changes back into Nebet Het-Nit, the Sistrum Goddess
The Lady of Joy and the Lady of Beauty
On the Winter Solstice
This is the Distant Goddess Myth
For Nebet Het-Nit

Nit is the Daughter of Sobek
Or His Consort, or His Mother
Depending on the temple and time period
She is Self-Created as the Mother of Creation
She is the consort of Ptah-Nun
She is the Daughter of Ra and His Mother
She is the Consort of Set

Nebet Het is the Daughter of Geb
She is the Daughter of Nut
She is the Wife of Wesir
She is the Mother of Heru and Ihy
She is the consort of Hemen and had a child with Him
She is the Daughter of Ra and His Mother
She is the Wife of Set

Psychopomp, Warrior
Goddess of the Graves
Nebet Het-Nit
Nebet Het and Nit
Nebet Het is the Wife of Set
And had a child by Him
Nit is the consort of Set
And Their son Sobek came out of Their union
Nebet Het wields the bow and arrows
Nit wields the bow and arrows
As the Goddess of War
The weapons of war belong to Nebet Het-Nit
As the Wife of Set,
As the Lady of the Grave
As the Lady of War

Nebet Het-Nit
Is the Creator of the World
Is the Goddess of War
Is the Flaming Eye of Ra
Is the Lady of the Graves
She is the Creator
She is the Warrior
She is the Guide to the Dead
And Guardian of the Graves.

Nebet Het-Nit: *Uraeus* and Guard

by Chelsea Luellon Bolton

Nebet Het is with Nit
The Arrow's Goddess
Lady of the Bow, Ruler of Arrows
Lady of Lower Egypt, Royal Lady
Guide of the Dead,
Guardian of the Graves
Nebet Het and Nit can meet here.
Nit mourns Wesir, as She is his Mother
Nebet Het mourns Wesir as his Sister
They meet here as ones who loved Wesir.
They are Daughters of Ra, they are His Eyes
Avenging Lioness, Avenging Leopard
Uraeus, Cobra, Snake Goddess
They are Daughters, Wives and Mothers of Ra
As Mehet Weret, as the Heavenly Cow
As the Creator and Mother of Ra.
As the *Uraeus*, they spit flame
As the *Uraeus*, they wield the bow and arrows
As the *Uraeus*, they protect and avenge
As the wielders of the power and magic of creation.
They are wives of Set.
For they wield the weapons of war
Nit is the Guardian of Soldiers
Nebet Het is the Lady of War
Nit is the precise Goddess, the Strategist
Nebet Het is silence
Silence of waiting to be attacked
The Silence of the Dead
Both guard the graves
And protect Egypt for all eternity.

Nebet Het-Nit-Seshat

by Chelsea Luellon Bolton

Nebet Het:
I guard the shrine
Dwelling in the edges
Of the Desert
Of Space
Of Life
Striking Cobra, Fiery Queen
Flames burn shackles away
Your own boundaries I break
Change is my mission
Sorrow its wake
The dead my companions
Kite's wailing is my song
Silently swift as a Leopard
I am there and then I am not
I am standing at the Gate,
The threshold is my domain
The last breath exhaled is Mine

Nit:
I am creation
Life-giving Waters
Of Bovine Form
Precise as Arrows
I hunt
I fight
I guide the path as the Wolf Lord
Hissing cobra, Stinging Bee
Lotus of the Water
I am the beginning
All start with Me

Seshat:
I am the Scribe
Lady of Panthers

Knowledge is my Way
Books, sacred implements
What is written
I record
I build Holy Houses
So that We may Know you

Nebet Het-Nit-Seshat: Three as One

by Chelsea Luellon Bolton

I am Nit, of the Celestial Cow,
I am joined with the Scribe,
and the potter and the widow.
We are three as one.
We are three as One.
Nebet Het is the Goddess of dissolution.
Nebet Het is the Goddess of the end.
She is Death,
Personified.
And I am life,
as Nit, the primordial mother.
I am the Life-Giver,
I am the one with the voice,
to shatter millions.
I am the One whose veil,
Conceals all time.
Yesterday, Today, and Future Days,
Morning, Noon, and Night
I am the Scribe, the Mourner, and Widow,
the one who brings you life.
I mourn your passing
and I record your deeds.
And this is the path of the Three Goddesses,
as Nebet Het-Nit
as Nebet Het-Seshat
as all Three as One.

Nebet Het-Nit-Seshat: Three Poems

by Chelsea Luellon Bolton

Nebet Het: Home, Shrine, and Grave
Nebet Het
Lady of the House
Lady of the Home
Lady of the Shrine
Lady of the Temple
Lady of the Tomb
Lady of the Grave
She Whose Flame is Painful
She Who Wipes Away Tears
Lady of the Nile, Lady of Rain
Goddess of Mourning
Lady of Magic, Lady of the Ancestors
Guardian, Guide and Guard to the Dead
With Her son, Yinepu
Wife of Wesir, Daughter of Ra
Wife of Set, Daughter of Nut, Daughter of Geb
Eye of Ra, Leopard Goddess,
Panther Queen, Mistress of Renewal
She Who Guards Against Impurity
Sopdet, the Star of the New Year
Celestial Cow, Mother of Ra
Lady of Writing, Lady of Words of Power
Lady of the Home, Shrine, and Grave

Nit: Creator, Warrior and the Guard of the Graves
Nit,
The Female Wepwawet
Who Opens all the Pathways
Who Opens the Way in all Her Places
The Guide and Guard to the Dead
Of those who died in war
Of all the deceased
She guards the graves
As a warrior, guide, and guard

Mother of Sobek, Daughter of Sobek
Consort of Ptah-Nun, He is South of His Wall
She is North of Her Wall
Self-Created One,
Mehet Weret, Celestial Cow, Mother of Ra
Female Nun, Nunet
Creator Goddess, Lady of Water,
She gives birth to Ra every day at dawn
She Opens the Paths of the Sun
Lady of the Sky, Lady of the Night Sky
Lady of War, Eye of Ra, *Uraeus*
Lioness Goddess,
Lady of the Bow, Lady of Arrows
Lady of the Shield
She is the Creator, the Warrior and the Guard of the Graves

Seshat: Wisdom, Words, and Writing
Seshat,
Goddess of Wisdom
Lady of Writing,
Lady of the Library
Lady of Knowledge
Lady of Science
Lady of Record-Keeping
Lady of Accounting
Lady of the Seven-Points
Lady of the Leopard Skin
Lady of the Stars and the Night Sky
Female Scribe
Wife of Djehuty,
Daughter of Djehuty
Paired with Djehuty, She is Lady of the Crescent Moon,
She Who Wears the Two Horns
Lady of Words, Wisdom and Writing
Lady of the Archives
Lady of Builders
She Who Builds the Temples with the Cord
Lady of Astronomy, Lady of Astrology
Mistress of the House of Books
Lady of Wisdom, Words, and Writing

Nebet Het-Hethert: Lady of Beauty

by Chelsea Luellon Bolton

Do not disregard the Goddess of Beauty,
Do not disregard Her in your life.
For Aset is a Goddess of Beauty,
so is Her sister, Nebet Het.
She is the Lady of Beauty,
Do not disregard Her so easily.
She is not just Nebet Het.
She is not just Seshat,
for an organized house is a beauty all its own.
She is not just Aset-Herself
or Aset-Hethert too.
She is Nebet Het-Anuket,
for all Goddesses have beauty of some kind.
all have some beauty of Their own to share
with the world.
She is Nebet Het-Hethert,
When She is patron of the arts,
Patron of music and dance,
Patron of drinking and revelry,
Patron of laughter and joy.
The Lady of Joy.
The Lady of Drunkenness.
Lady of Music and Dance.
For one honors Nebet Het with a tambourine.
one honors the Lady of Beauty,
with a *sesheshet*, a sistrum with a shape like a *naos*.
with a *sekhem*, a sistrum with a shape like a hoop.
Shaking the rattle to bring joy.
Shake the sistrum.
Shake the sistrum.
And see Our beauties flow.

Nebet Het-Mehet Weret: Nebet Het, the Celestial Cow

by Chelsea Luellon Bolton

What is right, dear child?
What is wrong, dear child?
Do you not have what you desire?
Do you not have what you need?
Do you not have what you want?
Listen, child.
for I am the world mother,
who records all names.
I am the one who names the faces.
I am the one who names the gods.
I am Nebet Het of the River.
I am Nebet Het of the primordial waters.
I am Nebet Het of primordial time.
I am Mehet Weret
I am the Cow of the Waters.
I am the one who births the sun.
I am the one who owns the stars.
I am the Star Goddess.
I am the Twilight.
I am the First Dawn.
I am the First Light.
I am the First Voice.
I am the First Breath.
I am the Celestial Cow of Creation.
I am the Mother of the Gods.
I am the Cobra, I am the Sun's Eye.
I am the Mother of the Sun God.
Ra.
Nut gave birth to Him,
but so did I.
For I am also Mehet Weret.
so is Hethert.
so is Aset.

so is Nut,
and so too, am I.
I am the Goddess of the Starry Heavens,
I am the Goddess of the Night Sky
and I am the Lady of the Stars.
and I am the Lady of the Vault of Heaven,
and I am the veil between the Two Eyes.

Nebet Het-Nut: Heaven, Nile, and Underworld

by Chelsea Luellon Bolton

I am with Nut
As Nebet Het-Nut
As the Lady of Heaven
As the Goddess of the Stars,
As the Celestial Cow and the Mother of Ra
I am with My Mother
As *Amenti*, as Lady of the West
As a Goddess of the Underworld
As the starry vault of Heaven is the
Land of the Dead.
This is *Amenti*.
I am the Goddess of the Rain-Storm
As Nut weeps for Geb,
When She was separated from Him
As Nut weeps for Wesir,
When He was slain
So too do I weep for My beloved, Wesir
As rains fall, We weep
As storms rage, We wail
As the Nile floods, We mourn
Our rage and Our sorrow
Is quelled by the tambourine
And the sistrum
And the offerings of the People
I am Nebet Het
I am Nut
I am Nebet Het joined with Nut
I am Nebet Het-Nut
As the Goddess of Heaven, the Nile, and the Underworld

Nebet Het-Nut: Sky

by Chelsea Luellon Bolton

Nebet Het-Nut is the Star Goddess
Lady of the Night, Lady of the Sky
Lady of the Stars,
Cow Who Gave Birth to Ra,
Lady of the Ancestors
Lady of the Tomb
The Celestial Cow holds the dead in Her embrace
She contains Wesir and Ra
She contains the multitudes of the dead as stars
She is the Sky, within Her is *Amenti*
She is the Lady who watches over all
She is the sky above,
Look up:
She is there.

Names and Syncretisms: A Poem

by Chelsea Luellon Bolton

Nebet Het
Lady of Mourning, Eye of Ra
Lady of the Ancestors, Wife of Wesir
Daughter of Ra, Wife of Set
Nebet Het *Kherseket*
She Who Wipes Away Tears
Mourning Lady, Comforter of the Bereaved
Nebet Het *Merkhetes*
She Whose Flame is Painful
Eye of Ra, Protector of Wesir and Heru
Lioness, Leopard and Cobra
Nebet Het-Aset
Two Sisters, Two Mourners
Two Widows, Two Wives
Lady of Magic, Lady of Strength
Sopdet, Eye of Ra, Great of Magic
Guile, Wit and Wisdom
Twin Goddesses, who mirror each other
One is a Lioness, the other a Leopard
One is a Cobra, the other a *Uraeus*
Lady of the Sky, Earth and Underworld
Lady of the Nile, Sun and Star
Nebet Het-Nit
Creator and Warrior, Lady of War
Who tends the graves of the fallen
Lioness Goddess, Eye of Ra
Nebet Het-Seshat
Lady of the Library, Female Scribe of the Gods
Lady of the Astronomy and Astrology, Lady of Writing
Panther Goddess,
Nebet Het-Hethert
Lady of the West, Sycamore Goddess
Lady of Beauty and Dance, Solar Eye of Ra
Lioness and Cobra
Nebet Het possesses all these attributes Herself

And yet also when merged with other Goddesses
May Her names be known
May Her aspects be recorded
May Her manifestations appear
Where ever She wishes.

Poetry of Nebet Het and Set

Red Lady and Lord

by Chelsea Luellon Bolton

I am the Red Lady,
He is the Red Lord.
We are a duality here.
In this space.
My husband and I.
He is Set.
I am Nebet Het.

He is the Lord of the Oasis,
and I am the Lady of the Oasis.
He of the Falcon-Head and Double Crown.
Lord of the Oasis, Lord of the Marshlands
I am here, as His husband.
Lady of the Oasis,
Lady of the Marshlands.
I am the Lady with Her Name as Her crown.

We are here as defenders,
We are here as protectors.
We aid the Sun in its journey.
We destroy the Nameless One,
as We travel in the Boat of Ra.
Set wields the weapons of war,
while I wield arrows.
I am the Strong One, the Strong-Armed.
He is the Great of Strength,
this Lord of the Oasis and the Red Lands.
We are here to grant Our blessings.

Lord and Lady
Lady and Lord,
of the Red Lands,
Who rule the Oasis.

Light in Darkness

by Chelsea Luellon Bolton

Nebet Het speaks through silence,
through whispers
through hushed crowds
and silence born of darkness
of twilight
of creation
of the light streaking out at dawn.

I can be bright
as I illuminate shadow
as I peer into darkness
with My two bright Eyes
My Flame is that of an Eye of Ra
I am the Cobra
I am the leopard
I am the lioness as well

Though I am dark
I can be bright
Though I am silent
I can be loud

But My voice deafens
My voice shatters illusion
Why do you think I am a Wife of Set?
He makes the Sky shake
Tremble with Power
Thunder God
Red Lord
That is My husband
He is the One who keeps the Uncreated at Bay
My Sister helps Him as do I

Who warns of danger in darkness?
Who illuminates what is hidden?
I do.

I give Set the *Abdu* Fish
to warn of the Uncreated's approach
So He and My Sister may slay it

Each day this is My task
Remembered each Year
For the Festival of Lights for Me and My Husband
What time has forgotten, I remember
Light the Lamps on My Day
help Me keep the Uncreated at bay

Flood, Rain, and Storm

by Chelsea Luellon Bolton

Set:
I am Set, Great of Strength,
I am the Lord of the Oasis,
the Great God,
Slayer of the Serpent.
I am the God of Strength
without compromise or excuses.
I am the one who gets things done,
in the time when it needs doing.
I am the God of Strength,
I do not come to those
who cater to their excuses.
I come to make you strong.
So be strong.
Get your stuff done.

Nebet Het:
I am the Lady of Strength.
I am the Goddess of War,
when needed.
I am the Lady Who Guards Boundaries,
I am She who guards the thresholds
and liminal spaces.
I wield a scimitar and flame,
I wield magic and tears,
I wield the transformation
of storms and rain.
I come before My husband,
as the One Who wields lightning
as the Lady of Storms and Rain.
I transform.
Through floods and trenches,
Through bright flame and smoldering embers,
Through candlelight,

Through light in darkness,
I come.
So heed My words now,
I am the Goddess of Rain and Storms,
I am the Goddess of the downpour,
I am the One Who burns brightly,
in darkness,
and in light.
For when I burn,
I am bright and fierce,
along with My husband,
as Lady and Lord of Storms.
Along with My husband,
Who Shakes the Sky,
Thunder-God,
Set, Lord of Storms,
God of Lightning and
the Chaos which brings change.
Which brings Me.
For I am transformation.
I am the one illuminating the darkness,
I am the one making your hidden selves
known.
I am the one flashing in the sky,
as lightning.
I am the Goddess of Twilight
and illumination.
Those that come to Me,
must change.
Those that come to Me,
must transform.
For I am the Goddess of the Pathways,
the Goddess of Revealing what is Hidden,
even hidden from yourselves.
So come to Me and change
and be transformed,
with the power of flood, rain and storm.

Land's Purge

by Chelsea Luellon Bolton

Set:
Wind, Rain, and Storm,
Are My blessings
and My cure,
for stagnation
for entropy
for death.
For the land must be purged
For the land to be cleared,
of all entropy
of all stagnation
in order for plants to flourish.
I bring stagnation's end,
I bring change with a purpose,
I bring the end of one way,
to begin anew.

Nebet Het:
I am Nebet Het,
I am death and decay,
I am the Bringer of Life
From the dead.
All who live, are nourished by death.
All who live, are nourished when
Stagnation is cleared away.
I bring this transformation,
Along with My husband.
He strips away what needs to be purged
And I cleanse what is left,
so that transformation can begin.
And this is the process of renewal.
I cleanse what My husband clears away.
My husband clears away what must be cleansed.

Rain Renews the Land

by Chelsea Luellon Bolton

Set:
I am the Storm
I am the Rain
I am the Clouds
I am Thunder,
Which Shakes the Sky.
I am the One who Thunders in the Sky.
He Who the Sky Shakes,
I am the Storm God,
I am the Storm Bringer,
I bring the Hurricanes, the Tornados,
The Snow and Rain,
The Ice and Sleet,
I bring all storms and all weather
in My wake.

Nebet Het:
I am the Storm Bringer
I bring the Storm as well.
I am the Wife of the Red Lord,
Set is His Name.
I am the Rain Goddess,
as He is its Lord.
I bring rain for the Nile's flood,
He brings rain to honor His Brother.
For the rain to fall,
For the crops to grow,
For the land to be renewed.

Great of Strength, Lady of Strength

by Chelsea Luellon Bolton

Set:
I am the Storm Bringer
I am the Storm God,
I am Set, the Sky-Shaker,
I make the Heavens Tremble
at My command.
I bring the rain,
I bring the snow
I bring the thunder and lightning,
I bring the winds and gales
I bring the darkness with the cloud covered sky.
I bring transformation through death,
of the Self.
I bring change through hardship
I bring strength from despair,
I bring strength from pain,
And I bring strength to those who ask.
So ask,
I bring strength from hardship.
You are stronger than you believe
You are more capable than you ever dreamed.
So ask for My aid,
I am Set, the Great of Strength,
God of Storms

Nebet Het:
I am Nebet Het,
Lady of Strength,
Goddess of Storms
I am Nebet Het,
Great of Magic,
I am Nebet Het,
The Strong Armed.
I am the one who aids the disenfranchised.
I am the one who aids those who ask.
So ask,

And My strength will come.
You will endure.
You will endure.
You will endure.
Any hardship, any grief,
And you will come from this death,
This transformation
Healed from your heartache and pain.
I am Nebet Het, Lady of Strength,
Goddess of Transformation

Call on Us

by Chelsea Luellon Bolton

Set:
Set, God of Storms
Set, God of Life
For to be strong is to live
Those who are weak die
In their own minds
In their own ways
They break
Burdens weigh them down
Too proud or stubborn
Or lost in their despair
To seek aid
So I will tell you now
Those who call upon Me
I will give them strength
I will give them mental fortitude
I will give them power to wield
And they will be their own savior
Along with any who wish to aid them
It takes strength to ask for help
So ask, dammit.
So ask for help
And I will get you the help you need
It can be a counselor
Or medicine
Or family and friends
Whatever you need,
I will try to help you
So get up
Get off your ass
And ask for My aid.

Nebet Het:
I am honored among other Gods
I am honored among My siblings

And My husband, too
I am honored with Set of the Oasis
I am honored with Set, God of Storms
I am honored with Set, My brother and husband
I am honored with Him
In times of loss or sorrow,
When you need aid
Call on Me, Call on Us
And We will aid you
I am the Goddess of sorrow
I aid and comfort when you despair
I am there when you are hurting
I am there when you are in pain
As Set is the God of Strength,
I am the Goddess of Fortitude
I am the one who endures
I am the one who perseveres
Despite hardship
Despite pain
Despite sorrow
Despite rage
Despite grief
I endure
And so will you
I am steadfast
I am strong
And so are you
I have suffered
I have mourned
And so have you
So listen,
if I can make it
if I can work through this turmoil,
So can you
For My strength is your strength
For My pain is your pain
For My grief is your grief
My fortitude is yours
My strength is yours
We will get through this

I am the Strong Armed
He is Set, the Great of Strength
And We will help you
Our power is yours
Ask,
With an offering
and you will receive it

Choose Your Life by Set and Nebet Het

by Chelsea Luellon Bolton

Set:
Your strength comes from fear
This is wrong
This is not true power
This is a fallacy
You put yourself in a box
So you won't be scared
So you won't be terrified
So you won't be near Me
I am the Outsider
I killed Wesir
All the Gods know this
And hold Me accountable
And I hold them accountable
For what they've done;
And We will hold you accountable for what you've done
All of you.
Because your actions are who you are
Your deeds are who you become
Do you want to be someone?
Who coasts through life with no plan or destination?
Do you want to be mediocre?
Do the minimal required things?
Do you want to survive or barely get by?
Or do you want to be ambitious and strive for your dreams?
Do you want to accomplish your aspirations and goals?
Do you want to be grand, and help the world
On a global scale?
This is your life.
This is your chance to change.
What do you want to do!
Decide this
And then do it.
If you need to change,
In order to reach your goal,

Then do it.
And become who you are.

Nebet Het:
Strength comes from rage
But it is temporary
Like the flame of a candle
It flickers and is snuffed out
By the smallest wind or water
It can't endure
It will burn itself out.
Eventually, rage will do the same.
And all that is left is despair
Why?
Because it is unfulfilled rage
It had no outlet to express itself
So it transforms into tears
So, then it will be heard in the
Wailings of your heart
And this is where it sits
To fester and boil
As rage is like flame
It burns hot
So it boils the water
And it leaves you dried out
Like a simple husk
And thirsty
For now you have nothing to feed on
No water
No flame
So where is your spark of life?
And where is your movement through your limbs,
So you live?
And where is the water which flows through your veins?
And where is the fire which ignites your life-force?
And where is your *ka*?
And where is your heart, your *ib*?
And where is the manifestation of your heart?
And where is the manifestation of your power, your *ba*?

Align your *ka* and *ib*
Align your life-power and heart
To manifest your power
And choose your own life.

Firestorm and Lightning

by Chelsea Luellon Bolton

Nebet Het is the Wayward Daughter
She marries the Red Lord
Of the Desert Lands
She marries Him
And Their love is eternal
They bring change and sorrow
They bring transformation
The change He brings is Swift, Brutal
Unyielding
You can't turn away
From the lies you tell yourself
Or the hidden truths you wish to keep locked away
You cannot hide from your desires
With a slew of excuses
You don't have time?
Make time.
You don't have money?
Ask for help.
You'll do it later?
Don't procrastinate.
You feign indifference when you say you have a dream.
Stop hiding from your desires.
Stop being complacent in your life.
Take steps and get your tasks done.
These are the lessons of Set.
Don't let excuses or complacency stop you
from living out your dreams.
Nebet Het's change is no less brutal
But Her change is internal to ourselves
As we cry,
As we sob,
As we wail,
As we mourn,
It is the sorrow when we experience loss

It is the rage when someone wrongs us
It is the grief when someone dies
It is the emotional turmoil,
When change tears our world to shreds
Any normalcy, any complacency
Any excuse — is swiftly rebuked
Enough
Enough
Enough
The change at my door will not destroy me
The sorrow in my heart will not lead me to harm myself
The grief in my soul will not lead me to suicide
I will get through this
I will live through this
I will triumph over my fear and my pain
With the strength of Set
With the fortitude of Nebet Het
I will rise
I will wipe away my tears
I will stare down my fears
And with a smile, I will say:
Is that all you've got?
And your strength will rise in you
Like a firestorm
Like a lightning storm
And you will say:
I will get through this.
How about you?

Change Brings A Little Death

by Chelsea Luellon Bolton

Nebet Het's time
Nebet Het's wake
is the storm bringer
Wife of Set, Lord of Storms
Wife of Set, Lord of Change
Wife of Set, Lord of the Desert
This is Her time
She Who brings healing from Despair
She who heals doubt and fear
She who quells anger
Nebet Het, *Kherseket*
She who wipes away your tears
Lady of Set,
The one who weeps
As He brings His change
This sorrow, this self
Being torn asunder
Heart ripped apart
Stomped on, beaten
Wheezing and gasping for breath
For life
Tears flow, Sobbing, Crying,
Wailing and Keening
Change has come
And Death follows;
For with every change is a little death
Set comes
And Nebet Het comes
One as the God of Change
And one as the Goddess who mourns the loss it brings
But with each little death
Comes strength and hope
For a better tomorrow
With the sunrise

Poetry of Nebet Het, Aset, and Ra

Power of My Light

by Chelsea Luellon Bolton

I am a Bright Goddess
as well as My sister;
I am the sunbeam while She is radiant light
I am the shadow flickering off candle flames.
This is Who I am.
I am a whisper
I am an echo.
I am the sound that is silence
I am the light of dawn and dusk
I am twilight.
Peering into the darkness,
I reveal Mysteries.
Peering into the twilight,
I see the God rise at dawn.
My Father Ra.
My Sister Aset and I,
aid Him during His transition
between day and night
for His travels in the *Duat*
is His travel of transformation.
He is the God who renews Wesir in the *Duat*
Just as My Sister and I do.
We are all light.
I am the Solar Goddess and the Star Goddess
as well as My Sister.
Night is sacred, as is Day.
I am the transformation from day to night.
I am the one who renews and transforms the dead.
With the light of stars.
I renew with water and flame.
But I am not Aset.
I am Her companion.

Her transformation is different than Mine.
My water secretes poison,
purging toxins from the body and soul.
My fire burns away
things no longer needed.
I purge all things that do not serve the self.
I am Bright when My Sister is dark
I am dark when My Sister is Bright.
I am the Bright One
at dawn, in dusk;
in darkness;
I can be luminous
And I can be light,
but My light shines in darkness.
I am the Lady who reveals the shadows,
I see what is hidden in their depths,
I illuminate secrets and Mysteries
in the night.
I am the light at night.
Dawn breaks and darkness recedes
this is the Power of My light.

Fire and Magic

by Chelsea Luellon Bolton

I am the Red Lady,
He is the Red Lord.
I am the Diadem of My Brother.
He is the Defender of My Lord.
We defend Ra, the Lord of All.
We defend Ra, the Lord of All.

I am the Eye Goddess,
I am a Lioness and a Serpent,
I am the cobra which sits on His brow,
I am the Goddess who blinds and burns the enemies of Ra.
I am the Goddess who wields the scimitar.
I am the Goddess who shoots arrows.
I am the Goddess who defends Her people,
with flame and magic.
I am She who knows Her spells.
Just as Aset does.
For I am Her sister.
For I am Her twin.
And this magic is Mine to command.
For I am Nebet Het, of the Two Sisters.
I wield My magic well.
My voice shatters illusions,
My voice dispels entropy,
clearing and cleansing it away.
My sister beguiles,
My sister commands,
Yet, I am the unseen avenger,
I sneak and slip in, unnoticed,
until I strike.
There is no entropy in My wake.
My sister and I,
command Our magical power,
command Our fiery might,

and We walk here together,
as Goddesses
who wield Our spells and weapons of might,
against the disturber.
We enchant to destroy,
the enemies of Our brother,
the enemies of Our son
and the enemies of Our Lord, Ra.

Poetry of Nebet Het and Wesir

Nebet Het, Wife of Wesir

by Chelsea Luellon Bolton

So you want to honor Nebet Het,
the Wife of Wesir.
Do you know Her cycles,
as a Mourner, Widow, and Wife?
Do you know Her as a Weeper?
Do you know Her as the Royal Lady?
Do you know Wesir,
Her husband?
Do you know Her cycles
as the Widow, who mourns the slain God?
as Sopdet, who heralds the New Year
and the torrents of rain which flood the Nile?
These are Her Mysteries, along with Aset.
These are the Weeper, the Mourner, and the Widow.
These are the Mysteries of Wesir,
as the ones who bring transformation.
as the ones who bring life from death.
as the ones who mourn Wesir.
as the ones who weep for the slain God.
Along with Aset, She searched for Wesir.
Along with Aset, She found Him.
Along with Aset, She revitalized Him.
Nebet Het and Aset searched for Wesir.
The Two Sisters are with Wesir in the Hall of Two Truths.
as His sisters, widows, and wives.

With One Who Grieves

by Chelsea Luellon Bolton

Sister of Aset
Wife of Wesir
These are the titles of the Goddess of Transformation.
Nebet Het, the Sister of Aset
Nebet Het, the Wife of God.
These are Her aspects,
These are Her forms,
as the Royal Lady,
as the Wife and Widow,
as the Mourner and Avenger,
of the God.
Nebet Het, the Companion of Aset
Nebet Het, the Mourner of Wesir
These are the titles of the Goddess of Transformation,
through tears and rain,
through storms and flood.
For these are the cycles of the Goddess,
who weeps and wails,
who mourns and rages,
for the avenger is also the mourner here.
for both come in tandem,
with one who grieves.

King and Lady of the Dead

by Chelsea Luellon Bolton

Nebet Het of the Crossroads
Nebet Het of the Dead
The Psychopomp
Mistress of the Dead
Lady of Waiting for those who die
This is Nebet Het
Of *Amenti*
Of the Land of the Horizon
The Land of the *Duat*
The Afterlife
Lady of the West Who brings home
Those who are in tears
Those who have had a good life
Go to *Amenti*
Or the place of their choosing
If not Egypt;
But,
For those who honor the Egyptian Gods
We will judge you first
And then We will see
What will become of you.

Wesir is the King of the *Duat*
Wesir is the King of the Dead
He is invoked here
As the God of Judgment
As the King
As the Benevolent Ruler
As the Benevolent King
Aset is His Queen
Nebet Het is His Lady
We judge the Living
As best We can;
For when they die
They join the multitude of stars
In the Belly of Nut

Nebet Het is the Lady of the Dead
Wesir is the King of the Dead
Here, they judge those who are worthy
They award those who are great;
They permit those to pass
Who pass the Heart and Feather test of Wesir
Yinepu balances the scales
Djehuty records the outcome
And those who pass are welcome
In Our Halls

Offering Sacrifice to Nebet Het and Wesir

by Chelsea Luellon Bolton

Fruit is laid before the Goddess,
Milk and honey placed at Her shrine.
Offerings and libations given,
to the Lady of the Festival,
to the Lady of the Shrine.

To the Lord of the Festival,
to the Lord of the Shrine,
Libations and offerings are given to the God.
Fruit, honey, water and milk are given to this God.
In ancient times, Lord Wesir and Lady Nebet Het,
were given these offerings on this day,
Offering Sacrifice to Nebet Het and Wesir.
On this day, the 13th of the month of September,
on this day, They are honored.
on this day, They are given offerings.
on this day, They are given sacrifice.
By Egyptians, Greeks, and other devotees.
So give offerings to this Lady and Lord,
let their blessings flow.

Brother, Husband, and King

by Chelsea Luellon Bolton

Wesir:
Nebet Het is a goddess of the Mountain
The *Benben* stone.
The first light
The first breath
The first dawn
Became here.
Lighting up the sky,
In the form of the *Bennu*, the Heron,
The Sun God's form as the Phoenix
Here She is as an Eye of Ra,
as the *Bennu*,
the Bird of the Eternal Flame,
which is as old as the Creator.
She is His protector here,
As flame, as fragrance
As breath, as light.
The Creator is born as the *Bennu* Bird
The light which suffuses His being,
Permeates all of creation as the *Ka*,
as the vital essence of all things.

I am Wesir,
And here I sit,
On the *Benben* stone,
With My sister and mother,
Nebet Het and Nut,
Both goddesses of dawn and dusk,
Of twilight,
Of the Lands between.
This point of creation is the dawn
This point of creation is the horizon,
In which Ra and Wesir meet
In the *Duat*.

Here the sun and underworld
Coalesce,
as the sun permeates the Unseen Realm.
Giving life to the Weary One,
And the Ancestors.
This light of the living,
Permeates the land of the dead.
The solar rays give life to those in the *Duat*.

Nebet Het:
I am in the *Duat*.
I am in the Underworld.
I am the Queen of the Dead.
I am Wesir's Wife.
I am the one whom He loves.

Wesir:
I am the Husband.
I am Wesir.
I enable the sun to permeate the *Duat*.
This is My Land.
I am its King.
Aset and Nebet Het are the Queens, here.
I am Wesir.
I am the King of the *Duat*.
I am its Lord.

I am the Husband.
She is the Wife.
She is Aset.
She is the Wife.
She is Nebet Het.
I am here between My Two Sisters,
as Brother, Husband, and King.

Lord of the Oasis

by Chelsea Luellon Bolton

Wesir:
Lord of the Oasis
This is My role
as the God of Vegetation
and the Water's flow.
I am the God of the Oasis
I am the God of Life
I am Lord of the Oasis
I am the Lord of Life.
I am Wesir of the Oasis.
I am Wesir of the Marshlands.
I am Wesir of the Waterfall
The Cataracts, the Nile's flow.
I am Wesir of the Marshlands.
I am Wesir, God of Life.

Aset:
I am Aset of the Marshlands
I am Aset of the Riverbanks
I am the Wife of Wesir, Sister of Nebet Het.
Goddess of the Nile,
Lady of the River
And the Goddess of Vegetation
I am the Goddess of Life
I am the Goddess of Rain
And the Nile's flood
I am the Wife and Mourner of Wesir.

Nebet Het:
I am Nebet Het, Sister of the God
Sister of Wesir, Sister of Set
Wife of Wesir, Wife of Set
I am the Goddess of the Marshlands
I am the Goddess of the Oasis.
And all that reside in the Heart of Egypt.

All life is sacred.
All life is precious.
As Wife of Set, I am a Protector Against Evil
I am an Avenging Goddess
I am a Holy Queen.
As a Wife of Wesir,
I am a Mourner and an ally for the Dead.

Set:
I am Set of the Oasis
I am Set, of the Marshlands.
I am the Husband of Nebet Het.
We destroy the Reviled Serpent
We destroy the Evil One.
I am the God of the Oasis.
And My Wife and I
protect Our devotees
against evil
against harm
in all its forms.
I am the Falcon God
I am the Set-Animal.
I am the Lord of the Desert
And the Oasis too
I am the God of the Marshlands
And I will protect all of you.

Wesir:
Wesir of the Oasis
Wesir of the Tree
I am Wesir of the Marshlands
I am God of the River
I am the God of the Streams
I am the God of Vegetation
I am the God of Life
in all its forms.

Aset, Nebet Het, and Wesir

by Chelsea Luellon Bolton

Aset and Wesir
Goddess and God
Lord and Lady of the Oasis
Lord and Lady of the *Duat*
Aset and Wesir
Lord and Lady of the Oasis
Aset and Nebet Het
Wives of Wesir
Nebet Het, Lady of the Oasis
Mourner and Queen of the Dead
Nebet Het, Queen of the Oasis
Lady of Juniper, Lady of Berries
Lady of Vegetation
Nebet Het, Lady of *Isheru*
Lady of Streams and Stars
Nebet Het, Lady of the Oasis
And all of the land,
From Heaven to Earth.

Wife and Mourner of Wesir

by Chelsea Luellon Bolton

I am the Wife
I am the Mourner
I am the One Who Weeps
I am the Widow of the Slain God
for Wesir is My husband,
along with My Sister Aset.
I am Nebet Het of the Graves
I am Nebet Het of the Nile
I am Nebet Het of the Tomb
I am with My Sister here
and We are both with Wesir.

Poetry of Nebet Het and Yinepu

Guide of Souls
by Chelsea Luellon Bolton

Nebet Het of the Stars
Nebet Het of the Sun
Nebet Het of the Flame
Nephthys of Fire
Lady of Light
With Yinepu, the Lord of Light

Yinepu:
I am Yinepu
I am Anubis
I am the Star Lord
With My Mother, Nebet Het
And Aset
I am the God of Darkness
And Pathways
I guide with light
Alongside Aset and Nebet Het
We guide souls through the light
The light of stars
And through starlight
To dawn
We guide the light of the path of the soul
We guide with light
And show the way
To the path of the stars

Son of Ra and Nebet Het
by Chelsea Luellon Bolton

We are the Parents of Yinepu
Anubis is Our son
The Son of Ra and Nebet Het
The Son of Ra and Nephthys
He is Our son
He is Our beloved son
Our royal child
He is a guide and guard
He is a protector of Ra
He is the Jackal of the Cemeteries and the *Duat*
He is the Embalmer and the Undertaker
He is the Lord of the Dead
Yinepu, the Son of Ra and Nebet Het

Poetry of Aset and Nebet Het

The Twins, The Dyad

by Chelsea Luellon Bolton

I am the Twin of My sister,
I see as well as She.
I am the Sorceress and the Healer.
I am the Goddess of the Tree.
I am the Goddess of the Underworld,
I am the Goddess of the Night,
I am the Clandestine Lady,
of magic only revealed in the dark.
I am the Goddess of Magic,
invoked here.
I am the Lady of Mystery and Might.
I am the companion to My sister,
We Two Goddesses, We Two Twins,
We complement each other,
in all that We do.
I am bright, when She is dark.
I am dark, when She is light.
I am close to My sister
and She is close to Me.
We are twins,
We are a dyad,
We are the Ladies of the Tree.

Way of the Two Sisters

by Chelsea Luellon Bolton

Queen of the Road
Queen of your home,
Where I sit.
All who come to you
must go through Me.
All who come before Me
must go through My crucible.
All must do this.
No exceptions.
All must cry.
All must weep.
All must temper their rage.
For rage and grief are companions of death.
So all must do this.
Stand before Me when you cry.
Come before Me when you weep.
And when you rage,
go to My sister —
as the Lioness, as the Leopard,
as the Raging Goddess
as the Avenging Lady.
And She will help you.
She will guide you.
I am the Avenging Goddess.
Heru-sa-Aset is the Avenging God.
And Wesir is the one who was slain.
And Nebet Het is My companion,
who weeps with Me.
She is an Avenger too.
For She aids in the search for the body,
and She aids in His renewal.
And She is the Wife of Wesir in the *Duat*.
She is His companion as well.
I weep.
I wail.

I mourn.
As does My sister.
I burn in a rage.
I howl and yell in anger.
I screech.
I yell.
I shriek.
And My rage has voice.
My sister's rage has a voice.
It has a purpose.

So does yours.
Rage can only be conquered
with strength.
Rage can only be conquered
by giving it a voice.
by acknowledging its existence,
can you give it form and substance.
Once named, once realized,
anger will subside.
Give anger a voice of self-expression.
Listen to your rage.
And heal your heart with cleansing fire.
For this is the way of Aset and Nebet Het,
as the Two Sisters.

Way of the Heart

by Chelsea Luellon Bolton

Aset:
This is Aset.
Queen of the Road
Queen of your Home.
Queen of your Life.
This is not strife.
Be who you are.
Love who you've become.
A warrior, a priest, a lover
an artist, a writer, a scholar
an athlete, a parent, a worker
Love all that you do,
for that is a part of who you are.

Nebet Het:
This is Nebet Het.
Be the spaces in between each breath.
Be the ones who love in silence.
Be the ones who care without boasting.
Be the ones who help those who weep in silence.
Be the ones who aid those who weep in joy.
Be joyful, Little One.
Be mad with joy.
For We are here now beside you.
We have never left your side.
Be aware, dear child.
Be aware.
We are always where Our devotees reside.

Aset:
This is Aset.
Queen of the Road
Queen of your life.
Own who you are,
own all in your home.

Be who you wish,
Be who you've become.
Transcend the limitations you've put on yourself.
And build the life you desire.
with Me.
The Gods stand beside those
who honor Them,
who do Their work,
who ask for aid.
Do this and blessings will flow from the Gods to Their devotees.

Nebet Het:
This is Nebet Het.
The ones who call on Us for aid,
will receive it.
The ones who call on Us for strife,
will receive their own in return.
Listen.
Listen, well, O People.
Design the Life you wish you had
when you were three years old.
Design the Life you wish you had
when you were younger.
Remember the dreams that are unfulfilled.
Remember the hopes and desires
of your three-year-old self;
of your five-year-old self;
of your ten-year-old self;
of your twenty-year-old self;
of whatever age you were,
where you found something
that made your soul,
light up as bright as a star in the Heavens.
This is your heart's true desire.
And yes, there can be more than one.
But follow this light and its purpose.
Follow the light of your True Desire.
Pursue the dreams of your heart
and hear the voices of your soul.
Follow the path laid out by your True Desire.

For what you truly desire is the voice of your heart.
And the heart is the center of your soul.

Aset:
This is Aset.
Follow the Way of the Two Sisters.
Follow the Way of your Heart.
Follow the Way of the *Ka*.
Follow the heart of your soul.
And build a life worthy of Us and yourself.

The Two Sisters Call

by Chelsea Luellon Bolton

Nebet Het:
I am not the Goddess of change
But of transformation
I aid Wesir in the *Duat*
I aid My sister during Dawn and Dusk
I am Aset's Twin
I am Her Shadow.
I am Her epitaph
I am etched upon every stone
the names of the Dead,
committed to memory.
Each tear shed is Mine,
and Mine alone.
I am Aset-Nebet Het,
I am the *Ma'ati*,
the Lady of the Hall of the Two Sisters.
I am My sister here.
and She is Me.
We are One here.
We are Three.
The King Maker, the Cunning Magician;
The elusive Lady of Dusk and Twilight.
The Lady of the West.
We, Two Sisters here
We are the twilight.
We are in every dawn and dusk.
Every waking and sleeping.
This is Our time.
This is My time.
We weep.
We mourn.
We judge the deeds of the disturber.
We oversee the Judgment of the Dead.
We see your deeds and thoughts throughout your life.
We see all possibilities and the one path,

that must be taken,
that must be chosen.
This one path will lead you to Me.
All paths lead to Me in the end.
My hall.
Our gate.
All paths lead here.

So beware, when you come,
answer this:
Why did you ignore Our call?
Why did you embrace another's path,
besides Our Own?
Why did you forsake your heart's desire?

Sistrum-Goddess

by Chelsea Luellon Bolton

Aset
I am the Sistrum-Goddess,
I am the Lady of the Oasis
I am the Lady of Jubilation,
I am the Joyful One.
My son rests upon My throne.
He is avenged.
I am appeased.
The sistrum rattles,
and My rage disappears.
I have avenged My brother,
and the land is at peace.

Aset and Nebet Het
This is My role as the Sistrum Goddess.
I am Aset.
I am Nebet Het.
I am the one whose rage is cooled.
I am the one whose rage is appeased,
with the rattling of the sistrum
and offerings to the Gods.
to Me.
to Us.
To the Two Sisters,
Wives and Widows of Wesir.

This is Our journey as the Sun's Eye.
For We depart and return.
the Nile recedes and floods.
The star shines and departs.
And this cycle is Ours as Eyes of the Sun God.
And this cycle is Ours as Luminous Ones in the *Duat*.
For We are there.
Now. Now.
As Bright Ladies

as Noble Women
as the Two Sisters,
who renew Wesir
against decay and entropy.
We aid the Sun God,
in His nightly journey.
We slay the disturber.
And the enemy is felled.

The Stars illumine the sky.
And all is right in the world.
This is the cycle of the *Duat*.
Day by Day.
Year by Year.

Aset
For Yearly, I leave and depart.
I mourn and weep,
and search for My husband.
My sister accompanies Me.
We search and find Him.
And renew Him.
The waters flood and recede,
The star Sopdet, appears and departs.
This is Our cycle as an Eye of Ra.
For We are Wives of Wesir.
For We are Daughters of Ra.
For We are the Eye Goddesses,
filled with solar might and the power of stars.

Magic Gateway

by Chelsea Luellon Bolton

Aset:
I am the Goddess of your home,
I am the Goddess of your life,
I am the Goddess of your ancestral *ka* or lineage.
I am the energy in this space.
I am the Magic in breath.
I am the Goddess of *Heka*,
the connective magic of all creation and your life.
Everyone has this power, this might,
to do with as they will.
Plants bloom their flowers.
Birds fly.
Brooks flow with water.
Animals eat and thrive or die,
by My Hand.
People live when I say,
People come when I call,
and child,
You will be in My Hall.

Nebet Het:
I am Nebet Het, the Twin of My sister, too.
I am the Lady of the Shrine.
I am the Lady of the Home.
I am the Power that is unseen and unknown.
I am the goddess of strength and might.
I am the Goddess of what is right.
I am the Lady of Ma'at,
as well as My sister too.
I am the Goddess of the crossroads.
I am the Goddess of the Boundary ways
and altars.
I am the Goddess of Magic, unseen
I am the Goddess of powerful things,
I am the Lady of the Shrine,
where all power is divine.

The thrones of the gods, I guard,
I guard from impurity
and keep evil at bay.
I use magic and guile,
I use stealth
as invisible as the wind
and just as swift.
I use wards and talismans
to guard the shrine,
the power of My voice
the power of My words,
with My sister.

Aset and Nebet Het:
We guard this space.
We guard the shrine
where all magic is kept,
where all magic is divine.
The power here is creation itself
The power here is a God's wealth.
The power of the Gods in their shrines.

Nebet Het:
I am the gateway,
the doorway unseen,
I am the pathway,
both cluttered and clean.
I guard the entrance
I guard the gate,
I am the Goddess who guards fate.
I guide the souls
from here to there.
I guide them and lead them,
everywhere.

Aset:
I am the Goddess of the shrine,
I am the Goddess of the Home.
I am the Goddess of *ka*-power,
wherever you roam.

Enraged Widows

by Chelsea Luellon Bolton

My dirge
is strewn across the Heavens.
I am the Wife and the Widow.
I am the Sister and the Mourner.
I weep and wail.
Inconsolable sorrow is My lament.
I am the Widow of Wesir.
I am with My sister here,
as We mourn for Him.
We are the Two Widows,
We are His Two Wives.
Our keening can be heard
for miles.
Our shrieks can deafen,
Our wails can terrorize,
Our laments can frighten,
We mourn,
lamenting Our sorrow.
We mourn and yet,
We are enraged.
We are fiercely bright,
We are cobras
We are Lioness and Panther.
We wield scimitars
We wield bows and arrows.
We are enraged.

So We hunt for the disturber.
So We search for Our prey.
We slay the one who took Him from Us,
We slay his allies.
With magic and flame,
With weapons and knives.
We slay, We butcher,
We enchant the enemy,
and slay them.

We destroy the disturber.
And We weep and rejoice.
For the enemies are felled,
but too late.
The deed is done.
Wesir has died.

And We are alone,
as Widows and Wives
of the slain God.

Savior Goddesses

by Chelsea Luellon Bolton

Nebet Het:
I am Nebet Het, the Savior Goddess,
I am Nebet Het, the one who enchants,
I am the one who beguiles,
by moonlight.
I am the one who aids the throat,
causing it to breathe.
I beguile, I ensnare,
I enrapture the ones
who gaze upon Me,
Just a glimpse, Just a second glance
and I disappear into the night.

Aset:
I am Aset, the Sorceress,
I am Aset, the Enchantress,
I am the one who beguiles,
I am the one who enchants,
by starlight.
I am the one who causes breath,
I bring breath to the nose and mouth,
I speak and words vibrate across creation,
My voice is My magic,
for words are My source of power.
I beguile and enchant,
I am the Sorceress, who will not be ruled.

Aset and Nebet Het:
We are the Two Magicians,
We are the Great of Magic,
We are the ones who are skilled in magic,
We are excellent of speech and words.
We enchant with spells and incantations,
We ensnare with guile and cunning,

with spells to entrap or conceal.
We bring the evil doer to their knees,
felled beneath Our feet.
We are the ones who slay the disturber.
We are the ones who enchant and beguile,
We are the ones who use Our spells
to ward off evil,
as the Savior Goddesses,
who help, aid, and protect the people.

Throne and House Goddesses

by Chelsea Luellon Bolton

Aset:
Aset is the Mistress of the Throne
The Seat of the *Ka*-Power of the Lineage of Kings
The Magician's Seat, the Seat of Authority and Power
Mastery of the Self,
Queen of the Ancestors, Lady of the West, Aset *Amenti*
Queen of the Underworld, the Royal Wife of Wesir
Lady of the Sycamore

Nebet Het:
Nebet Het is the Mistress of the House, Temple, Palace and Tomb
Queen of the Ancestors,
Lady of the West, Nebet Het *Amenti*
Lady of the Underworld, the Royal Wife of Wesir
Lady of the Sycamore

Aset:
Aset, the Throne Goddess
Seat of Power, of the Beautiful Throne
Lady of *Amenti*,
Lionesses encircle the throne
On which Aset sits
On which Ra sits
On which all Kings sit
Because of Aset, the Lioness,
The Queen and the Mother of the Throne.

Nebet Het:
Nebet Het is the House Goddess
Lady of the Sacred Enclosure
Lady of the Temple, Palace, Home and Tomb
Beautiful *Amenti*,
Leopards encircle the beautiful palace,
The beautiful home, the beautiful temple,
The beautiful tomb,
As flagstaffs, they guard the entrance and gate.

Lady of the Crossroads

by Chelsea Luellon Bolton

Aset and Nebet Het:
We are the Goddesses of the Shrine
in your home and in your life.
We are the Goddesses of Crossroads,
of Boundary spaces, of Between-Places.
Liminal spaces are where We reside.
We are the Goddesses of your life.

We are the Goddesses of Boundary Spaces,
in Between-Places and Homes.
We are the Ladies of God,
We are the Ladies of Goddesses,
We are ones who are the Flagstaffs
as one enters temples and shrines.
We guard the boundary
between the sacred and mundane.
We are the Ladies of the Roads here,
where three ways meet,
the boundary itself,
the temple
and the street.
We are the Ladies of the Crossroads,
where three ways meet.

Rhyme for the Two Goddesses

by Chelsea Luellon Bolton

We are the Royal Ladies,
We are the Royal Wives,
We guard, bless and protect
your lives.

Just as We protect Ra,
We protect you,
We protect all people,
We Goddesses, Two.

We are the Wives of Ra,
We are His daughters too,
We are snakes and scorpions,
We protect even you.

We are Wives of Wesir,
We are His Widows too,
We mourn and weep,
That's what We do.

We are Powerful Ladies,
We are Powerful Wives,
We are Goddesses,
Who watch over your lives.

We are Goddesses of Magic,
We are Goddesses of Might,
We are the Flaming Ones,
Who are burning, fiercely bright.

We are the Goddesses of Plenty,
We are Goddess of Lives,
We are Goddesses of Wealth,
Who will help you always thrive.

We are Ladies of the Dance,
We are the Ladies of Music too,
We are the ones with the tambourine,
Play for Us, won't you?

We are the Ladies of the Sistrums,
We are the Ladies of the Dance,
We are the fierce Goddesses,
Care to take a chance?

We are Goddesses
We are Wives,
We are Ladies,
Who own Our lives.

We are Goddesses,
Can't you see?
We are here
to help you with your plea.

We are the Ladies of the Graves,
We are the Goddesses Who Weep,
We are Ladies of the Tomb,
We listen as you speak.

We are the Two Lionesses,
of Magic and Might,
We are Sun Goddesses,
Who shine fiercely bright.

We are the Two Leopards,
the Panthers, of night,
We are the Two Ladies,
Whose stars shine light.

We are the Two Ladies,
We are the Female Hounds,
We guard and guide
those who need to be found.

We are the Two *Uraeii*,
We are the Cobras Divine,
We are the Daughters of Ra,
Ladies, appeased with wine.

We are the Two Goddesses,
We travel with Our Lord,
We are the Goddesses of Sunbeams,
Who protect Him, wielding swords.

We are Aset and Nebet Het,
We are Egyptian here
We are Goddesses, who hear prayers,
We are always, ever near.

We are Goddesses of Magic,
We are Goddesses of Night,
We are star Goddesses,
Whose burning flames are bright.

We are the Ladies of Life
in all its forms,
We are the Two Sisters,
Since We were born.

We are Aset and Nebet Het,
We are the Two Sisters, here
We are the Two Goddesses,
Whose love is always near.

We are the Two Ladies,
We travel with Our Lord,
We are the Twin Goddesses,
Who are always adored.

Throne and Throne Shrines

by Chelsea Luellon Bolton

Nebet Het:
I am the Goddess of Kings
I am the Goddess of Thrones.
I am the Goddess of the Throne,
which bears My Name.
I am the Liminal Lady,
of boundaries, and spaces in between.
I am Nebet Het, *Kherseket*.
I am the Lady of Temples.
I am the Building of which They are made.
I am the Lady of Temples, Shrines, and Home.
I am the Lady of the Palace,
I am the Lady of the Royal Power.

Aset:
I am the Goddess of Kings,
I am the Royal Wife,
I am the Throne Goddess
who sits upon Her Seat.
I am the Lady of Royal Power
through succession from King to King.
I am the Lady of the Throne,
I am the Lady of My Name.
I am the Lady of Royal Power
and Magical Power of the *Ka*.
This power and this magic
is passed down through kingly lineages
and family lines — of all people.
I am the Goddess of the Temple,
I am the Lady of the Shrines.
I guard the entryway and the altars.
All shrines are the thrones
of the Gods and Goddesses
who dwell in them.
This is My domain.

My Sister makes the Temple.
My Sister guards its gates.
My Sister is the enclosure.
My Sister is Lady of the Temple.
She is the Lady of where I reside.
If I am the throne of Kings,
and She is the Palace deified,
then I am protected by My Sister,
as I am the throne and throne-shrine,
and She is the Palace and the Temple,
Then She is the protector of
where Kings and Gods reside.

Veiled Magic

by Chelsea Luellon Bolton

Veil of Tears
Sorrowful Wailings
Shrieking in the Night
Mystery so Profound
To Utter it would shatter reality
This Name,
Becoming who you most desire
Spoken with intention
For what comes forth will manifest
When your will matches Mine.

Aset-Nebet Het

by Chelsea Luellon Bolton

I am Aset-Nebet Het.
I am the *Ma'ati*.
I am Aset as Nebet Het.
I am both of Us
combined into one being.
I am Aset, Herself
and I am joined with Nebet Het.
My Sister is with Me here.

We come together
as Black Kites
as Falcons
as Gold Vultures
as Cobras
as Felines.
One as a Lioness,
One as a Panther.
One as both.

We rule the Celestial Waters
as the Great Mother of All the Gods.
We are *Amenti*.
We are the Creator who gave birth to the Sun.
For He rests between Our horns.
And We are the Great Mother,
who envelopes Him as He dies each day.
For We are the Star Goddess,
We are the Milky Way,
with its expansive array of stars.
We are the Queen of *Amenti*,
the Hidden Land where the Dead reside.

Now. Now.
We come to you
as Sisters and Wives of the Star God.

He is Wesir.
He is the Lord of *Amenti*.
Our Lord.
Our King.
Our Husband.
We call out to you for aid.

Honor your Dead.
Honor your ancestors.
Honor your teachers who have passed on.
Honor the Gods of Egypt.
Honor the Goddesses of Egypt.
Honor Us all.

For We are the Queen of *Amenti*
We are the Ladies of the Sun Barque.
We are the Ladies of the Sunrise and Sunset.
We are the Goddesses of the West.

We rule here,
as Wives
as Queens
as Widows
as Mourners.
We reside here.
We come from the *Duat*
to reside with the King of the Gods.

Wake of Sorrow and Rage

by Chelsea Luellon Bolton

And yet, and yet,
I am the undertaker.
I am the one who knows Her spells.
as My sister does.
as We are the Two Magicians,
We are the Two Wives of Wesir,
We are the ones who mourn and weep,
We are the ones who sing the dirge.
We are the ones who cause transformation.
We are the Voice which shatters,
We are the sound which invokes terror,
We are the ones lamenting those that have died.
We are the keening-women,
We are the mourners,
and We lament,
and We shriek and keen,
so loud that worlds shatter.
Ears deafen, Sight diminishes
as you clutch your ears
and shut your eyes,
as Our song makes you tremble
with fear and awe.
As Our dirge, resounds
in the wake of sorrow and rage.

We are Breath

by Chelsea Luellon Bolton

I am Aset-Nebet Het,
I am the Awakener,
from life and death.
I am the one who
chills you to your core.
I am the one who leaves
you breathless,
gasping for air.
I am the one who is married to Death.
I am the one who is married to Life.
For I am in both these places.
I am Aset.
And I am Nebet Het.
We exist here,
between the Two Realms.
between this and that,
here and there.
We are in between and everywhere.
We are wind and breath.
We are gales and whirlwinds.
We are wherever you breathe.
We are everywhere.
Do not think you can escape Us.

Partners and Twins

by Chelsea Luellon Bolton

Nebet Het is the Lady of the Dead and Creation
Aset is the Lady of Creation and the Dead
As a *dyad*, as a pair
They come as twins
They come as partners
They come together

In all forms and all names
We are Ourselves
And yet,
When We appear as One
We are One
We speak and act as one
We are twins
We mirror each other
We complement each other
One is dark, one is light
Now it changes
The other is dark, the other is light
Aset and Nebet Het
Are the Two Sisters
Mirroring each other
As Twins
As partners
As complementary opposites
Like Set and Wesir;
We mirror each other
We complement each other
We are complex and simple
We are the Two Sisters
Who — like Our brothers
Have a dynamic cycle
From light to dark
From dark to light
For We are the Two Sisters of the *Duat* and the Oasis

Life from Death

by Chelsea Luellon Bolton

Nebet Het and Aset
Aset and Nebet Het
Lady of Life
Lady of Death
The corpses and the shadow
The reaper and the keener
The one who rages at death
The one who holds death accountable
For ending life;
The End and Beginning
Another Beginning
And an End
These are the ways of death
Change and Transformation
With the one who cause decay
And desolation
And the ones who pry
Life from death

Call on the Two Mourners

by Chelsea Luellon Bolton

Nebet Het, of the Roads
Like Her Sister
Like Aset
She peers into the pathways
And sees all outcomes
All fates, all possibilities
And sees the path that must be taken
Based on what has come before.
Your actions speak of someone who is hurting
You are bereft and alone
You were abandoned
You were left to die
Alone
You are angry at Us
You thought We'd left you
We hadn't
We were always here
We have always been here
We have never left you
We do not abandon Our devotees
Honor Us
And We will help you
And not abandon you
You were not abandoned
You are not alone
You are not alone
You have friends and family
And the Egyptian Gods and Goddesses
Aset and Nebet Het, especially
We will help you
For you are going through
The Death of Wesir
You are going through a great transformation
A little death
In your life

That is impacting you
As much as His death affected Us
So call on the Mourners
The Two Sisters
The Two Wives
The Two Lovers
And We will help you
We love you
Do not ever forget that
Always

Creation's Goddess

by Chelsea Luellon Bolton

I am Death
I am War
I am Rain
I am Tempest
I am what makes you face your fears
I am the courage a coward seeks
I am the strength a warrior knows
I am the will to keep fighting
The will of fire
The will of flame
is to keep burning
or streaking through the sky as lightning
I am the will to keep going
I am the will to never die
I am the cradle of creation
I am the cauldron of knowledge
Of primordial water, ink, and scrolls
I am the speech of the First Creation
Goddess and God
God or Goddess
Goddess, only
God, only
However creation transpired
Wind and Rain
Air and Water
Lightning as fire
Light as flame
These are creation's markers
There are creation's gifts
Nature is creation's bounty
You are its speech
I am Aset, the Firstborn Daughter of Geb
I am Nebet Het, the Second Daughter of Geb
We are Daughters of Ra

We are Daughters of Nut, the Sky Goddess
We are the Daughters of Creation
We are Goddesses
We are Scribes
We are the Words of Magic and Life
Decay and Death;
We are the Daughters of the Earth God
And Daughters of the Scribe
We are Daughters of Heaven and the Sky
And the Starry Night;
We are Daughters of Creation
And heirs to the throne of Life
We are the Daughters of Geb and Nut
Of Ra;
And We are the will to keep living
And never die

Goddesses of Creation

by Chelsea Luellon Bolton

Aset is the North Wind and West Wind,
Nebet Het is the East Wind
She is your breath;
She is there as you breathe,
As you speak,
As you sing,
As you wail,
As you scream,
She is there with you in joy and sorrow.
Breathe and She is with you.

She is the Sky above you
She is Mehet Weret
The Starry Heavens, the Night-time sky
The Dusk and Dawn are Her domains
As the Star Goddess and Lady of Night
She is the Celestial Cow
She is the Creator and Mother of Ra
She is Aset
She is Nebet Het
She is the Mother of All the Gods

She is the Nile
And the water you drink
She is the rain which pours down from Heaven
She is the rainfall
She is the downpour
She is the storm
She is the water which nourishes all living things
She is the water of creation which sustains life
She is Mehet Weret, She is Nut
She is Nit, She is Nunet
She is Aset
She is Nebet Het

She is the Tree
She is the Earth beneath your feet
Her father dwells there and Her husband
As the land is the realm of Geb
As the dead are laid to rest here
So Wesir is here as their King
And the Lady of the Sycamore
Nourishes the deceased with water and fruit
She is *Amenti*, the Lady of the West
She is Aset, the Queen of the Underworld
She is Nebet Het, the Queen of the Underworld
And She is the earth which bestows its bounty
As the rainfall nourishes the crops, the plants and animals
And land below
She is here as the Lady of the Harvest
The Lady of Flowers and the Lady of Animals
And the Goddess of the Dead

She is Sunlight
She is flame
In the darkest hour
Look to the stars and bask in the starlight
Look to the solar rays and bask in their light
She is the Eye of Ra
She is the Solar Goddess
She is the Lady of Dusk
She is the Lady of Dawn
She is the Lioness, the Cobra and the Leopard
She is the fire in your eyes
And the star in your soul
As joy and rage flow through you
She is here in your rage
She is here in your joy
And She is here to carry you through
She is here as the Lady of Fortitude
She is here as the Lady of Strength
She is the Leopard
She is the Lioness
She is Nebet Het
She is Aset

She is the roar which speaks your name
Listen to the words of the Lioness
Listen to the words of the Leopard:
You are strong enough,
Did We not make you?
Did We not mold you in Our tears?
You people are Our creations just as much as Our Father's.
The Tears of Ra made humankind
The Eyes of Ra made humankind
And once you were formed,
Did We not love you?
Did We not give you magic?
Did We not give you life?
Look all around you, child.
Creation is Our gift
Life is Our gift
We are all around you
In every facet of your world
In every breath, in every drop of water
In every tree, in every light
In every land,
We are always there
We are always with you
We are woven through the tapestry
Of your life
Know these four things:
Our love is eternal
Our strength is with you
Our magic is in you
And you are never alone.

Watch Over Your Life

by Chelsea Luellon Bolton

Nebet Het of the Marshlands
Nebet Het of the Oasis
Aset of the Marshlands
Aset of the Oasis
We are Wives of Wesir
We are the Lady of the Sycamore
Lady of the River
Lady of the Stream,
Cataracts too
We are the Two Ladies
Who have come to you.
We come bearing a message for all who will ask
We are the Twins
We are the Goddesses
We are the Ladies of Life
We are the ones who are invoked
For protection from evil and strife
We are the Goddesses
Who protect all who ask
We are the Goddesses
Who give you a task
We want you to be faithful
To all that you are
We want you to respect yourself
And your tribe
We want you to know
That We will watch over your life
In all that you are
In all that you do
Aset and Nebet Het
Isis and Nephthys
Will always watch over you
As you grow and change
We are here
As you live and breathe

We are here
We are always by your side
Throughout all of your life

Manifest Your Power

by Chelsea Luellon Bolton

Heru of Egypt
Nebet Het of the Two Lands
This is about Kingship
And owning your power
As a God, As a Goddess
Own your power
As if a God or Goddess
Is with you, at all times
The strength of Nebet Het is yours
The strength of Aset is yours
To do with as you will,
But remember, you are responsible for the power you wield
You are responsible for your actions and deeds
Both good and bad
We are the Ladies of Strength
We are the Willful, Determined,
Strong Ones
We wield the blades, the scimitar,
We aim with the bow and arrows
We strike as lionesses, as panthers
We are swift as cobras
We wield Our words as weapons —
to ward off harmful events
We wield Our magical power
With strength, knowledge, and reverence
We wield Our power
as We wield Ourselves
We are responsible for Our actions
We are responsible for what We do
as you are,
as you will be once you die
So listen,
This power is here inside
You are not helpless
Take one moment

Take one breath
Exhale and Inhale
So now you are still
and calm
So from this place of serenity
Make a choice
Exert your power
Manifest yourself and your desire
And join with your desire
And manifest your power

Solar Cycle as a Star

by Chelsea Luellon Bolton

I am the Sistrum Goddess
of beauty and rage.
I am the Lioness here,
I am the Cobra,
I am the Goddess whose anger cannot be appeased.
The rattle of the sistrum calms Me.
The sound of music quells My anger.
I am appeased with the sound of the sistrum.
I am appeased with the sound of your voice,
singing praises in My Name,
singing hymns long forgotten.
Recite the names
of My deeds.
Recite the names
of My family line.
Recite the names
of My ancestors.
Recite your names.
Recite the names
of your dead.
Recite the names
of the Gods and Goddesses.
Recite the names,
for I am the Wife of Wesir.
I am enraged at His passing.
I am enraged at His death.
And I leave and depart,
to Nubia,
to the *Duat*,
as Sopdet,
as the Star in the Heavens.
This is My myth of the Distant Goddess.
This is My Solar Cycle as a Star.
I am Aset, here.
I am Nebet Het here.

We are together, here.
in all years.
in all time.
of this festival
of the Re-Awakening of Wesir.

Blazing Goddess of the Star

by Chelsea Luellon Bolton

I leave and return
as Sopdet,
I arrive and depart
as Sopdet.
I arrive as the Blazing Goddess
of the Sun and Star.
I arrive and I bless the people,
during the New Year time.
I bless the people
throughout My cycle
as the Goddess of the Starry Heavens.
I see the people
with their faces toward the sky.
I bless all the people
who gaze upon Me.
I bless all the people
as the starlight beams down,
as the sunbeams brighten the earth,
I bless the people
with My rays.
For I am Aset-Sopdet,
Ruler of the Northern Skies.
I am Aset-Nebet Het,
as I gaze upon the Earth.
My sister sails with Me,
across the Northern Heavens.
I arrive and depart,
I appear and vanish,
Just like My sister does. .
She too is Sopdet.
And My search for Wesir
My renewal of the People
both living and dead,
as the star that brightens the sky,

is the journey
of the Two Sisters
and the Widows of Wesir.
And this cycle is Hers,
and also Mine.

Burning Fiercely Bright

by Chelsea Luellon Bolton

Aset and Nebet Het:
I am Aset.
I am Nebet Het.
I am the Two Sisters, here.
I am the Lady of the *Duat*.
I am the Lady of Tears.
I am the Goddess,
who burns ever bright.
I am the Goddess,
who shines fiercely bright.

Aset:
I am the Star Goddess,
of Dawn.
I am the Star Goddess,
of Night.
I am the Lady,
ever, burning,
fiercely bright.

I am the Goddess of the Star,
I am the Lady of Light.
I am the Queen of both
Day and Night.

I am the Lady of the Star,
I am the Lady of bright light,
I am the Star Goddess
burning, fiercely bright.

I am with My husband,
and My son.
and My sister,
in the sky.
I am Sopdet,

along with My sister.
He is Orion.
My son is Sah.
We travel throughout the night,
in the *Duat*,
and the Heavens,
We burn,
Fiercely bright.

Nebet Het:
I am the Goddess of the Sky
and of the Stars at night.
I am the Lady of Sopdet,
burning, fiercely bright.
I am the hidden star,
I am the hidden light,
yet, when I shine,
when I glow,
I burn, fiercely bright.

Aset:
We are the Goddesses
of night.
We are the Goddesses
of stars.
We are the Fiercely Bright Ones,
shining at night.

Uraeus

by Chelsea Luellon Bolton

So you want to get to know the *Uraeus*,
the one who wept at creation,
filling the world with men and women?
So you want to honor the Goddess,
who made the first sunrise?
So you want to know of the Goddess,
who sits on top of Ra's brow?

What can be told of such a Lady?
She of the Cobra and Panther?
The slithering serpent of flame and magic.
The Primordial Goddess of the First Light.
The First Dawn.
Creation's Mother and Daughter
as Ra's Eye.

She is the Panther Goddess
of Stars and Night.
The Leopard's spots are the stars of Heaven.
She is the Goddess of the Solar Light
and Starlight.
She is the Fierce Lady,
who roars and hunts
throughout the night.
She Who devours the King of the Gods,
to give birth to the dawn.

Solar Lady,
Stellar Light,
She brings the dawn
and births the Light.
Every day is Her creation.
Every day is Her renewal.
She is the primordial Goddess

of the Dawn.
Water and Starlight,
are Her powers
which bring about transformation.

She is the *Uraeus*,
the coiled cobra on His brow.
She is the *Uraeus* of Ra,
She is the Cobra of Geb.
She is the Serpent Who protects the shores of Heru.
She is Aset, the Eye of Ra.
She is Aset, the Lioness.
She is Aset, the Panther,
the Leopard Goddess of the Stars.

She is the *Uraeus*,
the coiled serpent on His forehead.
She is the *Uraeus* of Ra,
She is Nebet Het, the Eye of Ra.
She is Nebet Het, the Cobra of Ra.
She is Nebet Het, the Panther Goddess,
the Leopard of the Starry Heavens.

These Two Sisters
Wield flame and magic here,
of creation and destruction
and protection
born of the fiercest love,
the love of all of creation.

Star Goddess, Eye of Ra
by Chelsea Luellon Bolton

I am the Lioness,
I am the Leopard,
the Panther Goddess.
My sister is the Panther,
We are both Eyes of Ra.
We are both *Uraeii*
We are both lionesses
of the Day and Night.
We are the Goddesses of Dawn and Twilight.
We are the Ladies of the Western Skies.
We are the Ladies of the *Duat*.
and Queens of Heaven.
We are Ladies,
and We have a Lord.
He is Wesir of the *Duat*.
He is Our Husband.
He rules the Dead as King.
He is the Bright Lord, the Star Lord
as We are the Bright Ladies and the Star Ladies.
We rule the night,
We travel the realms
as Sopdet in the Sky.
We follow Wesir.
The Heavens reveal Our journey,
with the Wolf and Jackal Lord at Our side.

Nebet Het is the Lady of the Stars.
as Sopdet, along with Me,
for We are the Ones,
who rise at dawn,
during the New Year.

And We are the Bright Ones
in the Sky as Solar Goddesses
and as Star Goddesses
of the Night and Day.

We are the Brightest of Goddesses
of Starlight and Flame,
Feline Goddesses,
Who massacre enemies
and protect those We love,
and Goddesses who will
bring light to the darkest of days.

We will dispel darkness with Our light.

Celestial Goddess

by Chelsea Luellon Bolton

Aset, the World-Bringer
Aset, the World-Shaker
Aset, the Lady of the Sky
Aset, the Lady of Heaven
Aset, the Lady of Rain
Aset, the Lady of the Stars
Star Goddess, Lady of Light
Mistress of the Constellations
Lady of the Planets
Lady of the Stars

Nebet Het, Lady of the Sky
Lady of Rain,
Lady of the Constellations
Lady of Heaven, Queen of the Road
Mistress of All the Gods.

Ladies of the Celestial Realm
Ladies of the Stars
Ladies of the Constellations
Ladies of the Light of Heaven
Ladies of the Light of Ra
Star Goddesses
Ladies of the Night Sky filled with Stars

Eye in the Storm

by Chelsea Luellon Bolton

Aset:
I am there when the sky darkens,
I am there when the clouds roll in,
I am there when thunder
shakes the sky.
I am there when lightning ignites,
shooting across the sky.
In My anger, in My rage,
I scream as wind howls,
I wail as birds screech,
I mourn, I weep,
as rain floods the river,
as rain floods the earth.
I cry and wail
I scream so loud
My voice is thunder.
My tears are rain.
My wind is a wail.
And the sky,
shakes.
My rage resounds across the Heavens,
Lightning blazes across the sky.

My rage is not appeased,
as the Goddess of Heaven.
As the Goddess of the Darkened Sky.
I am enraged.
I am the one who brings the storm to flood,
the Nile's banks overflow,
and crops and people drown.
I burn so brightly as Sopdet,
yet I am the one who brings the storm,
which floods the river and earth below.
And I am the Storm Bringer,

and I am the one who owns the sky.
For I am the Goddess of Rain-Clouds,
and I am the Goddess of the Flood.
I bring the wrath of Heaven
to the Earth below.

The sky trembles,
as I appear in My form of Sopdet.
The sky shakes,
and the Storm Bringer comes,
for I am the one who knows the Name
of the one who controls the sky,
the Lord of Heaven.
For I am the one who knows all
and sees all,
from My Heavenly Seat.

I am the one who brightens the sky,
as the clouds roll in,
I am the one who wails
as thunder resounds.
I am the one who weeps,
as rain falls.
I am the one who wails,
as wind howls.
I am the one who screeches,
as I keen.
I am the Storm Bringer,
as the one who brings the flood.
The river overflows,
plants and people perish below.

Yet, I am not appeased.
I wail, I weep
I mourn, I keen.
Rain falls from My eyes
I am the Eye of Ra,
I am the Avenger.
Instead of scorching heat,
I bring the Storms,

I bring the rain,
I bring the flood of rivers and trees,
I bring you to Me,
in the *Duat* as the Sycamore
or as Sopdet
as She appears and departs from the sky.

And I weep in the Heavens,
as the Goddess enraged,
by My husband's death,
by My husband's murder,
and yet,

I am appeased by the Goddess of the Starry Sky,
I search and follow Him,
throughout the sky,
Orion and Sopdet.

I am only appeased,
as the Star Goddess,
brightly illuminating the Northern Skies.
I am Aset, the Storm Goddess,
I am Aset, the Rain Goddess,
I am Aset, the Fiercely Bright One.
I am Aset-Sopdet.
I am Aset, Lady of the Stars.
I am Aset, the Solar Goddess of the Night.
I am Aset, Queen of Heaven.
I am Aset, Lady of the Sky.

Nebet Het's lightning is barely seen,
dancing among the clouds.
Her wind is a gale or a whirlwind,
Blowing away entropy.
Her tears are the rain
Her rage is the thunderstorm.
The sky shakes at Her command,
and thunder vibrates throughout the lands,
as Her rage pummels the earth,
with pellets of water.

Nebet Het:
The howl of the wind,
is My dirge.
My lament transforms into song.
I wail and sing
of My brother slain.
and the sky sings along.
He who makes the Earth-Shake,
He who makes the thunder roar,
see the tear-drops fall from My eyes.
and I mourn.
The sky trembles as I pass
The sky is ablaze,
with the fire from My eyes
as thunder shakes and sky,
as lightning flashes
as rain pellets fall,
and the wind howls a dirge.
I am Nebet Het, Wife of the Storm Bringer,
I am Nebet Het, Widow of Wesir
I am Nebet Het, Lady of the Sky,
I rule the Heavens in the night.
I am the Eye of Ra.
I am the Lady, enraged.
I am the one who calls the Storm,
I am the one who quells its rage.
I am Nebet Het, Lady of Storms,
the sky trembles at My approach.

Her Wrath

by Chelsea Luellon Bolton

Her storms bring the tears of God
Her storms bring the wrath
of the disturber.
Her storms, His storms
Bring transformation amidst rage.
Transformation amidst sorrow.
Transformation among the Eyes of God.
Aset and Nebet Het, Wives of Wesir.
Sopdet, shining
peering through the clouds of the darkened sky.
Lightning illuminates the night.
Rain floods the river.
Rain floods the river.
Banks overflow and people and plants die.
No one is nourished.
No one is saved,
in this flood fueled by rage.
Rage at the Disturber.
Rage at the Death of Wesir.
Rage enough to flood Egypt.
Rage enough so the Oasis holds no refuge
for those fleeing from the Wrath of God.
Yet, wait — the storm is quelled.
The anger appeased.
She has found Orion, the Star of Wesir.
Sopdet and Orion.
Race to the Heavens,
traveling among the stars of the Blessed Dead.
To renew the cosmos — one more year.

Eyes of Ra

by Chelsea Luellon Bolton

It is I who introduce the Gods,
It is I who gain Their favor.
I am Aset.
I am Nebet Het.
We Two Sisters, here.
We encircle the sun
as *Uraeus*, as *Uraeii*
protecting the sun on His journey.
We protect Him,
for We are His daughters.
Not His sons.
We do not inherit the land,
but We did inherit the Heavens,
the Sky God and the Sky Goddess,
We inherit the Heavens from Our Mother,
Nut, the Lady of the Sky.
We are Goddesses of the Earth,
from the Earth God, Geb.
We inherited the land with Wesir.
The crops are His and My husband's,
as They grow the plants
from their soil.
With Our Light,
with Our Rays,
with Our Sunbeams.
And We replenish the Earth,
with Our rain,
with Our flood,
with Our water flow.
And We inherited Our sunbeams,
from Our Father, Ra,
Lord of the Sky,
and God of the Sun.
He is Our Father
and Lord of All.

He commands
and We create.
He commands,
and We defend.
He commands
and We protect.
As the Two Goddesses,
as the Two Widows,
as the Two Wives.
as the Two Daughters.
We protect creation,
with the Power of Our Voice,
with the Power to command,
with Our magic,
with the Power to destroy,
with Our flame and weapons.
We command.
We destroy.
And We defend.
As consorts,
as daughters
and as Eyes of Ra.

Nut, Our Mother

by Chelsea Luellon Bolton

The Goddess Nut
is Our Mother,
the Sky Goddess
is Our Mother.
The Starry Heavens
The Starry Sky,
is filled with stars.
For Our Mother.
She is the *Duat*,
in the Sky.
This is where Wesir lives,
This is where the Two Sisters,
live as Sopdet.
The Star Goddesses,
the Twin Sisters,
mirror each other.
As We speak as One.
As We speak as Two.
as We speak together.
We are the Star Goddesses
of the Night Sky,
because of Nut, Our Mother.

Geb, the Earth God

by Chelsea Luellon Bolton

The Earth God, Geb
is Our Father.
We are the Ladies of the Two Lands.
We are the Ladies of the Fields.
We are the Ladies of Crops and Plants.
We are the Ladies of Papyrus, Lotuses
and Roses.
We are the Ladies of the Graves,
for We bury Our dead Wesir
in the ground of Our Father.
And He rules the Blessed Dead.
in the ground,
in the Earth,
buried in land of Our Father.
Geb and Wesir,
Our Kings here,
of the Land,
of the Rocks,
of the Dead buried within the ground.
We are Wesir's Beloveds,
We are His Wives
We are His Mourners,
We weep and the plants
of Our Father grow.
We weep and the plants
of Our Husband grow.
We weep the tears Our Mother
shed when Geb was taken from Her.
We weep the tears We shed,
when Wesir was taken from Us.
For this is the cycle of the renewal
of the Earth.
This is the cycle of Our Father,
and Wesir.
This is the cycle of the Earth God.

Ra, Our Father

by Chelsea Luellon Bolton

Ra:
Eye of Ra,
Lord of the Sunbeams,
Lord of All.
Who beams down
on fields,
causing the crops to flourish.
With My daughters.

Aset and Nebet Het:
We are the Wives of Wesir
We are the Daughters of Ra,
We the slay the serpent
to protect Our Father,
in the *Duat*,
to protect all of creation,
so that life may continue
so that life may exist.
We protect the Gods of *Kemet*.
and Our Father,
Who is the King of the Gods.
He commands,
and We slay,
the enemies of Our Father
and all of creation.
We destroy,
with flame and magic.
We destroy,
with the Power of Our Might.
We are Ladies of Strength.
We protect the Sun God,
in all He does,
throughout His journey,
in the Sky,
both day and night.

Wesir, Our Husband, the Fiercely Bright

by Chelsea Luellon Bolton

Wesir:
We are the Creators
of the World.
We are the Gods
who made humans —
both women and men —
equally.
And yet, And yet,
Humans defile Us,
Humans reject Us,
Humans disown Us.
And yet, We thrive,
We live,
We breathe,
We own Ourselves.

Wesir:
I am Wesir,
King of the Underworld.
I am Wesir,
God of Gods, King of Kings,
I am Wesir,
who died.
I am in the *Duat*.
I am Wesir,
the Lord of Lords.
I am Wesir,
of the *Duat*.
I am Wesir,
of the Night.
I am Wesir,
of the Moon.
Burning, fiercely bright.

Aset:
I am the Wife of Wesir,
I am the Woman of the Home,
I am the Lady of Ladies,
I am the Queen of the Road.
I roam as Sopdet,
the shining star.
I roam with My sister,
where ever We are.
My sister and I,
We are the stars at night.
We are the Two Goddesses,
burning, fiercely bright.

Nebet Het:
I am the Goddess of the East and West,
I am the Goddess of the final rest.
I am the Lady of here and there,
I am the Goddess of everywhere.
I am the Lady of the Tomb and Grave,
I am the Lady,
who calls to you in your final hour.
I am Nebet Het,
Lady by the graveside,
leaving offerings,
leaving boons,
leaving flowers,
by the tombs.
I am the Goddess of the Sun,
I am the Goddess of the Star,
at night.
Burning, fiercely bright.

Wesir:
We are the Fiercely Bright Ones,
in the *Duat* now,
We are the Fiercely Bright Ones,
as the Moon,
as the Stars,
and the Two Sisters, as the Sun.

Those Who Renew

by Chelsea Luellon Bolton

Wesir:
I am Wesir,
Lord of the *Duat*.
I am with My wife, Aset,
and My second wife, Nebet Het,
We are the Family here.
We are the Husband and Wives.
We are alone here,
in the *Duat*.
in the night.

Aset:
I am Aset, Goddess of the Night Sky,
I am with Wesir here
as *Amenti*,
as the West.
I am the Lady of the West,
Goddess of the Northern Mountains,
Lady of the Lake of *Isheru*.
I am the Goddess who
renews My Husband.
I am the Goddess of the Brightest Star,
Sopdet, the Second Sun.
I renew all of creation
and Wesir,
with My blazing light.

Nebet Het:
I am Nebet Het,
Lady of Starlight.
I am Nebet Het,
Lady of Renewal.
I renew Wesir,
I renew the Dead,
through starlight.

I am the Brightest Star,
at night.
I am *Amenti*,
along with My sister.
We are the Two Sisters,
Who burn, fiercely bright,
in the *Duat*.

Wesir:
I am Wesir, in the *Duat*,
along with My Two Sisters,
along with My Two Wives,
We are the Gods of the *Duat*,
forever in Our cycles,
throughout time.

Guide and Guard

by Chelsea Luellon Bolton

Aset:
Wepwawet is My Son
Wesir is His Father
The Wolf and Jackal Lord
He is the Lord of the Crossroads
All roads leading to here or there
He is the one to call upon when you are lost
He will guide you home to safety
He is the warrior, the magician
And the one who leads the way
As a scout, guide, and guardian

Nebet Het:
Yinepu is My son
He is the guide of the deceased
He is the one of the funeral shroud
He is the Master of Secrets
For the rites of the dead;
He is My son as the son of Ra
He is the Royal Child
The shining God
Guiding the way through sunlight and starlight
Both night and day
He is a guide and a guard
He is My son
As the one who aids Wesir

Yinepu is My son
As a royal child
As a royal descendant
He is My son
For I am from a royal lineage
I am the one who cares for the deceased
Yet My son is the one who buries them
He is the one who appeases their souls

As they pass
He is the one who weighs
Their heart against a feather
In Hall of Ma'at
So that judgment can occur.
And I am one of judges
He is the one who oversees mummification
He also mummified Wesir
He did the burial rites for Wesir
I am the mourner who wails for the deceased
Do you see now?
He is My child
I am Death
And He is My Guide

Aset and Nebet Het:
Lord of the Crossroads
Lord of the Ways
These are the Two Jackal Gods
Our Sons
The Two Sisters' Sons
Aset's son is Wepwawet
Nebet Het's son is Yinepu
They guide and guard
They protect Wesir
They guide the dead as well as the living
We are the Wailing Women
And They are the ones who guard the God
As they are the Two Dogs
Two Jackals
And the Two Lords
Who guide, guard, and protect
Their loved ones

Lioness and Leopard

by Chelsea Luellon Bolton

Of Dust and
Shattered Tears
I walk
Crumbling embers beneath my feet
Crack

I fall

Taste bitterness in my mouth
Defeat mixed with Fear

I spit
Expel those shadows deep
I cry, I wail
I shriek
Though no one hears
The keening of a Mourner

My voice is gone
Throat dried up
Water does not flow from my eyes

I brush the dust from my face
I stand
A word rumbles from inside my Being
I roar
And the sky trembles

Light of the Panther Goddess

by Chelsea Luellon Bolton

Leopard Goddess, Panther Queen
I am the star-strewn sky
I herald the dawn and the year
as a star
I am the light in every twinkle
in every flame across creation
All light is Mine
I am seen and known
I am a light in the dark
I banish shadows
with each dawn
I bring the light

Light of the Dawn
I bring
Along with My Sister
We are the Lioness,
We are the Leopard
On top of the brow of Ra
We are His Eyes
We are His protectors
We protect both gods and men
We protect both gods and women
For We are the Goddesses of Women
We protect all mankind, all women-kind
All humans everywhere
Not one is excluded from Our protection and love
Not one
We protect those who honor Us
We are the Leopard as the Star Goddess
We are the Lioness as the Solar Flame
We protect those who honor Us
So, honor Us
And see Our blessings flow.

Soul-Bringer

by Chelsea Luellon Bolton

Sorrow is not meant to be permanent
It is a transient state.
You grieve and weep
and then your pain transforms
You transform — as someone who holds this pain
Forever changed.
No one can rescind the jaws of death,
nor comfort the mourners at the wake.
But you learn to live with these —
little deaths —
these events that happen —
out of your control
or within your control,
it does not matter which,
for you are forever changed,
when death comes.
Every change is a mark upon your soul
for good or ill.
Change happens and comes.
I am sorry you are hurt.
I am sorry that you suffer,
but child,
some of this is your doing
some of this is your choice
and some of it is not.
Much of it is out of your control.
And yet you cling to pain as if it's breath,
for what else do you have?
You are alone.
You are afraid.
You are enraged.
And yet, these little deaths
throughout your life —
have shaped and changed who you are —
for better or worse.
But at the end of this pain,

and at the end of this changed self
is someone else.
Someone new.
This is the self you must reach
to become who you want
to become who you desire
to become who you are.
And this is the lesson of the soul-bringer,
for the ones who own themselves,
must know who they are.

This is Your Star

by Chelsea Luellon Bolton

You need Nebet Het
For compassion,
For transformation
For fortitude
For She is Aset's counterpart
She is Her mirror
And She is your twin;
Your twin souls mirror the Two Sisters.
Light and Dark
Night and Day
Kind and Enraged
These are the cycles of your soul.
You are the Daughter of the Star Goddess
And the night sky;
You are the Daughter of the Solar Eye and Lunar Eye
You are the Daughter of the Fiercely Bright One
The Lioness, the Leopard, the Panther
Aset, the Lioness
Nebet Het, the Panther, the Leopard
Aset, the Panther, the Leopard
Nebet Het, the Lioness
Shining brightly in the dark
Shining brightly in the light
This is you
This is where you shine
With the celestial bodies
As Venus, as Aphrodite
The Morning Star which shines at Daybreak and Dusk
The Goddess of Joy, Beauty and Love
As Aset, as Nebet Het
This is what you need;
As Sopdet is Aset's star
You too, have your own;
It is love you need
It is joy you need to thrive;

Creativity and Joy of creating are what you need;
Writing is your passion.
Do it.

Aset-Serqet, Nebet Het-Serqet: Expeller of Poison

by Chelsea Luellon Bolton

I am the goddess of the shores,
I am the goddess of the river,
I am the water and the rain.
I am wet and sleek like a flowing river,
I am rain, pouring down, filling the water.
I am the waves which excrete poison,
toxins I dispel,
in My waters holy and divine.

I am Serqet, the Scorpion,
I am the venom in the Cobra's fangs,
I excrete poison, I expel venom
from those who call to Me.
I am Nebet Het, the Scorpion Goddess,
I am Nebet Het-Serqet.

And I dispel the poison
from My son and My brother,
for I dispel the poison,
from anyone who asks.
I am like My sister,
in this way, I am like My sister.

Yet, She is the Scorpion of Nubia,
She is Aset-Serqet.
And I am Nebet Het of the Flaming Eyes,
My tail is coiled, ready to strike.
Yet, I am the one who expels poison.
And I am the one who causes the
poison and venom to wash away.

Hymns, Prayers, and Adorations

Awaken in Peace, Nebet Hwt

by Jonathan Sousa

Awake, Nebet-Hwt, lover of silence!
Awake, Nebet-Hwt, Mistress of the House!
Awake, Nebet-Hwt, Dark Sister of Auset the Savior!
You who know what it is to suffer, be with us!
You who – most importantly – know what it means to triumph, have mercy!
Nebet-Hwt, Bride of Sutekh the Mighty, let us be the Eye of the Storm!
Nebet-Hwt, Beloved of Wesir,
Mother of Yinepu who guides and upholds – be our bridge to the Stars!
Nebet-Hwt, Wise Woman, known also as Seshat – constant companion of Djehuti –
may our memory aid us in coming forth!
Awake, awake, Nebet-Hwt, awaken in peace!

Prayer to Nephthys I

by Rebecca Buchanan

nephthys
beautiful one who exists
mistress of the house of the west

i descend into the darkness
on your barque of night

suckle me at your left breast
oh reckoner of lives
nephthys

Hymn to Nephthys I

by Rebecca Buchanan

the hawk of night,
she glides
above
the dark
river, mourning

Twenty-One Adorations of Nephthys

by Rebecca Buchanan

Daughter of Starry Sky and Dirt
Wife of Storm
Mother of the Jackal
First Priestess
Mistress of the Sacred House
Lady of the Gateway
Lady of the House of the Sistrum
Sanctifier of Beer
Navigator of the Barque of Night
She Who Makes Visible That Which Is Hidden By Moonlight
Lover of Deepest Night
Bird of the River of Night
She Who Stands Upon the Perilous Edges
Composer of the Songs of Lamentation
Mistress of the Bed of Life
Overseer of Putrefaction
Lactating Mother
Hawk of Mournful Cries
Guardian of the Bennu-Bird
She Who Breathes the Flames of the Bennu-Bird
She Who Speaks Silence

Descend With Me

by Amanda Artemisia Forrester

"Descend with me"
She calls my name
And holds out Her hand

I am afraid.
I don't want to go.
I'm not ready —
I don't know
What lies below.

The night-barque glitters
Like a thousand stars
The Lady's long hair swirls
Around Her beautiful face.
But behind Her is only inky blackness.
I cannot see where She means to take me.

I am afraid.
I don't want to go.
I'm not ready —
I don't know
What lies below.

"Descend with me"
She calls my name
And holds out Her hand

I am fearful.
The blackness will surely swallow me whole.
But I reach out anyway.
I don't even know why.

I am afraid.
I don't want to go
I'm not ready —

I don't know
What lies below.

Her strong, cool hand grasps mine
And She pulls me into the night-barque
I open my mouth to scream
But before I can
She enfolds me in Her embrace
Her hands are no longer cool, but warm
Her feathered wings wrap me tight as a mummy
Warm in my cocoon of Goddess wings.
……..Or are they bandages?
I am washed in a wave of contentment
Warm as the salt sea in the desert sun.

I'm not afraid any more.
I don't know why.
I don't need to know
What lies below.

She'll keep me safe
Through the night
Though the long journey
And aid Ra against Apophis' might

Tonight I'll descend with Nephthys
In the morning I'll arise with Isis.

You Are Welcome Here
by Amanda Artemisia Forrester

Nephthys
Darker Sister
Hidden One
Veiled Goddess
You walk between the worlds
Comforting the dead
Appearing in dreams
In instinctual intuition
Lady of Rebirth
Mother of Anubis
Wife of Seth
With Your bright sister You searched
For the pieces of Osiris's body
With Your sister You stood
Side by side
As She resurrected the brother
That You both loved
Your lessons are darker than those of Isis
But You are necessary
For all men pray for Your presence
When they realize their end is near
O Nephthys, sad-eyed and forlorn
I see You lurking outside, hiding in the dark,
Wondering if You'll be let in.
Come, Goddess, I invite You into my home
Share my bread and beer
For You are most welcome here.

Nephthys, In Five Senses

by Amanda Artemisia Forrester

I hear You speak in the silence between soft sighs
I see You in the red eyes of weeping mothers at the funeral home
I smell You in the wet, damp earth piled on a freshly dug grave
I taste You in the coppery sharpness of my own blood
I feel you in the slowing pulse of a dying man

Hail Nephthys, merciful comforter of the dead!

To the Two Sisters

by Amanda Artemisia Forrester

I sing a song to the Two Sisters
The Two Ladies
Dual Goddesses
Light and dark
Night and day
Contending
But balanced
Unity in duality
Hail to You,
Two Ladies of Aigyptos
Divine sisters, daughters of Nuit
Isis and Nephthys
I will remember You both

A Call to Nephthys

by Tina Georgitsis

I call to you Daughter of the earth and sky
Whose place in the ennead is high
I call to you

I call to you
Mistress of the house
Counterpart to your barren spouse
I call to you

I call to you
Protectress of those in labour
Safeguard scavenge like the vulture
I call to you

I call to you
Goddess of the air
Hapi guide whose breath protects his lair
I call to you

I call to you
Underworld living companion
Bask in the Nile rain dominion
I call to you

I call to you
Goddess of mourning, death and decay
Uttering words of power who holds sway
I call to you

I call to you
Sister of A'set,
helper of resurrection
Like the hawk your power is ascension
I call to you

I call to you
Winged Goddess with head of basket
Cotton strips infused with Heka placed upon the casket
I call to you

I call to you
O Great Nephthys
I call to you

Evocation to Nephthys

by Frances Billinghurst

The following invocation is an evocation I wrote dedicated to Nephthys a number of years ago to help me to establish connection with her and to understand her power. It can be used in a ritual specifically created for understanding the power and energy of Nephthys:

I am Nephthys – the daughter of Geb and Nut
I am Nephthys – the sister of Isis and Osiris
I am Nephthys – the sister/wife of Set and the mother of Anubis
I am Nephthys – the Mistress of the House, the home of the Sun God Horus

I guide the newly dead and comfort their family
I am called the Queen of Magick, of secret knowledge and prophecy
I am the teacher of religion as well as ritual
I am a Goddess of Ma'at
I am that part of you that guides you, that influences you
That part that threatens you, that makes you feel inadequate, even ashamed.

I am the darkness to Isis's light
I am death, I am decay and immobility
Without me, you will never experience the true power of my sister's strength
Without me, you will never know how to appreciate life
For the two of us must be.

I am there to greet you at the beginning of your life
And although you may forget me,
I await for you at the end.

I am Nephthys – the silent one
I am Nephthys – the dark one
I am Nephthys. I am Nebt-het.

Nebthet

by Taqerisenu

In the blue bowl of the sky,
she collects stars,
each as precious as a tear
shed over the funerary bier.
In the threshold of the house,
she stands,
draped in before-dawn gray and dusk purple,
arms and door open,
welcoming in.

The Sorrows of Nebet-Het
by Rev. Anna Applegate, M.A.

It seems long overdue
The blotting of my lapis blood in the expanding indifference of cobalt skies
Inky forgetfulness
A yearning for erasure
Reabsorption into the arching vault of the Womb of My Mother, Nut
Where the seed-souls of those who have long gone before
And those who have yet to come after
Gleam with perfection
Illumined contrasts
To the lingering murk of near-suffocating sadness
Marsh-enshrouded mass of my shame

And yet, to ascend, one must first sail my waters
Ra Himself knows this,
Greets me as *Nebet Amenti* [Lady of the West],
Tanet-pa-Shai [The One of the Lakes],
For I am *Mesketet,* the Evening Boat of Ra,
The coffin that sails limitless waves of darkness
Darkness lapping upon darkness
Keku Keku Keku [Darkness],
I come to Thee, O King,
Uncoiling my raiment,
Adorning Thy face with strips of white, green, bright and dark red linen,
My tresses
As Thy body is wound, from the terrors of the *Duat* Thou art unbound
My kisses, salt and water
Copious libations of tears
I am the Kite of Mourning, *Djeryt*
My cries loudly ring out in the marshes
Freewheeling overhead
Guardian of the hidden head,
Diadem of Ausar
With My Good Sister, The Lady of the Words of Power,
Poised at the feet

Nebet-Het behind you, Aset before you

Cigarette burns on my forearms
Swiftly yank my roaming *ka*
I cry out and shudder
I am once again moored
A twisted grin in milk-white skin before me
Under the lamplight, green eyes transfix me with such foulness
Red curls coil tightly
As if to spring
Like his anger
Upon the unwary
I yelp in pain, acknowledging the anchoring to this body
He nods in cruel assent
And walks off with a brisk pace
Certain now that I have no choice but to follow
His heels *click-clack* against the strange pavement of this alien metropolis
One arid landscape exchanged for another
My gentle son, Anupu, ever-watchful and responsive,
Unfetters a yelp to echo mine — Sacred Mirror —
He trots behind me at safe distance, trepidatious loping,
Ears perked but fearful,
Tail semi-coiled between his legs and his back almost as arched as that of his Grandmother,
Scenting his uncle's crimson eruptions
Rage upon the wind

Nit behind you, Serqet before you

He is drunk again,
My wholly unwholesome sibling and spouse,
Sutekh [The Drunken One], for speak not his name,
Yet the ale he imbibes dulls not his senses,
Grants him instead fixed purpose
Fearsome to behold
He makes spitting images once again:
Mighty, forceful, he spits onto the pavement
And the white liquid masses take shape,
Almost like *ushabti*, but with limbs fully moving
They dart ahead of him, an army of *muuet,* spirits of the angry dead,

Sent to hunt down scores upon scores of his enemies
(He has no shortage of those)
His laughter of victory, hollow-sounding peals like a slap on a hollowed-out trunk
(Wherein lay the minced pieces of Our Brother?)
Rounding a corner, the laughter abruptly stops
Greek graffiti, crudely sprawled on a wall:
"I have discovered a secret: Nephthys having intercourse with Osiris!"

I know what is going to come
I project my *ka,* swift as lightning,
Just as the first blow lands on my cheek
With frightening force
My face takes on the hue of the heavens above
At the onset of twilight, a swelling mixture of indigo and violet
Hot words, ubiquitous hurt: *"I shall teach this whore a lesson!"*
Now a kick in the stomach
My vessel, on the verge of breaking
And he takes me there,
Refashions my inert clay to his will,
As with his spittle, so with his seed:
These white droplets take the forms of asps
But no matter how much they sting,
Failure is his: The key of life cannot turn in my womb
Not when I flee like this
My *ka* soars now, escapes this strange, barren land

Sekhmet behind you, Bastet before you

As the Red One thunders against his own impotency,
I find oasis in the sycamore tree rooted firmly in the marshes
Here is where I join my sister,
Nebet-Shesep, the Bright Lady,
In wandering, mourning, and gathering Fragments of the Holy
Sections of a Splintered King
Missed most mightily
Our Beloved Brother, Ausar

Someday, you will behold me coming from the West,
Coming from the House of Beautification,

True of Voice in the Region of Silence,
I will come to you at twilight, uncoiling my raiment,
Adorning your face with strips of white, green, bright and dark red linen,
My tresses
As your body is wound, from the terrors of the *Duat* you are unbound
My kisses, salt and water
Copious libations of tears
For I am *Nebet-Hotep*, Lady of Offerings
I am the Lady of Watchfulness, *Nebet-Resh*,
Who will stand at the head of your coffin, your *hen,* with My Sister at your feet

Nebet-Het behind you, Aset before you

And you will sink into darkness, for I am the Night-bark who grants you safe passage
Though no one has ever granted it to me
You will sail my still, silent waters
As Ra Himself does
Waves of darkness lapping upon darkness
Keku
Keku
Keku

Prayer to Nebet-Het

by Robin Penn

Hidden One, whose "head is hidden," assist the disabled, chronically ill, and neurodiverse in our lives and healing journeys.

Let no hurtful institutions, false charities, or hateful hearts who would erase and destroy us speak in our names. Let not our needs be left out or behind.

Let us access the tools we need to continue our lives in joy, comfort, and in peace. Let no child, no wounded heart, and no wronged soul die by their own hand, or the hand of another's abuse or neglect.

Let us find the determination to live to guide another through the dark night of the soul, where we have walked, crawled, and wheeled before.

Let our pains be heard, that they may be honored and addressed — let our joys be heard, that they may be shared and multiplied — let us rejoice in our loving communities, that they may foster hope, spread awareness, and create solidarity in difference.

Hymn to Nephthys

by Hearthstone

To Nephthys, great friend of the dead, I offer my praise.
Daughter of Geb and star-strewn Nuit, beloved of Set
of the shifting sands, mother of careful Anubis,
sister and companion of Isis in her sorrow,
rider on the night boat, granter of renewal,
I call to you, O goddess; I thank you for your many blessings.
O youngest of the Ennead, well-honored in Heliopolis,
you hear the laments of the mourning; you are the solace
of those who weep, the comfort of the bereft.
Yours is the care of those who grieve; yours is the care
of the dead. O lady of the household, mistress of the house,
yours too is the warding of women, within and without the home;
yours is the tending of mother with child, the easing of travail.
At life's beginning and at life's end, yours is the hand
that guides us; I praise you, O Nephthys, I honor your calling.

Poetry of Nebet-Het

by Robin Penn

"Lady of the House,"
of the body,
of the Gods Housed Inside Us.
Of intuitive knowing,
High Priestess,
our mirror,
our Internal Voice.
Our labors of love,
our Devotion,
our daydreams and
our myths.
Our internal stories of our lives
our inspiration,
our hope,
our Faith.
Our sacrifice,
our endurance,
our Dedication,
to the values we hold,
and the people we love.
To ourselves,
as Gods,
of light,
and love,
in the dark.
Holding each other and
pressing kisses to our tender faces.
"Beauty Inside, Divine,
I Love You.
I See You.
I Know You."

Fiction

The Queen of the Birds: an Egyptian Tale
by Darius Matthias Klein

The daughter of Pharaoh had fallen ill. As the days passed, she began to waste away, until it was feared that she would soon die. One by one, Pharaoh summoned all of the healing priests and *savants* to his palace in Awanu, the royal city, to cure his daughter of her malady. But all of them were forced to admit that it was beyond their power to help her.

All, that is, but one. "My Lord," declared Nitocris, a priestess of Nebet-het in the Great Enclosure of the Gods,[193] "it is exactly as I had suspected when I first heard the rumors of your daughter's affliction. Your daughter requires nothing but the touch of a feather from the breast of Azoth, Queen of the Birds. This alone will expel the unclean spirit which possesses her."

Now, Nitocris was very learned in all of the mysteries of the healing arts. But whereas all of the other *savants* whom Pharaoh had summoned all enjoyed excellent reputations for their abilities, Nitocris and her powers were little known in Egypt; so Pharaoh was immediately suspicious of her.

"I have never heard of this queen," Pharaoh said, his eyes narrowing. "Where is her kingdom, and where can she be found?"

The priestess said, "I know of her existence only from sacred scrolls in my possession which pertain to the gods and their holy rites. The Queen of the Birds is no ordinary queen, but an image of living stone. It is written that she can be found in a cave in the Mountains of Iah, the Moon, which lie far beyond Kush and fabled Punt, at the world's southern extremities. It is in this cave, according to the sages, that the goddesses Nebet-het and Aset restored the body of the divine Wennefer to life. Nebet-het then created the image from the vivifying substance with which they effected their enchantment and erected it there; and this image is the Queen of the Birds.

---

[193] i.e., the great temple.

"Unless the princess receives the touch of such a feather," the priestess went on, "she will shrivel up into a dried colocynth-pod within a matter of days, then perish altogether; for that is the power of the unclean spirit which possesses her."

"In that case," Pharaoh said, his countenance glowering, "I command you to obtain a feather from this Queen – and by tomorrow morning. If you fail to do so, I will extirpate the worship of Nebet-het, whose adoratrix you are, from all of Egypt; aye, and destroy all of her devotees as well!"

Nitocris received this mandate with a heavy heart. Beyond all doubt Pharaoh's demands were impossible to fulfill. All of priestesses of Nebet-het knew of the Queen of the Birds in the Mountains of Iah, but, to the best of their knowledge, no mortal had ever been traveled there to look upon her. In any case, the Mountains of Iah lay at such a great distance that to travel there and back, even if one did not take into consideration the perilous and uncertain conditions to be found in the desert wastes of the intervening lands, would be a journey of two or three years at least.

So Nitocris returned that night to the Great Enclosure and informed the other singers and adoratrices of the goddess of the terrible news. All of those who received the news began to wail in despair, since none of them believed it would be possible to obtain a feather from the breast of the Queen of the Birds in such a short time.

Among those to whom Nitocris spoke was one of her disciples, Seshat. Seshat was only a neophyte among the priestesses of the goddess, but was already well-versed in her mysteries. The young girl spoke at once.

"Have all of Nebet-het's devotees," she cried, "abandoned their divine mistress, that they have given up hope so easily? Have you all forgotten that Our Lady is the protectress of the powerless and the oppressed, and patroness of those who must work in secret, far from the pitiless eyes of their enemies?"

The priestess asked her disciple what she meant. Seshat explained that on that very morning, she had dreamt that a falcon had come in from the desert and perched in her window. It spoke to her in a human voice and said that it would soon lend its wings to her *ka* – the soul of her intellect – as the goddess had commanded it to do.

"There must be one among the priestesses of Nebet-het," Seshat went on, "who knows the enchantment of the separation of the *ka* from the living body. Flying on the wings of the spirit, the *ka* will be able to travel to the Mountains of Iah and obtain a feather from the breast of the Queen of the Birds in the twinkling of an eye."

Nitocris confessed that she knew the words of the enchantment which would effect the separation. Although the separation of any part of the soul from the still living body was a potentially hazardous undertaking, it was evident from her daughter's prophetic dream that that was what the goddess wished them to do, in order to avert catastrophe.

Seshat and Nitocris then withdrew into the inner sanctum of the goddess' shrine. Trembling, the elder spoke the words of enchantment over the younger. Presently Seshat slipped into a deep sleep. Nitocris then observed the *ka* rising from her brow – a tenuous creature borne on the diaphanous wings like those of a falcon; she flew through the walls of the sanctum as if they had not even existed, then made her way into the nighttime sky, now unseen by human eyes.

The *ka* winged its way in a southward direction with such haste that it seemed only a few moments before she had passed the high ramparts of the cities of Kush and the watery wastes of fabled Punt, to arrive at the lofty peaks of the Mountains of Iah at the world's end. Beyond the mountains lay only the vastness of the firmament and the heavenly bodies it contained.

Recalling that she must return to Seshat with the feather before sunrise, the *ka* flew about the mountains in a hurry, hoping to find the mouth to the cave as quickly as possible. When she at last sighted an opening in the highest of all the peaks, she flew toward it.

As she was about to enter the cave, a strange and imposing figure emerged from it. Seshat's *ka* instantly recognized it as a guardian spirit, inasmuch as it bore the divine *uraeus* on her brow, while her countenance shone with a divine radiance.

"I am Sefa, one of the elemental spirits brought into existence when Shu and Tefnut fashioned the Earth and Sky at the beginning of time," the being announced. "I admit into the cave only those whom Nebet-het permits; all others are deemed impertinent and turned back, if the goddess even allows them to live at all. It was I who spoke to you in your dream; and even now you fly with my wings, which the goddess ordered me to loan you."

"You know, then," Seshat's *ka* replied, "that I have come to obtain a feather from the breast of the Queen of the Birds. I only ask that you do not take back your wings now; for I have only a little time left to get the feather and return to Egypt."

Sefa assured the *ka* that the effect of the enchantment would only return the wings to their rightful owner once her separation from the living body had concluded.

She then led the *ka* into the recesses of the cave, where they stood before the image of Queen of the Birds. The *ka* was nearly overcome with awe. The image stood fully twelve cubits high. Moreover, although it had been carved from stone, or a kind of mineral, it nevertheless appeared to be composed of some living and liquescent matter. The substance of the image thus appeared to perpetually flow, yet still subsist in the regal bird-form in which the goddess had cast it in primordial times.

Trembling, the *ka* stepped up to the image of Azoth and plucked a feather from its breast. The feather was heavy and dense, like stone, yet moist and pliant to the touch. A delicious fragrance wafted forth from it.

Sefa ordered the *ka* to hurry on her way, if she wished to return to Seshat before sunrise. Wasting no more time, the *ka* flew back the way she had come. The rays of the Sun were just beginning to shine over the eastern horizon when Nitocris, who had kept a wakeful vigil over the neophyte through the night, observed the *ka* fly into the sanctum through the walls and return to Seshat, dissolving into her brow like a fine mist.

Seshat opened her eyes, and then held out her hand to the elder priestess. In her hand she held the feather of Azoth!

The two priestesses made their way to the royal palace. Nitocris presented the feather to Pharaoh, who was nearly beside himself with joy. He took the aromatic feather himself to where his daughter lay and brushed it lightly against her cheek. She opened her eyes immediately; the unclean spirit that had possessed her flew out of her mouth and back to the desert wastes from which it had come. Within an hour the princess' recovery was complete, and she was taking food and water as if nothing had occurred.

Thereafter, Pharaoh not only refrained from the persecution of the devotees of Nebet-het, but contributed endowments to their orders, so that for many years they were able to feed the poor and the destitute of Awanu, and compile scrolls of the enchantments they used to heal the sick and expel the unclean spirits that afflicted the Egyptians.

As for Pharaoh's daughter, she maintained a bond of friendship with Seshat throughout her life, and herself became an adoratrix of the goddess. She never tired of hearing Seshat tell and retell the enthralling story of how her *ka* had traveled to the Mountains of Iah to obtain the feather from Azoth's breast; for the perceptions and experiences of the *ka* during the separation had become Seshat's once it had reunified with her, so that Seshat could narrate the events of the journey just as if she had undertaken it herself.

THE END

Epilogue

Appendix A

Festivals of Nebet Het
Compiled by Chelsea Luellon Bolton

No Dates Recorded
Nebet Het and Set's Lighting of the Lamps Festival in Letopolis[194]

Monthly Lunar Festivals
Chronokrater: Day Festivals
8th Day of the Lunar Month – Sacred to Nebet Het[195]

Festivals
9th Day of the Lunar Month-Sacred to Nebet Het[196]
10th Day of the Lunar Month-Sacred to Nebet Het[197]
21st Day of the Lunar Month-Sacred to Nebet Het[198]

Yearly Festivals
1st Akhet/Thoth/August
Chronokrater: Day Festival
19—Nebet Het[199]

Festivals
1-Wep Ronpet/Opening of the Year[200]

---

[194] Meeks, Dimitri. Mythes et Légendes du Delta: d'après le papyrus Brooklyn 47.218.84. (IFAO, 2006) 18 and 230. Thank you to Edward Butler for bringing this to my attention.
[195] Siuda, Tamara L. The Ancient Egyptian Daybook. (Stargazer Design, 2016), 304.
[196] Morgan, Mogg. The Wheel of the Year in Ancient Egypt. (Mandrake of Oxford, 2011), 208. From the Astrological Frieze from the Temple of Heru at Edfu.
[197] Tripani, Luigi and Amentet Neferet. Egyptian Religious Calendar: CDXV-CDXVI Great Year of Ra (2015 CE). (Amentet Neferet, 2014), 36.
[198] Tripani, Luigi and Amentet Neferet. Egyptian Religious Calendar: CDXV-CDXVI Great Year of Ra (2015 CE), 44.
[199] Siuda, Tamara L. The Ancient Egyptian Daybook, 61.
[200] El-Sabban, Sherif. Temple Festival Calendars of Ancient Egypt. (Liverpool University Press, 2000), 57.

10-Procession of Nebet Het[201]
14-Speech of Weret Hekau[202]
16-Speech of the Lady of the Temple[203]
22-Speech of Weret Hekau[204]
29-Speech of the Lady of the Temple[205]

2nd Akhet/Paopi/September
Chronokrater: Day Festivals
3—Nebet Het, Lady of the Embalming House/Lady of the Annals of Ra's Power[206]
4—Aset and Nebet Het[207]

Festivals
3-Feast of Weret Hekau[208]
11-Speech of the Mistress of the Uraeus[209]
13-Offering Sacrifice to Nebet Het and Wesir[210]

3rd Akhet/Hethara/October
Chronokrater: Day Festivals: None

---

[201] Siuda, Tamara L. The Ancient Egyptian Prayerbook. (Stargazer Design, 2009), 145; and Siuda, Tamara L. The Ancient Egyptian Daybook, 54.
[202] Cauville, Sylvie. Dendara XV: Traduction. (Peeters, 2012), 111. Translated by Chelsea Bolton. Weret Hekau or Great of Magic is a title of many goddesses, including Aset, Hethert, and Nebet Het.
[203] Cauville, Sylvie. Dendara XV: Traduction, 110-111. Lady of the Temple is one way to translate Nebet Het's name.
[204] Cauville, Sylvie. Dendara XV: Traduction, 109. Translated by Chelsea Bolton.
[205] Cauville, Sylvie. Dendara XV: Traduction,108-109.
[206] Siuda, Tamara L. The Ancient Egyptian Daybook, 76.
[207] Siuda, Tamara L. The Ancient Egyptian Daybook, 77.
[208] El-Sabban, Sherif. Temple Festival Calendars of Ancient Egypt, 157; and Siuda, Tamara L. The Ancient Egyptian Prayerbook, 146.
[209] Cauville, Sylvie. Dendara XV: Traduction, 119. Translated by Chelsea Bolton. Nebet Het can be the Uraeus and the Mistress of the Uraeus.
[210] On the 13 of Boedromion (Mid-September). Alvar, Jaime. Romanising Oriental Gods: Myth, Salvation and Ethics in the Cults of Cybele, Isis and Mithras. (Brill Academic Pub, 2008), 313-314. A cockerel and fruit were offered; milk and water mixed with honey were offered as libations. Barley and wheat were scattered as is Greek custom.

Festivals
17-Lamentations of Aset and Nebet Het[211]
24-Appearance of Aset and Nebet Het in Jubilation[212]

4th Akhet/Koiak/November
Chronokrater: Day Festivals
25—Nebet Het[213]
28—Nebet Het, Sister of God[214]

Festivals
1 to 6-Procession of Nebet Het of Per Meru (Komir)[215]
18 to 30-Mysteries of Wesir[216]
22 to 26-Festival of the Two Female Kites (Aset and Nebet Het)[217]
25-Festival of the Twin Goddesses (Aset and Nebet Het as *Netjeryt*)[218]
28-Speech of Nebet Het, the Sister of God[219]

1 Peret/Tybi/December
Chronokrater: Day Festivals: None

Festivals
14-Weeping of Aset and Nebet Het[220]
19 to 2 Peret 4 (Solstice)-Festival of She is Led Back/Return of the Eye[221]

---

[211] El-Sabban, Sherif. Temple Festival Calendars of Ancient Egypt, 58; Siuda, Tamara L. The Ancient Egyptian Prayerbook, 148.
[212] Brier, Bob. Ancient Egyptian Magic. (William Morrow and Company, 1980), 233; and Siuda, Tamara L. The Ancient Egyptian Prayerbook, 148.
[213] Siuda, Tamara L. The Ancient Egyptian Daybook, 130.
[214] Siuda, Tamara L. The Ancient Egyptian Daybook, 133.
[215] Sauneron, Serge. Esna V: Les fetes religieuses d'esna aux derniers siecles du paganisme. (Institut français d'archéologie orientale, 1962; 2004), 15; El-Sabban, Sherif. Temple Festival Calendars of Ancient Egypt, 162 and Siuda, Tamara L. The Ancient Egyptian Prayerbook, 149.
[216] El-Sabban, Sherif. Temple Festival Calendars of Ancient Egypt, 58.
[217] Siuda, Tamara L. The Ancient Egyptian Daybook, 127.
[218] Siuda, Tamara L. The Ancient Egyptian Daybook, 130.
[219] Cauville, Sylvie. Dendara XV: Traduction, 131. Translated by Chelsea Bolton.
[220] Brier, Bob. Ancient Egyptian Magic, 236.
[221] Siuda, Tamara L. The Ancient Egyptian Daybook, 137, 141-142 and 153; and Levai, Jessica. Aspects of the Goddess Nephthys, Especially During the Graeco-Roman Period in Egypt. (Brown University Dissertation, 2007), 61-62.

22-Feast of the Two Goddesses (Aset and Nebet Het)[222]
25—Establishment of the Celestial Cow[223]

2 Peret/Mechir/January
Chronokrater: Day Festivals: None

Festivals
17 to 18—Defending the Akhet Eye[224]

3 Peret/Pamenot/February
Chronokrater: Day Festivals: None

Festivals
17-Speech of Weret Hekau[225]

4 Peret/Parmuthi/March
Chronokrater: Day Festivals: None

Festivals
1-Feast of Ra and the Eye of Ra[226]
21-Speech of the Mistress of the Sycamore[227]
28-The Heart of Nebet Het is Joyful[228]

---

[222] Nelson, Harold H. "The Calendar of Feasts and Offerings at Medinet Habu." in Work in Western Thebes 1931-33. Harold H. Nelson and Uvo Holscher, ed. (University of Chicago Press, 1934), 18; and Schott, Siegfried. "Feasts of Thebes." In Work in Western Thebes 1931-33, 89.
[223] El-Sabban, Sherif. Temple Festival Calendars of Ancient Egypt, 175; Brier, Bob. Ancient Egyptian Magic, 236; Siuda, Tamara L. The Ancient Egyptian Prayerbook, 149-150; and Siuda, Tamara L. The Ancient Egyptian Daybook, 156. Nebet Het can be the Celestial Cow along with Hethert, Aset, Nut, and other goddesses.
[224] Siuda, Tamara L. The Ancient Egyptian Daybook, 171-172.
[225] Cauville, Sylvie. Dendara XV: Traduction, 151. Translated by Chelsea Bolton.
[226] El-Sabban, Sherif. Temple Festival Calendars of Ancient Egypt, 171.
[227] Cauville, Sylvie. Dendara XV: Traduction, 157. Translated by Chelsea Bolton. Nebet Het is the Lady of the Sycamore along with Nut, Hethert, Aset, and Mut.
[228] Siuda, Tamara L. The Ancient Egyptian Daybook, 217, referencing Papyrus Wilbour, Dynasty 20 and Lexicon der Aegyptologie entry for Edfu.

1 Shomu/Pachons/April
Chronokrater: Day Festivals
22-Nebet Het[229]

Festivals: None

2 Shomu/Payni/May
Chronokrater: Day Festivals
29—Nebet Het, Savior of the Gods[230]

Festivals
1-Appearance of Nebet Het[231]
21-Day of the Living Children of Nut[232]

3 Shomu/Epiphi/June
Chronokrater: Day Festivals: None

Festivals
Solstice—Departure of the Wandering Goddess/Eye of Ra[233]
26-Speech of the Uraeus[234]
30-Burning the Widow's Flame[235]

4 Shomu/Mesore/July
Chronokrater: Day Festivals: None

Festivals

---

[229] Siuda, Tamara L. The Ancient Egyptian Daybook, 237.
[230] Siuda, Tamara L. The Ancient Egyptian Daybook, 257.
[231] Siuda, Tamara L. The Ancient Egyptian Daybook, 245.
[232] Brier, Bob. Ancient Egyptian Magic, 244.
[233] Siuda, Tamara L. Ancient Egyptian Daybook, 137, and 140-142; and Levai, Jessica. Aspects of the Goddess Nephthys, 61-62.
[234] Cauville, Sylvie. Dendara XV: Traduction, 179.
[235] El-Sabban, Sherif. Temple Festival Calendars of Ancient Egypt, 178 and Siuda, Tamara L. The Ancient Egyptian Prayerbook, 156. Burning the Widow's Flame is a Hethert Festival which includes Aset, the Widow. Nebet Het can also be the Widow of Wesir so I'm including this festival in her calendar.

18- Speech of the Lioness[236]
22-Children of Geb and Nut in Festival[237]

Days upon the Year
Chronokrater: Day Festivals
4—Nebet Het, Powerful of Heart[238]

Festivals
5-Birthday of Nebet Het and Speech of Nebet Het, the Excellent, Sister of the God[239]

---

[236] Cauville, Sylvie. Dendara XV: Traduction, 187. Translated by Chelsea Bolton. Aset and Nebet Het are called Young Lioness at the Temple of Dendera. So I'm including this for Nebet Het.
[237] Brier, Bob. Ancient Egyptian Magic, 251.
[238] Siuda, Tamara L. The Ancient Egyptian Daybook, 300.
[239] El-Sabban, Sherif. Temple Festival Calendars of Ancient Egypt, 11, 173; and Cauville, Sylvie. Dendara XV: Traduction, 177.

Her Correspondences
by Chelsea Luellon Bolton

In my experience, Nebet Het is an obscure Lady. She is quiet. She doesn't speak often. She often communicates kinesthetically — using feelings, instinct, and images in the mind. I find She is indirect. She won't tell you outright a straight answer. You'll get the answer — just not the way you expect. Her presence to me can be as subtle as a breeze or strong enough to make you tremble. I have found that She is possessive of those She considers Hers and those devoted to Her are few and far between.

She is a goddess of twilight and liminal spaces. She is the pause between words and the balance of dark and light. She is a goddess of silence. She is a goddess of stillness.

She can be honored with any number of the ancient Egyptian deities, most notably members of her family or within a group honored together in an ancient nome or city. Some honor Nebet Het in a triad along with Set and Yinepu. Some honor her only with Set or Yinepu. Some honor her with Aset and Heru. Sometimes, Nebet Het is just honored with her sister Aset since they make up a complementary dyad.

Her Altar
Items
- Image or Statue of the Goddess
- Two Candles
- Incense or Essential Oil
- Bowl and pitcher for water libations
- Altar Cloth

Colors
- Purple
- Black
- Pink
- Gold
- White
- Red

- Green
- Dark colors in general

Incense or Scent
- Myrrh
- Frankincense
- Iris
- Jasmine
- Kyphi/Kapet
- Florida Water
- Rose Water

Stones
- Amethyst
- Carnelian
- Garnet
- Jasper (especially leopard print jasper)
- Lapis Lazuli
- Obsidian
- Onyx
- Turquoise
- Dark Gemstones in General

Flowers and Plants
- Palm Branches
- Pink Flowers
- Purple Flowers
- Orchids
- Roses
- Violets

Liquid Offerings
- Water
- Milk or Chocolate Milk
- Red Wine
- White Russian Cocktail

- Beer
- Grape Juice
- Cranberry-Grape Juice
- Pomegranate Juice
- Raspberry Juice

Food Offerings
- Vegetables
- Fruits; Strawberries
- Bread
- Pastries; Cookies; Cakes; Brownies; Donuts
- Strawberry Flavored Pastries
- Chocolate
- Cheesecake
- Cheetos
- Coca-Cola or Sprite
- Junk Food in general

Meat Offerings

- Beef and other red meat
- Chicken
- Duck

Taboos

- Pork (as Wife/Widow/Mourner of Wesir)
- Fish (as Wife/Widow/Mourner of Wesir)
- For colors: Yellow

What to Ask For
- Compassion
- Comforting the Bereaved
- Healing
- Divination

- Magic
- Mysteries
- Relations with Ancestors
- Revealing What is Hidden or Unknown
- Cleaning and Maintaining the Home
- Protection from Impurity
- Protection from Negative Forces
- Inner Strength and Fortitude
- Writing

Family of Gods
- Wesir (brother or consort)
- Set (husband)
- Heru Wer (brother)
- Aset (sister)
- Yinepu (son)
- Heru (son)
- Ihy (son)
- Nut (mother)
- Geb (father)
- Ra (father or consort)

Appendix B

Gods and Goddesses Name List

- Aset, Auset (Isis)
- Bast, Bastet (Bubastis)
- Djehuty, Tehuti (Thoth)
- Hethert, Hetharu; Hwt Hrw (Hathor)
- Heru-pa-Khered (Horus the Child; Harpocrates; Harpokrates)
- Heru-sa-Aset (Horus, son of Isis; Horus, the Younger; Harsiese)
- Heru Wer (Horus, the Great; Horus, the Elder; Haroeris)
- Menhyt (Menhit)
- Mut, Mout (Muth)
- Nebet Het, Nebt-Het; Nebet Hwt (Nephthys)
- Nebetuu (Nebtu)
- Nit, Net (Neith)
- Sekhmet (Sachmis)
- Seshat, Sesheta (Sefkhet Abwy)
- Set, Sutekh (Seth)
- Sobek, Sebek (Suchos)
- Sopdet (Sothis; Sirius)
- Tefnut, Tefenet
- Wepwawet, Upuaut (Ophois)
- Wesir, Ausar, Asar (Osiris)
- Yinepu, Anpu, Inpu (Anubis)

By Names

- Wennefer (Onnophris): A title or epithet of Wesir (Osiris) meaning "He Who is Good/Good One."
- Wentnefert/Onnophret: A title of Nebet Het (Nephthys) meaning "Female Onnophris."

Contributor Biographies

Rev. Anna Applegate, M.A. is proud to be a native Chicagoan, imprinted from childhood's earliest hours by the numerous spirits of land, river, lake, and concrete and steel in this magical crossroads of a world-class city. She has been active in Chicago's Pagan community for 18 years. Legally ordained as a Priestess of Nebet-Het, Hekate Khthonia, and Bast in the worldwide Fellowship of Isis (FOI), Rev. Anna is the Founder of the FOI-chartered Iseum of Rekhet Akhu, whose mission is to highlight the interrelatedness of the communities of the living and the dead and to cultivate transfigured spirits *(akhu* in ancient Egyptian*)* in human form. Additionally, Anna provides holistic support to families experiencing the transition of a loved one in her work as a certified Death Midwife, helping the dying birth themselves into the Spirit World. Anna is also an initiate in the West African-derived religion of Ifá, which centers on worship of the Orisha and the cultivation of one's *Orí* (Destiny) in this lifetime. You can read about Anna's diverse array of esoteric adventures at her blog, *Amor et Mortem* ("Love and Death"), at amoretmortem.wordpress.com, where she writes under the *nom de plume* of Katakhanas.

A writer by trade and for pleasure, Anna holds an MA degree in English Literature from Loyola University Chicago. Her Pagan poetry appears in the Scarlet Imprint anthologies *Datura* (2010) and *Mandragora* (2012). She also serves as Executive Editor of *Isis-Seshat,* a quarterly journal for the Fellowship of Isis. Anna and her husband live on the northwest side of Chicago with three felines and a serpent.

Frances Billinghurst is a prolific writer with an interest in folklore, mythology, and ancient cultures. Her articles have appeared in various publications including Llewellyn's *Witch's Calendar, The Cauldron, Unto Herself: A Devotional Anthology to Independent Goddesses, A Mantle of Stars: A Devotional to the Queen of Heaven, Naming the Goddess, Witchcraft Today: 60 Years On,* and *The Faerie Queens.* She is the author of *Dancing the Sacred Wheel: A Journey through the Southern Sabbats* and *In Her Sacred Name: Writings on the Divine Feminine*, as well as the editor of *Call of the God: An*

Anthology Exploring the Divine Masculine within Modern Paganism. When she is not writing, Frances is attempting to replicate the Hanging Gardens of Babylon on her patch of Australian dirt, and journeying between the worlds. More information about Frances can be found through her writer's blog (francesbillinghurst.blogspot.com.au).

Chelsea Luellon Bolton has a BA and MA in Religious Studies from the University of South Florida. She is the author of *Lady of Praise, Lady of Power: Ancient Hymns of the Goddess Aset; Queen of the Road: Poetry of the Goddess Aset;* and *Magician, Mother and Queen: A Research Paper on the Goddess Aset.* Her other books are *Lord of Strength and Power: Ancient Hymns for Wepwawet;* and *Sun, Star and Desert Sand: Poems for the Egyptian Gods.* She is both the editor of and a contributor to this anthology, *She Who Speaks Through Silence: An Anthology for Nephthys.* Her other latest book is *Mother of Magic: Ancient Hymns for Aset.* Chelsea's current projects include *Lady of the Temple: Ancient Hymns for Nephthys* and *Flaming Lioness: Ancient Hymns for Egyptian Goddesses.* Her poetry has been previously published in various anthologies. She lives with tons of books and her anti-social feline companion. You can find more of her work at her blog, fiercelybrightone.com.

Rebecca Buchanan is the editor of *Eternal Haunted Summer*, a Pagan literary zine. She is also editor-in-chief of Bibliotheca Alexandrina. She has been published in a wide variety of venues, including *Bards and Sages Quarterly, Cliterature, HEX Magazine, Nebula Rift, New Realm, witches&pagans,* and many others.

Amanda Artemisia Forrester, formerly Amana Sioux Blake, is currently in transition from the Indiana/Michigan area to the Missouri homestead of her dreams. She is the author of *Ink In My Veins: A Collection of Contemporary Pagan Poetry,* and *Songs of Praise: Hymns to the Gods of Greece.* She is working on the forthcoming *Journey to Olympos: A Modern Spiritual Odyssey.* A self-labeled history geek, she has taught classes on Greek Mythology, contacting spirit guides, and has written and taught the coursework for "Olympos in Egypt," an introduction to the unique hybrid culture and spirituality that arose in Alexandria, Egypt in the

Hellenistic Age. In a few years when the homestead is up and running, she may make it her goal to begin teaching again and holding rituals on her 5-acre property, Artemis Acres, and to reestablish the Temple of Athena the Savior in Missouri. Amanda's blog is at templeofathena.wordpress.com. She also runs a Cafepress store, OtherWorld Creations, which is located at cafepress.com/other_world .

M. Isidora Forrest is the author of *Isis Magic: Cultivating a Relationship with the Goddess of 10,000 Names* and *Offering to Isis, Knowing the Goddess through Her Sacred Symbols,* as well as numerous articles in a variety of anthologies and journals. Isidora has been devoted to Isis ever since the Goddess told her, in no uncertain terms, that she was not yet ready to be Her priestess. (Isidora respects a Goddess Who doesn't coddle.) More than twenty years — and a lot of research, ritual, agony and ecstasy — later, Isidora has earned the title of Prophetess in the House of Isis. She is also a priestess of the international Fellowship of Isis, a Hermetic adept, a maenad for Dionysos, and a founder of the Hermetic Fellowship, a religious non-profit devoted to education in the Western Esoteric Tradition. Isidora lives and works in the not-at-all-Egypt-like climate of Portland, Oregon with her husband, Adam Forrest, a curious black cat, and both a Temple of Isis and a grape arbor sacred to Dionysos in the backyard. Contact Isidora at www.isiopolis.com .

Tina Georgitsis is regular writer on Kemetic, Hellenic, Wiccan, and occult subjects. She edited her first book, *Sekhmet Daughter of the Sun: A Devotional Anthology in Honor of Sekhmet* in 2015. Tina is an Arch Priestess Hierophant in the Fellowship of Isis (Lyceum of Heka), a Hereditary Folk/Hermetic Witch, an Initiated Wiccan Priestess, a Reiki/Seichim/ Sekhem Master, and also a Tarot Councillor (ATA) who has worked professionally as a reader, healer, purveyor of magickal items, and as a teacher of workshops in various metaphysical and occult subjects.

Hearthstone has been a multi-faith, semireconstructionist pagan and polytheist for 25 years or so.

Emily Jones is a Certified Professional Tarot Reader and eclectic Wiccan High Priestess in the Temple of Witchcraft tradition. She is always looking for new ideas, events, and practices to continue informing her lifelong spiritual journey. She began studying with Christopher Penczak, one of the founders of the Temple of Witchcraft, in April 2006, and received ordination through the Temple in June 2011. She believes in working with Tarot and magick to empower yourself and craft the life you envision. Working with the Egyptian pantheon is one of the cornerstones of Emily's spiritual and magickal practice. In addition to working with the Egyptian pantheon and the Tarot, Emily also works with Egyptian healing rod energy tools, performs ministerial services as a legally ordained High Priestess, does energy clearing of people, places and objects, clears and balances chakras, offers ritual and manifestation coaching, works with shamanic practices, facilitates open public rituals, and teaches classes on a variety of metaphysical subjects such as Tarot, witchcraft, working with crystals, moon magick and more.

Darius M. Klein is a translator, writer, and independent scholar living in the Seattle area. His works of creative mythology have appeared in *Eternal Haunted Summer, Beyond the Pillars,* and *Niteblade*.

Robin "Perennia" Penn is a nonbinary Kemetic pagan and author of the *The Heart Road* blog (theheartroad.wordpress.com), who works primarily with Nebet-Het and Set. Ze is also Autistic, has C-PTSD, and loves hir friends and gods very dearly.

Secondgenerationimmigrant: Nonbinary Italo-Brasilian biomedical researcher. Intermittently pagan since 1997, walking the Kemetic/Levpag path seriously since 2015. Late Bronze Age nerd, devotee of Seth, Anat, Asherah, Ash, Ra, and Nebt-Het. Antifascist.

Tamara L. Siuda is a Ph.D. candidate in religion (ABD; expected 2018) at Claremont Graduate University. She holds an MA in Egyptology with a specialization in Egyptian philology (2000) from the University of

Chicago and a second MA in Coptic Studies (2008) from Macquarie University Sydney. Tamara is also the founder and spiritual leader (Nisut) of the Kemetic Orthodox Religion, a modern polytheism derived from ancient Egypt's religious practices. She is a frequent lecturer on Egypt-related subjects, has appeared in and consulted to documentaries, and has authored numerous articles and books, including *The Neteru of Kemet* (1994), *The Ancient Egyptian Prayerbook* (2009), *Nebt-het: Lady of the House* (2010), *The 42 Purifications* (2010), *The Ancient Egyptian Daybook* (2016), *The Hourly Ritual of Osiris* (2017), *The Ancient Egyptian Daybook Planner (2018)*, and *100 Gods of Egypt* (2019). tamarasiuda.com – patreon.com/tsiuda – @tamarasiuda on Twitter and Facebook.

Jonathan Sousa is a Priest/ess of the Goddess Diana, whom he serves through the initiatory framework of Italian Traditionalist Witchcraft (Stregoneria) and Hellenistic Sorcery. A prolific writer, his books are available via Amazon.

Taqerisenu is a museum professional living in Seattle. She is a Shemsu-Ankh of the Kemetic Orthodox Religion and has loved ancient Egyptian mythology and culture ever since she was a toddler, when her mother had to pull her away from the television where she'd been enraptured by a recording of *Aida* on the local PBS channel (Egypt > bedtime, clearly). She likes to think deeply about time travel, digital technology as a tool for informal learning, mythology, ancient cookery, and Sherlock Holmes.

References

- Allen, T.G. The Book of the Dead or Going Forth By Day: Ideas of the Ancient Egyptians Concerning the Hereafter as Expressed in Their Own Terms, Studies of Ancient Oriental Civilization #37. Illinois: University of Chicago Press, 1974.
- Alvar, Jaime. Romanising Oriental Gods: Myth, Salvation and Ethics in the Cults of Cybele, Isis and Mithras. Brill Academic Pub, 2008.
- Arundale, Francis, and Joseph Bonomi. Gallery of antiquities selected from the British Museum. J. Weale, 1842.
- Bakir, Abd el-Mohsen. The Cairo Calendar No. 86637. Cairo, 1966.
- Baring, Anne and Jules Cashford. "Isis of Egypt: Queen of Heaven, Earth and the Underworld." in The Myth of the Goddess: Evolution of an Image. Anne Baring and Jules Cashford, eds. New York: Penguin, 1993, pp. 225-272.
- Bergman, Jan. "Nephthys découverte dans un papyrus magique." In Melanges Adolphe Gutbub. Institut d'égyptologie Université Paul Valéry, 1984, pp. 1-12.
- Betz, Hans Dieter. The Greek Magical Papyri: In Translation including the Demotic Spells, Vol 1. London: University of Chicago Press, 1996.
- Bleeker, C.J. "Isis and Nephthys as Wailing Women." In Numen 5 (1958), pp. 1-17.
- Bunsen, Christian Karl Josias, and Samuel Birch. Egypt's place in universal history: an historical investigation in five books. Vol. 1. Longman, Brown, Green, and Longmans, 1848.
- Brier, Bob. Ancient Egyptian Magic. New York: William Morrow and Company, 1980.
- Bresciani, E. and S. Pernigotti. Il tempio tolemaico di Isi ad Assuan. Pisa: Giardini Editori E. Stampatori, 1978.
- Borghouts, J.F. The Magical Texts of Papyrus Leiden I 34. Leiden: E.J. Brill, 1971.
- Boylan, Patrick. Thoth, Hermes of Egypt: A Study of Some Aspects of Theological Thought in Ancient Egypt. Oxford University Press, 1922.

- Cauville, Sylvie. "Chentayt et Merkhetes, des avatars d'Isis et Nephthys." in Bulletin de l'Institut Français d'Archéologie Orientale Le Caire (BIFAO) 81 (1981), pp. 21-40.
- Cauville, Sylvie. Dendara II: Traduction. Leuven: Peeters, 1999.
- Cauville, Sylvie. Dendara XV: Traduction: Pronaos de Temple d'Hathor. Leuven: Peeters, 2012.
- Cauville, Sylvie. Le Temple de Dendera: La Porte d'Isis, Dendara, Cairo: IFAO, 1999.
- Cauville, Sylvie. Dendara: Le Temple de Isis. Vol 1. Traduction. Leuven: Peeters, 2009.
- Cauville, Sylvie. Le Temple de Dendera: Les Chapelles Osiriennes, Part. 1: Transcription et Traduction, BdE 117, Cairo: IFAO, 1997.
- Cauville, Sylvie. Offerings to the Gods in Egyptian Temples. Brian Calcoen transl. Peeters, 2012.
- Clark, R.T. Rundle. Myth and Symbol in Ancient Egypt. New York: Thames and Hudson, 1959.
- Coppens, Filip. The Wabet: Tradition and Innovation in Temples of the Ptolemaic and Roman Period. Prague: Czech Institute of Egyptology, 2007.
- Cintron, David A., "Aspects of Nephthys: Lecture delivered at the annual ARCE 2004 Meeting," from http://www.cintronics.com/cintronics/pdffiles/AspectsofNephthys.pdf (29.11.2006), 2004.
- Dennis, James Teackle. Burden of Isis: Being the Laments of Isis and Nephthys. London: J. Murray, 1918.
- Dijkstra, Jitse H.F. and Eugene Cruz-Uribe. Syene I: the figural and textual graffiti from the temple of Isis at Aswan. Phillip von Zabern, 2012.
- Doxey, Denise M. "Nephthys." In The Ancient Gods Speak: A Guide to Egyptian Religion, edited by Donald Redford. New York: Oxford University Press, 2002, pp. 275-276.
- El-Sabban, Sherif. Temple Festival Calendars of Ancient Egypt. Wiltshire: Liverpool University Press, 2000.
- El-Saghir, Mohamed and Dominique Valbelle. "Komir. I. – The Discovery of Komir Temple. Preliminary Report. II. – Deux hymnes aux divinités de Komir : Anoukis et Nephthys." in BIFAO 83 (1983), pp. 149-170.

- Faulkner, R.O. The Ancient Egyptian Pyramid Texts. London: Oxford University Press, 1998.
- Faulkner, R.O. The Ancient Egyptian Coffin Texts Vol 1-3. England: Aris & Phillips Ltd., 2004.
- Faulkner, R.O. The Ancient Egyptian Coffin Texts Vol 1: Spells 1-354. England: Aris & Phillips Ltd, 1973.
- Faulkner, R.O. The Ancient Egyptian Coffin Texts Vol 2: Spells 355-787. England: Aris & Phillips Ltd, 1977.
- Faulkner, R.O. The Ancient Egyptian Coffin Texts Vol 3: Spells 788-1185. England: Aris & Phillips, Ltd, 1978.
- Faulkner, R.O. An Ancient Egyptian Book of Hours (Pap. Brit. Mus. 10569). Oxford: Printed for the Griffith Institute at the University Press by Charles Batey, 1958.
- Goyon, J.-Cl., Confirmation du pouvoir royal au Nouvel An: Brooklyn Museum Papyrus 47.218.50, BdE 52, Cairo: IFAO, 1972.
- Grenier, Jean Claude. Anubis Alexandrin et Romain Vol. 57. Leuven: Brill, 1977.
- Griffith, F. Ll. and Herbert Thompson, eds. The Leyden Papyrus: An Egyptian Magical Book. New York: Dover Publications, 1974.
- Griffiths, J. Gwyn. The Isis-Book: Metamorphosis XI. Brill Academic Publishers, 1997.
- Hill, Marsha and Deborah Schorsch. "A Gilded-Silver Pendant of Nephthys Naming Mereskhonsu. [PL. I-II]." In Revue d'Egyptologie, Vol. 66 (2015), pp. 33-49.
- Illes, Judika. The Encyclopedia of 5,000 Spells. HarperOne, 2009.
- Illes, Judika. Encyclopedia of Spirits: The Ultimate Guide to the Magic of Fairies, Genies, Demons, Ghosts, Gods & Goddesses. HarperOne, 2009.
- Inconnu-Bocquillon, Danielle. Le mythe de la déesse lointaine à Philae. BdE 132. Le Caire/Cairo: IFAO, 2001.
- Junker, Hermann. Der Grosse Pylon des Tempels der Isis in Phila. Vienna: Kommission bei Rudolf M. Rohrer, 1958.
- Junker, Hermann and Erich Winter. Das Geburtshaus des Tempels der Isis in Phila. Vienna: Kommissionsverlag H. Böhlaus Nachf., 1965.

- Kockelmann, Holger and Erich Winter. Philae III: Die Zweite Ostkolonnade des Tempels der Isis in Philae. (CO II und CO II K). Verlag der Osterreichischen Akademie der Wissenschaften / Austrian Academy of Sciences, 2016.
- Kurth, Dieter. Die Inschriften des Tempels von Edfu. Abteilung I Übersetzungen; Band 1. Edfou VIII. Harrassowitz Verlag, 1998.
- Leitz, Christian, ed. Lexikon der Aegyptischen Goetter und Goetterbezeichnungen (LAGG). OLA 129, Band 8. Peeters, 2003.
- Lepsius, C.R., H. Brugsch, A.D. Erman, and L. Stern. Zeitschrift für ägyptische sprache und altertumskunde. Vol. 21. Leipzig: J.C. Hinrichs'sche Buchhandlung, 1883.
- Levai, Jessica. Aspects of the Goddess Nephthys, Especially During the Graeco-Roman Period in Egypt. Rhode Island: Brown University Dissertation, 2007.
- Levai, Jessica. "Nephthys and Seth: Anatomy of a Mythical Marriage." Paper presented at the 58th Annual Meeting of the American Research Center in Egypt, Wyndham Toledo Hotel, Toledo, Ohio, Apr 20, 2007. From http://citation.allacademic.com/meta/p176897_index.html
- Levai, Jessica. "Anat for Nephthys: A Possible Substitution in the Documents of the Ramesside Period." In *From the Banks of the Euphrates: Studies in Honor of Alice Louise Slotsky* (2008), p. 135.
- Lichtheim, Miriam. Ancient Egyptian Literature Vol 2: The New Kingdom. Los Angeles: University of California Press, 1976.
- Lichtheim, Miriam. Ancient Egyptian Literature Vol 3: The Late Period. Los Angeles: University of California Press, 1980.
- Lesko, Barbara. The Great Goddesses of Egypt. Oklahoma: University of Oklahoma Press, 1999.
- Lurker, Manfred. An Illustrated Dictionary of the Gods and Symbols of Ancient Egypt. New York: Thames & Hudson, 2006.
- Mariette, Auguste. Dendérah: description générale du grand temple de cette ville (Band 6): [Texte]. Paris, 1875.
- Morgan, Mogg. The Wheel of the Year in Ancient Egypt. Mandrake of Oxford, 2011.

- Nelson, Harold H. "The Calendar of Feasts and Offerings at Medinet Habu." In Work in Western Thebes 1931-33. Harold H. Nelson and Uvo Holscher, eds. University of Chicago Press, 1934, pp. 1-52.
- Nicoll, Kiya. The Traveller's Guide to the Duat. Megalithica Books, 2012.
- Nock, Arthur Darby. "Neotera, queen or goddess?" in Aegyptus 33, no. 2 (1953), pp. 283-296.
- Parker, Richard A. The Calendars of Ancient Egypt (The Oriental Institute of the University of Chicago. Studies in Ancient Oriental Civilization). University Microfilms, 1976.
- Piankoff, Alexandre. Mythological Papyri: Bollingen III Series. New Jersey: University of Princeton Press, 1957.
- Piankoff, Alexandre. The Shrines of Tut-Ankh-Amun: Bollingen II Series. New Jersey: University of Princeton Press, 1955.
- Piankoff, Alexandre. Tomb of Ramesses VI: Bollingen I. New Jersey: University of Princeton Press, 1954.
- Pinch, Geraldine. Egyptian Mythology: A Guide to the Gods, Goddesses and Traditions of Ancient Egypt. New York: Oxford University Press, 2004.
- Sauneron, Serge. Esna V: Les fetes religieuses d'esna aux derniers siecles du paganisme. Cairo: IFAO, 2004.
- Schott, Siegfried. "Feasts of Thebes." In Work in Western Thebes 1931-33. Harold H. Nelson and Uvo Holscher, eds. University of Chicago Press, 1934, pp. 63-90.
- Schorsch, Deborah. Gifts for the Gods: Images from Egyptian Temples. Metropolitan Museum of Art, 2007.
- Shalomi-Hen, Racheli. The Writing of Gods: The Evolution of Divine Classifiers in the Old Kingdom. Vol. 4. Harrassowitz Verlag, 2006.
- Siuda, Tamara L. (as Tamara Siuda-Legan) The Neteru of Kemet. Illinois: Eschaton, 1994. (2010 reprint)
- Siuda, Tamara L. Nebt-Het: Lady of the House. Illinois: Stargazer Design, 2010 (second edition).
- Siuda, Tamara L. The Ancient Egyptian Prayerbook. Illinois: Stargazer Design, 2009.
- Siuda, Tamara L. The Ancient Egyptian Daybook. Portland: Stargazer Design, 2016.

- Siuda, Tamara L. The Hourly Vigil of Osiris. Portland: Stargazer Design, 2017.
- Stadler, Martin Andreas. Théologie et culte au temple de Soknopaios: Etudes sur la Religion d'un Village Egyptien Pendant l'Epoque Romaine. Paris: Cybele, 2017.
- Te Velde, Herman. Seth, God of Confusion: A Study of His Role in Egyptian Mythology and Religion. Vol. 6. Brill, 1977.
- Tripani, Luigi and Amentet Neferet. Egyptian Religious Calendar: CDXV-CDXVI Great Year of Ra (2015 CE). Amentet Neferet, 2014.
- Tyldesley, Joyce. The Penguin Book of Myths and Legends of Ancient Egypt. New York: Penguin, 2011.
- Wainwright, Gerald A. "Seshat and the Pharaoh." In *The Journal of Egyptian Archaeology* 26, no. 1 (1941), pp. 30-40.
- Wilkinson, Richard H. The Complete Gods and Goddesses of Ancient Egypt. New York: Thames and Hudson, 2003.
- Wilkinson, Richard H. The Complete Temples of Ancient Egypt. New York: Thames and Hudson, 2000.
- Wilkinson, Richard H. Reading Egyptian Art. New York: Thames and Hudson, 1992.
- Wilkinson, Richard H. Symbol and Magic in Egyptian Art. New York: Thames and Hudson, 1994.
- Wilkinson, John Gardner. The Ancient Egyptians. New York: Crescent Books, 1988. (reprint)
- Wilkinson, John Gardner. The Manners and Customs of the Ancient Egyptians. Vol. 2. J. Murray, 1878.
- Willems, Harco, and Filip Coppens, Marleen De Meyer and Peter Dils. The Temple of Shanhur: Volume 1. Peeters, 2003.
- Zivie-Coche, Christiane M. Giza au Primier Millenaire: Autour du Temple d'Isis Dame des Pyramides. Museum of Fine Arts Boston, 1991.

Glossary

- Abu: (Greek: Elephantine) Khnum's sacred city on the First Cataract of the Nile.
- Abdju: (Modern: Abydos) This is the sacred city of Wesir and the place of the burial site of the first ancient Egyptian kings.
- Akh (singular)/Akhu (plural): the ancestors, or beloved dead.
- Alexandria: A metropolitan port city in the Ptolemaic period, where Aset (Isis) was honored in the Lighthouse of Alexandria on Pharos Island.
- Amenti: This is an alternative name for the Duat. The name comes from the Goddess Amentet, the Lady of the West. She is the Goddess of the sunset, the night sky, the deceased and the unseen realm. Amenti is a title and manifestation of the Goddesses Aset, Hethert, Nebet Het, and Nut.
- Amun-Ra: a syncretic deity who rose to prominence in the New Kingdom as a combination of Amun and Ra. He is the husband of Mut and father of Khonsu.
- Anuket: (Greek: Anukis) She is a Goddess who is associated with the Nile's inundation and whose sacred animal is the gazelle. Anuket was associated with the Nile as the waters receded, while Satet was associated with the Nile as the waters rose. She was worshiped at Elephantine along with Satet and Khnum, and at Komir she shared a temple with Nebet Het.
- Apep: (Ap-p; Greek: Apophis): a serpent who is the enemy of the Gods of Egypt. He wishes creation to be unmade. He is slain every night by Set and Aset and the Crew of Ra so that creation can last another day. This entity is not considered one of the Gods. Some modern Kemetics refer to It as the "Uncreated" or the "Serpent Enemy of the Gods."
- Aset: (also Auset; Greek: Isis): a Goddess of authority, sovereignty and kings. She is the Goddess of magic par excellence who owns Ra's Name. She is a solar Eye of Ra who wards off enemies from her husband, son, and the sun God. On

the Night Boat, Aset wards off Apep with her magic. She heralds the New Year rising in the sky as the star Sopdet. She is the wife of Wesir and the mother of Heru-sa-Aset.

- Antinoe: (Greek: Antinoupolis) Ancient city dedicated to Antinous, the deified lover of Emperor Hadrian who drowned in the Nile.
- Ba (singular)/Bau (plural): The eternal essence of a being; soul. The *ba* of a deity went into cult statues, and other theophanies were the manifestations (bau) of the deity on earth. A physical manifestation of a deity such as a cult statue, an animal or a natural force. The *ba* of a human is an eternal part of the soul.
- Bast: (Greek: Bastet) a lioness Goddess who protects her father Ra, is an avenging Eye of Ra, and is a Goddess of the yearly solar cycle. She is also a Goddess of joy and music like Hethert. In later periods, she became associated with the more domestic housecat.
- Behdet: (Greek: Apollonopolis Magna; Modern: Edfu) The city and temple are sacred to Heru Wer or Horus the Elder.
- Djedet: (Greek: Mendes) This city was sacred to the fish Goddess Hatmehyt and her consort, Banebdjedet.
- Djehuty: (Greek: Thoth) This is the ibis or baboon headed God of time, wisdom, math, science, scribes, recordkeeping, and the moon. In some inscriptions, Djehuty is the father or son of Aset.
- Duat: This word means sunrise and sunset and is often translated as the "Underworld." Duat is the Unseen Realm where the Gods and the dead reside. Another name for this place is Amenti.
- Geb: the earth God who was associated with the land itself and all that grows upon it. He is associated with all the minerals in the earth. He is associated with the dead since the dead are buried in the earth. In the beginning, he was separated from his wife, Nut, so that the earth and sky could be created. He is the father of Aset, Nebet Het, Set, Wesir, and Heru Wer.

- Gebtu: (Greek: Koptos or Coptos; Modern: Qift) a town in Upper Egypt sacred to Min, Aset, Wesir, and Heru-sa-Aset.
- Hebyt: (also Per-Hebitet; Greek: Isiopolis; Modern: Behbeit el-Hagar) An ancient sacred city to Aset. The ancient Egyptian name of this city means "House of the Festive Goddess." Her temple in this city is called the Iseion, or Temple of Isis in Greek.
- Heka: (literally, "magic"). This is both a God and a concept. The concept is a force of energy that resides in all things. It can be manipulated by deities and humans. It has been translated as magic, but it is really the power of the *ka* (life force) in motion.
- Hekau: a magician, a sorceror or sorceress, one who uses heka; or a plural form of "magic."
- Heru pa Khered: (Greek: Harpokrates; Horus the Child) a form of Heru-sa-Aset who is a child. He and his mother are mentioned together in many healing spells.
- Heru nedj itef: (Greek: Harendotes; Horus, Savior of His Father) the form of Heru-sa-Aset who has battled Set and won the throne of Egypt. He inherited the throne of his father.
- Heru-sa-Aset: (Greek: Harsiese; Horus son of Isis) the son of Aset and Wesir who can manifest in many forms such as a child, a warrior battling Set for the throne, and a triumphant King. He is the God of kingship and is proficient in magical spells because of his mother. He is a God of strength, leadership, and community. He is often portrayed as a hawk headed God with the Double Crown.
- Heru-sema-tawy: (Greek: Harsomtus; Horus, Uniter of the Two Lands) a form of Heru the Child who is the son of Hethert and Heru Wer.
- Heru Wer: (Greek: Haroeris; Horus the Elder) the sky God of kings and communities, whose eyes are the sun and moon. He is a protector and a warrior. He is the twin brother of Set, uncle of Heru-sa-Aset and the brother of Aset, Wesir, and Nebet Het. He

is often portrayed as a falcon headed God with the White Crown.
- Hethert: (also Hetharu; Greek: Hathor) a joyous Goddess of beauty, love, and fertility. She is an Eye of Ra and an avenging solar deity. She is also a Goddess who protects the dead.
- Het-Ka-Ptah: (also Mennefer; Memphis) The sacred city to the craftsman God Ptah. Its name means "House of the Ka of Ptah."
- Hypostasis: a distinct, seperate aspect within a unified God.
- Imet: (Modern: Tell Nabasha) A city that was sacred to Wadjet.
- Iunet: (Modern: Dendera) Sacred city of the Goddess Hethert.
- Iunu: (also On; Greek: Heliopolis) Sacred city of Ra and the Gods of his creation myth. The Ennead of this city consisted of Ra, Shu, Tefnut, Nut, Geb, Wesir, Aset, Nebet Het, Set, and Heru Wer.
- Ka (singular)/Kau (plural): the vital essence of a person or deity; the collective vital essence of a family line or kingly lineage
- Khent-min: (also Ipu or Apu; Greek: Chemmis or Panopolis; Modern: Akhmim) A city sacred to Min. In the Wesir Mythos, Aset takes her son to the marshes here to raise her son.
- Khmun (Greek: Hermopolis) This is the sacred city of Djehuty.
- Khnum: a Ram-headed God of the Nile's inundation, potters and a master craftsman. He creates the kau of humans on his potter's wheel. Khnum is also one of the creators of the world.
- Ma'at: (Greek: Mayet) a Goddess and a concept of truth, order and balance of the universe.
- Menat: (also Menet) a necklace used like a rattle in ritual. It is especially used for the Goddesses.
- Mehet Weret: (also Celestial Cow; Greek: Methyer) This is the cow Goddess of the primeval waters, creation, the birth of the sun God, and the heavenly sky. She is the caretaker of the dead since the stars fill the night sky. She is a manifestation of Nut, Nit, Nebet Het, Hethert, and Aset.

- Min: the ithyphallic God of fertility and procreation. Aset can be paired with him, as either her consort or her son.
- Mut: a Goddess of sovereignty, royalty, and an Eye of Ra. The wife of Amun-Ra and the mother of Khonsu.
- Nebet Het: (Greek: Nephthys) Her name can mean Lady of the House, Lady of the Temple, or Lady of the Tomb. She is a Goddess who protects boundaries such as the sacred from the profane or twilight lands during dawn and dusk. As a solar Goddess, she is an Eye of Ra and a protector of Ra and Wesir. She weeps with Aset, causing the flooding of the Nile. In some myths, Yinepu is her son. She can be consort of Set, Ra, or Wesir.
- Nefertem: (also Nefertum) A patron God of scents and fragrances, Nefertem is a God associated with the lotus and wears on upon his head. He also can be depicted as a child sitting on a lotus flower. He wards off evil in his leonine form. He is the son of Sekhmet and Ptah. He is also considered the son of Bast.
- Nekheb: (Modern: El-Kab) This is the sacred city of the vulture Goddess Nekhbet.
- Nekhen: (Greek: Hierakonpolis) This city is sacred to Heru of Nekhen, the God Khnum and the Goddess Nit.
- Nit: (Greek: Neith) The tutelary Goddess of Lower Egypt. She wears the red crown and holds bows and arrows. She is a primordial Goddess who began creation. She has a manifestation as the celestial cow where she is a creator deity, the lady of the primeval ocean and the night sky, holding the dead. She is a Goddess associated with protection of the dead, as she protects one of the canopic jars. She is a mother of Sobek and a consort of Set.
- Nut: The Goddess of the night sky filled with stars. She is the Goddess of the dead as their mother and caretaker. She gives birth to the sun God each morning and devours him each evening. As the celestial cow, she is the Goddess of the primeval

waters and the dead. She is the mother of Aset, Nebet Het, Set, Wesir, and Heru Wer.

- Of Iunu: (Greek: Heliopolitanos; of Heliopolis) This is normally translated as the Heliopolitan, or the one of Heliopolis or the city of Iunu in Ancient Egyptian. It is a common title of many deities.
- Per Bast: (Greek: Bubastis) The sacred city of the Goddess Bast.
- Per Hethert: (also Tepyhwt; Greek: Aphroditopolis; Modern: Atfih) A city sacred to Hethert.
- Per Medjed: (Greek: Oxyrhynchus) This city was sacred to Wepwawet in the New Kingdom (along with Aset and Hethert).
- Per Wesir: (or Djedu; Greek: Busiris) This city was sacred to Wesir.
- Pesdjet: (Greek: Ennead) a group of important deities of cities; their number could be nine, but was not limited to that number.
- Pharos Island: A small island in the harbor of the northern coastal city of Alexandria, where a Lighthouse once stood as one of the Seven Wonders of the World. Aset of Pharos (Isis Pharia) was honored here as its patron Goddess.
- Pilak: (also P'aaleq; Greek: Philae) The sacred temple and island to Aset during the Late through the Roman periods of ancient Egyptian history. The temple was relocated to Agilkia Island due to the construction of the Aswan Dam.
- Ptah: A creator God of Memphis who is the divine patron of craftsmen. He is the consort of Sekhmet and father of Nefertem.
- Ra: (also Re) He is the sun God who created the world and who rules among the Gods as their King. He is the father of many Gods and Goddesses, including Aset. Ra is one of the Gods associated with kingship and he is often portrayed as a man with the head of a hawk wearing a solar disk.
- Ra Heruakhety: (Greek: Ra Horakhty; Ra-Horus of the Two Horizons) A fusion of the Gods Ra and Heru Wer. He represents the sun's journey both by day and night. He is often

portrayed as a man with a falcon's head with a solar disk for his crown.

- Renenutet: (Greek: Thermuthis or Hermouthis) A cobra-headed Goddess of the harvest and the protection of granaries. She is a Goddess associated with fate and childbirth. She is a protective Eye of Ra Goddess who destroys enemies. She is the consort of either Sobek or Geb. She is the mother of Nehebkau.
- Satet: (Greek: Satis) a tutelary Goddess of Elephantine and the Nile's waters. She wears the White Crown encased in antelope horns. Her consort is Khnum and her daughter is Anuket. She can be syncretized with Aset.
- Shedet: (Greek: Crocodilopolis; Modern: Dime or Faiyum) The marshes sacred to the crocodile God Sobek. Aset, Wesir and Heru-sa-Aset were worshipped alongside Sobek in this nome during the Middle Kingdom through the Roman period.
- Shu: The primordial God of air and sunlight. He is the consort of Tefnut and father of Nut and Geb. He is often portrayed as a man wearing an ostrich feathered headdress or in leonine form.
- Sekhmet: (Greek: Sachmis) a lioness-headed Goddess who is the patron of healing and illness using magic and medicine to cure disease. As a daughter of Ra, she protects her Father from evil forces. Like many Goddesses, she is an Eye of Ra. She is a protector and a warrior who defends ma'at. She is the patron of healers and surgeons. She is the mother of Nefertem and her consort is the creator God Ptah.
- Senem: (Greek: Abaton; Modern: Bigeh) This island is near the Temple of Philae. A temple to Wesir was on that island, where Aset would honor her husband during weekly processions.
- Serqet: (also Selket; Greek: Selkis) a scorpion Goddess known for her healing abilities;
- Seshat: She is the Goddess of writing, scribes, record-keeping and recording the lives of kings. She was the patron of the "stretching the cord" ritual before a temple was built. As tutelary Goddess of scribes, Seshat can be depicted holding scribe

implements. She is often depicted wearing a leopard skin over her attire, and her head is adorned with a seven-pointed palmette with two bovine horns pointing downward.
- Set: (also Seth) He is the God of storms, the desert, foreigners, outsiders, and strength. He guards Ra's bark and kills Apep every morning. In some myths, he is also the one who slays Wesir and challenges Heru-sa-Aset for the throne.
- Shai: (Greek: Psais; Agathos Daimon) The God of fate, fortune, and destiny.
- Sobek: (Greek: Suchos) the crocodile God of the Nile waters, protection, strength, and the sun. In some locations such as the Faiyum, Sobek is the son of Aset and Wesir.
- Sopdet: (Greek: Sothis; Modern: Sirius) a form of Aset who brings the Nile's inundation and heralds the New Year as She rises in the sky. As the star Sopdet, Aset follows Wesir (equated with the constellation Orion) in the sky.
- Swenett: (Greek: Syene; Modern: Aswan or Assuan) A trade-city near Philae, sacred to the Goddess that the city was named for.
- Syncretic Deities: two deities who have fused to make a third, separate deity that still contains the uniqueness of the two deities, such as Aset-Tayet, Aset-Nut, and Aset-Mut.
- Tayet: (also Tait) a deity of purification and the linen wrappings of the dead. She can be syncretized with or considered an aspect of Aset.
- Ta-senet (also Iunyt; Greek: Latopolis or Letopolis; Modern: Esna) This city is sacred to the God Khnum and Nit.
- Tefnut: a lioness Goddess who is an Eye of Ra and a lady of moisture. She is a primordial deity as she was the first Goddess Ra created. She is the mother of Nut and the grandmother of Aset and her siblings.
- Tjebu: (Greek: Antinopolis) The city was sacred to Set.
- Uraeus: the fiery cobra who protects the sun God. Whose solar power is destructive toward enemies and protective for everyone

else. All Goddesses (and a few Gods) with the epithet Eye of Ra are associated with this cobra.
- Wadjet: (Greek: Buto) The patron Goddess of Lower Egypt. She is depicted as a Uraeus and can also be depicted as a cobra headed woman. She is associated with royalty and protection. She is also an Eye of Ra.
- Waset: (Greek: Thebes; Modern: Luxor) The sacred city of Amun, Mut, and Khonsu during the New Kingdom and beyond.
- Wepwawet: (also, Upuaut; Greek: Ophois) a Jackal God who is the Opener of the Way; he paves the way for armies, childbirth, the sun to rise, for rituals to the Gods, and for the dead to cross over. He is associated with the wolf by the Greeks. He is a son of Aset.
- Wesir: (Greek: Osiris) the God of vegetation and the king of the afterlife. Aset and Nebet Het mourn him after he is slain by Set. In some myths, he drowns in the Nile. Aset and Nebet Het search for him, find his body and bury it. Wesir is father of Heru-sa-Aset.
- Yinepu: (Greek: Anubis) the Jackal-headed God of embalming, a psychopomp for the deceased, and a guardian of tombs. Depending on the myth, the son or adopted son of Aset.
- Zau: (Greek: Sais) The sacred city of the Goddess Nit.
- Zawty: (Greek: Lykopolis; Modern: Asyut) This is the sacred city to Wepwawet.

About the Author

Chelsea Luellon Bolton has a BA and MA in Religious Studies from the University of South Florida. She is the author of *Lady of Praise, Lady of Power: Ancient Hymns of the Goddess Aset; Queen of the Road: Poetry of the Goddess Aset;* and *Magician, Mother and Queen: A Research Paper on the Goddess Aset.* Her other books are *Lord of Strength and Power: Ancient*

Hymns for Wepwawet; and *Sun, Star and Desert Sand: Poems for the Egyptian Gods*. She is both the editor of and a contributor to this anthology, *She Who Speaks Through Silence: An Anthology for Nephthys*. Her other latest book is *Mother of Magic: Ancient Hymns for Aset*. Chelsea's current projects include *Lady of the Temple: Ancient Hymns for Nephthys* and *Flaming Lioness: Ancient Hymns for Egyptian Goddesses*. Her poetry has been previously published in various anthologies. Chelsea lives with tons of books and her anti-social feline companion. Find more of her work at: https://fiercelybrightone.com .

Other Books by Chelsea Luellon Bolton

- Lady of Praise, Lady of Power: Ancient Hymns of the Goddess Aset.

- Queen of the Road: Poetry of the Goddess Aset.

- Magician, Mother and Queen: A Research Paper on the Goddess Aset.

- Divine Words, Divine Praise: Poetry for the Divine Powers.

- Lord of Strength and Power: Ancient Hymns for Wepwawet.

- Divine Beings, Earthly Praise: Poems for Divine Powers.

- Holy Mother, Healer and Queen: Papers on the Feminine Divine.

- Sun, Star and Desert Sand: Poems for the Egyptian Gods.

- Mother of Magic: Ancient Hymns for Aset.

- She Who Speaks Through Silence: An Anthology for Nephthys.

- COMING SOON: Lady of the Temple: Ancient Hymns for Nephthys.

Website:
https://fiercelybrightone.com/

Twitter
@Fiercelybright1

Printed in Great Britain
by Amazon